Matriliny and Migration

*Evolving Minangkabau Traditions
in Indonesia*

Matriliny and Migration

Evolving Minangkabau Traditions in Indonesia

TSUYOSHI KATO

Cornell University Press

ITHACA AND LONDON

First published 1982 by Cornell University Press.
Published in the United Kingdom by Cornell University Press Ltd.,
Ely House, 37 Dover Street, London W1X 4HQ

International Standard Book Number 0-8014-1411-3
Library of Congress Catalog Card Number 81-66647
Printed in the United States of America
*Librarians: Library of Congress cataloging information
appears on the last page of the book.*

To Ofukuro

Contents

Maps

Preface

In the mountainous region of western central Sumatra lies the cultural heartland of the Minangkabau, a people noted in Indonesia for their business acumen and their intellectual accomplishments. They are distinguished by three well-known social features: devotion to Islam, adherence to a matrilineal family system, and inclination to *merantau,* or migration. The Minangkabau have for a long time remained an enigma, a tangle of paradoxes to the outsider: ardent believers in patrilineally-oriented Islam yet tenacious followers of matriliny, well educated and enterprising yet upholding a seemingly archaic tradition, highly mobile and centrifugal in habit yet maintaining a strong sense of ethnic identity rooted in their homeland.

At the center of these paradoxes is the perseverance of matriliny. The Minangkabau matrilineal system, however, has been the subject of conflicting testimonies. Beginning in the middle of the nineteenth century, some outside observers diagnosed or predicted the disintegration of matriliny in West Sumatra: matrilineal extended families were being replaced by nuclear conjugal families; property, mainly land, was becoming individually owned rather than communally owned; inheritance was tending to be bilateral or patrilineal instead of matrilineal. Yet there are many accounts to the contrary.

In this book I will describe how, in comparison to the past, the matrilineal system is practiced in contemporary Minangkabau society and then explain how Minangkabau matriliny has been able to adapt to changing times and circumstances. The Minangkabau's strong tendency to migration is an important factor in the matrilineal system's adaptability. The key to understanding it is to grasp Minangkabau societal processes historically. Static analyses can capture only a part—or seemingly contradictory parts—of a dynamic and changing reality. Only by placing the interplay between matriliny and migration in a proper historical perspective can we comprehend how the Minangkabau have managed to maintain their matrilineal system. Unlike some other studies of social change, this is essentially a story of the resilience of tradition.

If I were to choose the single most important lesson I have learned from conducting field research and writing, it would probably be the realization of how much I owe others—for their work, advice, material and moral support, kindness, and generosity—in my efforts to carry out these tasks. I must first express my gratitude to three of my professors at Cornell University, Robin M. Williams, Jr., Bernard C. Rosen, and Lawrence K. Williams, who trained, influenced, and supported me in more ways than they themselves might realize. Whatever competence I have acquired in the fields of sociology and social psychology is a result of their guidance.

Special thanks are due to Benedict R. O'G. Anderson, who, as teacher and friend, taught me the importance of appreciating Indonesian society for itself rather than merely using it as a sample to theorize about. It is primarily because of his influence that I have written a book that is, in the terms of contemporary sociology, rather unconventional. He also spent countless hours carefully reading, editing, and commenting on the manuscript at various stages of preparation. Many of the ideas I have attempted to work out arose from suggestions he made or in the many stimulating discussions I had with him.

My field research in Indonesia (from January 1972 to July 1973) was carried out under the auspices of the Lembaga Ilmu Pengetahuan Indonesia (the Indonesian Council of Sciences) and financed jointly by a Humanities and Social Sciences Program Fellowship of Cornell University and by the National Science Foundation. The Cornell Southeast Asia Program and the Cornell Sociology Department supported the computerization of my field data. The assistance of these various institutions is gratefully acknowledged.

Some recent historical works on Minangkabau society have proved indispensable. Among them, the writings of Taufik Abdullah, Christine Dobbin, Elizabeth Graves, P. E. de Josselin de Jong (who kindly read my work and gave me some valuable comments), J. Kathirithamby-Wells, and Akira Oki have been especially useful. A number of friends helped, encouraged, influenced, and sometimes (pleasantly) annoyed me in the course of writing. I particularly welcome the opportunity to express my appreciation to Taufik Abdullah, Alison Davis, Judith Ecklund, William O'Malley, and Mildred Wagemann. Their aid and assistance went far beyond the simple yet tedious tasks of helping me understand Dutch material and editing my English. I thank them indeed, for everything.

Above all, I owe deep gratitude to the Minangkabau people from every walk of life whom I met in West Sumatra and in Pekan Baru in the course of my fieldwork. I was greatly honored that many of them embraced me as a relative; they said that according to legend one of three sons of Alexander the Great, Maharaja Diraja, became the ancestor of the Minangkabau, while Maharaja Depang, another son, became the ancestor of the Japanese. Without the generous cooperation of countless Minangkabau people, in IV [Empat] Angkat and other villages, and village heads from all over West Sumatra—a few of whom even walked all night to accommodate me (I only wish I had known that I was causing such trouble)—local government officials, friends, and friends of friends, my field research would have been impossible. I can only hope that this book has done no injustice to their kindness and helpfulness. Although so many people aided my field research, I would like to mention especially Sjahruddin Ans, Burhanuddin Pakih Kayo, Halimoen, Hasbullah Zen, Imran Manan, Mansur Jasin, Muhammad Nazif, Musnida Munir, the late Ratna Sari, Rafii Sa'adi, the late Amilijoes Sa'danoer, and Noerani Sa'danoer. They helped me to adjust to life in West Sumatra, to carry out research and interviews, and to understand Minangkabau society. A Minangkabau aphorism says: "Fish in the ocean, lime in the mountain, if destined, will meet each other yet." Although we are separated by a great distance, I hope we will meet again.

The following institutions were particularly helpful in supplying relevant information and data: the provincial government of West Sumatra at all levels (under then Governor Harun Zain), branch offices of various departments of the central government all over West Sumatra, Fakultas Hukum dan Pengetahuan Masyarakat of Universitas Andalas, Institut Keguruan dan Ilmu Pendidikan in

Padang, Akademi Pemerintahan Dalam Negeri in Bukittinggi, and
the West Sumatra Regional Planning Study of the Indonesian
Ministry of Public Works and Power and the University of Bonn.
The International College of Sophia University and the Center for
Southeast Asian Studies of Kyoto University provided me with time
and facilities to revise my work. The final version profited from the
excellent editing of Lisa S. Turner.

TSUYOSHI KATO

Kyoto, Japan

Note on Spelling

There are two types of Indonesian spelling, the old spelling (*ejaan lama*) and the new (*ejaan baru*):

Old	New
oe	u
j	y
dj	j
tj	c (pronounced ch)
ch	kh
sj	sy

In general I follow the new spelling. In the case of quotations from literature published before 1973, however, the old form has been retained. The same rule applies to the citation of authors' names and titles of materials published before 1973. In accordance with the Indonesian custom, no distinction is made between singular and plural for Indonesian or Minangkabau words.

Matriliny and Migration

*Evolving Minangkabau Traditions
in Indonesia*

The old adat, ancient heritage,
Neither rots in the rain,
Nor cracks in the sun
      —Minangkabau proverb

1 / Introduction

In West Sumatra, surrounded by the three mountains of Gunung Merapi, Gunung Sago, and Gunung Singgalang, there lies one of the most fertile lands in Indonesia. This region is called *darek,* the inner highlands, in contrast to the *rantau,* the outer areas or frontiers. *Darek* is the cradleland of the Minangkabau who, in their legends, trace their ancestry to Alexander the Great. Maharaja Diraja, one of Alexander's three legendary sons, and his retinue are supposed to have arrived by boat at Gunung Merapi when that mountaintop was only as large as an egg and when all other lands were still under the sea. What follows is an account of the people who created these legends—an attempt to understand their society, history, and tradition.

The Minangkabau are one of some 140 ethnic groups scattered over 3,000 islands in Indonesia.[1] According to the 1930 Dutch census, their share among the native population was only about 3 percent, yet they were the fourth largest ethnic group in Indonesia, outnumbered only by the Javanese (47 percent), Sundanese (15 percent), and Madurese (7 percent) (*Volkstelling 1930,* 5:179–180). The importance of the role the Minangkabau have played in the modern history of Indonesia is disproportionate to their numbers. Their national prominence, noticeable through the 1950s, covers many fields such as writing, politics, and business.[2]

1. As Hildred Geertz pointed out, the number of ethnic groups enumerated depends on how they are classified. The number represented here is adopted from the ethnic categories applied in the 1930 census (*Volkstelling 1930,* 8:44). Geertz (1967:24) herself gives a number of more than three hundred ethnic groups.
2. Of the fifteen major Indonesian writers in the 1920s and 1930s, nine were

The main habitat of the Minangkabau, the province of West
Sumatra, covers about 18,000 square miles of land extending from
north to south between the Indian Ocean and the Bukit Barisan
mountain range (see Map 1).[3] The interior (*darek*) of West Sumatra
mainly consists of mountainous highlands, with several enclaves of
plateau, while the narrow stretch of coastal area (*rantau pasisir*) is
a flat region dotted with marshes. The land in West Sumatra is
generally fertile and agriculture variegated. Wet rice is the major
agricultural crop. Rubber, copra, coffee, gambier, cinnamon, and
cloves are some of the important cash crops.[4] Such annuals as corn,
chilis, peanuts, and cabbages are also planted; they are usually
traded within West Sumatra. In addition to agriculture, artisanship,
for example, weaving, is widely practiced in some parts of the
interior, particularly around Bukittinggi.

According to the 1971 census, some 2.8 million people make
their living in West Sumatra. Although the area contains a substantial number of Chinese, Javanese, and Batak, probably close to 91
percent of this population are ethnically Minangkabau.[5] Reflecting
topographical conditions, the fertile central highlands are densely
populated. The northern and southern parts of the interior are
relatively sparsely settled. The population is still predominantly

Minangkabau (Graves 1971:3–4). The Minangkabau's contribution to Islamic leadership, both political and educational, was prodigious (Noer 1973:31–55). The
business acumen of the Minangkabau is well known. It is said that they are one of
the few Indonesian ethnic groups who can compete with the Chinese in business
(Robequain 1958:159; Furnivall 1967:47). In 1952, *Abadi,* a Jakarta daily news-
paper, conducted a public opinion poll to determine the most prominent persons in
contemporary Indonesia. Of the ten persons most frequently chosen, four were
Minangkabau: Mohammad Hatta, Mohammad Natsir, Haji Agus Salim, and Sutan
Sjahrir—all of them distinguished nationalists (Alamsjah 1952). The Minangkabau
filled 11 percent of the cabinet posts between 1945 and 1957 (Yasunaka 1970:116).
The prominence of the Minangkabau in these fields was due in part to the head start
in education they obtained during the Dutch period. By the 1950s, this educational
edge over other ethnic groups had begun to narrow. Furthermore, an abortive West
Sumatran regional rebellion in 1958 reduced the subsequent role of the
Minangkabau on the national scene.
   3. The islands off the coast of West Sumatra are not included.
   4. Gambier is used for betelnut chewing and also for tanning and dyeing.
   5. The figure is extrapolated from the 1930 Dutch census (*Volkstelling 1930,*
4:170) and applies only to the Minangkabau "in a narrower sense," the meaning of
which is explained in Chapter 4. The two censuses after independence (1961 and
1971) do not provide any data on the ethnic background of the population.

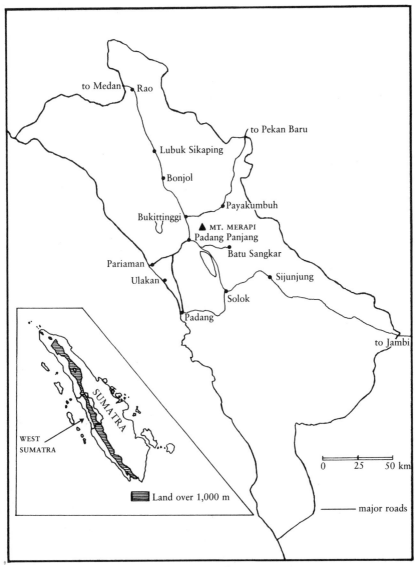

Map 1. West Sumatra

21

rural: 86 percent of the inhabitants live in villages. The largest city is Padang, the provincial capital, on the coast with a population of over 200,000 in 1971. Another city, Bukittinggi (about 50,000 people in 1971), is situated about sixty miles into the interior at an altitude of 2,700 feet above sea level. Padang and Bukittinggi are the two most important urban centers in West Sumatra and there a majority of the non-Minangkabau inhabitants are concentrated. Administratively, the rural areas of the province are divided into eight districts (*kabupaten*), seventy-three subdistricts (*kecamatan*), and some 510 villages (*nagari*). In addition, there are altogether six municipalities (*kotamadya*).

Other than a strong Islamic faith (in contrast to the more syncretic Javanese), the characteristics most often associated with the Minangkabau are *merantau* (out-migration) and *adat* (tradition, particularly matrilineal customs).

Merantau is a compound word, consisting of a prefix "*me-*" and a noun "*rantau.*" *Rantau* originally means shoreline, the reaches of a river, and "abroad" or foreign countries. *Merantau*, a verb, itself implies to go abroad, to leave one's home area, to sail along the reaches of a river, and so on (Echols and Shadily 1963). In the Minangkabau context, *merantau* is always understood in the second meaning of the term, to leave one's home village (in search of wealth, knowledge, and fame).

A Dutch scholar once described the Minangkabau, not without justification, as a people with wanderlust (Josselin de Jong 1952:9). Assuming 91 percent of the population in West Sumatra in 1971 to be ethnically Minangkabau, one is left with a rough estimate of 2.5 million as the number of Minangkabau residing within the province. Estimates of Minangkabau living outside of West Sumatra vary. Tentatively, I propose that some one million Minangkabau lived outside their native province in 1971 (for more details, see Chapter 4). This means that 30 percent of the Minangkabau population may be found outside West Sumatra. One estimate even suggests a figure of 400,000 Minangkabau in Jakarta alone, which would constitute approximately 10 percent of the population of the capital city.[6] The presence of "*orang Padang*" (Padang people), as they are often called outside West Sumatra, as merchants, office

6. "Djakarta Rantau Bertuah," *Tempo*, 15 January 1972, p. 37.

workers, and even as pickpockets, is a familiar phenomenon to most Jakartans.

The Minangkabau practice of merantau is not simply a product of the recent urbanization process but is deeply rooted in Minangkabau history. Local myths and legends telling of early Minangkabau settlers are found in many places in Sumatra: in Tapak Tuan and Meulaboh in western Aceh (Szekeley-Lulofs 1954:7–8), in the Karo Batak lands of North Sumatra (Neumann 1972:53), in Siak Sri Indrapura (Effendy and Effendy c. 1972:15–16) and Muara Takus (Schnitger 1939:39, 41) in central Sumatra, in the Riau inland areas (*daratan*) adjoining West Sumatra (Pemerintah Daerah Propinsi Sumatera Tengah c. 1955:n.p.), in Pangkalan Jambu in western Jambi, in Tungkal Ulu and Jambi in eastern Jambi (Kementerian Penerangan c. 1954:57), in Rejang in Bengkulu (Jaspan 1964:25), in Sekala Berak near Lake Ranau (Tsubouchi 1980:483), and in Paminggir settlements in Lampung (Funke 1972:36).[7] (For the locations of some of these places, see Map 2.) Their movement, moreover, reaches beyond the shores of Sumatra. In western Malaysia across the Straits of Malacca, one finds large Minangkabau settlements in Negri Sembilan (literally Nine States, including Sungai Ujong, Rembau, and Naning). This pattern of movement is believed to have started in the sixteenth or seventeenth century, and possibly as early as the fifteenth century (Josselin de Jong:9, 121). The Minangkabau do indeed seem ubiquitous. As one joke has it, astronaut Neil Armstrong, landing on the moon, found a Padang restaurant already established there.[8]

In addition to the prevalence of merantau, another characteristic often associated with the Minangkabau is matrilineal *adat* or tradition. The Minangkabau are probably one of the largest matrilineal societies in the world. Aside from the relative rarity of the matrilineal system itself, Minangkabau matriliny has been of special interest to scholars because of its combination there with patrilineally-oriented Islam: "How such a [matrilineal] system

7. The information on Pangkalan Jambu and Tungkal Ulu is based on my interviews respectively at Pangkalan Jambu and at Akademi Pemerintahan Dalam Negeri in Jambi, both in August 1973.
8. "Orang Minang dan Lapau Nasi," *Aneka Minang,* no. 4 (1972), p. 32. Padang restaurants, famous for their spicy cuisine, serve precooked food and charge only for what the customer eats.

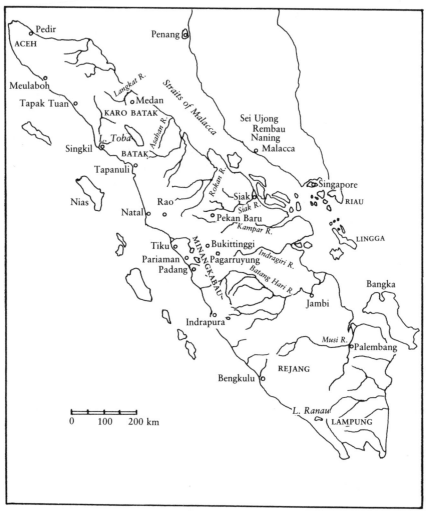

Map 2. Sumatra and Malay Peninsula. Based, by permission of author and publisher, on J. Kathirithamby-Wells, *The British West Sumatran Presidency, 1760–1785* (Kuala Lumpur: Penerbit Universiti Malaya, 1977).

could work in conjunction with the patrilineal Islamic legal framework has excited a good deal of speculation" (H. Geertz:80).[9] The seeming contradiction and conflict between adat and Islam have in fact induced many scholars to maintain that matriliny in West Sumatra faded as the Islamization of the Minangkabau society progressed. Particularly after the society weathered two powerful Islamic reformist movements in its recent history—the Padri zealots in the early nineteenth century and the Kaum Muda (Young Group) movement in the early twentieth century—and the resultant Dutch political control, penetration of a money economy, educational progress, and increasing mobility, such a conclusion has been widely entertained.

As early as in the middle of the nineteenth century, Francis, a Dutch official in West Sumatra, commented on the "bastardization" of the Minangkabau matrilineal system (Francis 1839:111). Since then, similar remarks have been made repeatedly by a succession of scholars, including Willinck, Joustra, Schrieke (Evers 1975:87), and de Moubray (1931), culminating in Maretin (1961), who diagnosed that the Minangkabau matrilineal system was being replaced by a more patrilineally-oriented system. Given the changes experienced by the Minangkabau society over the last 150 years, the diagnosis seems both plausible and credible.

Unfortunately, there has so far been little published material on the contemporary Minangkabau matrilineal system either to substantiate or to refute this diagnosis.[10] As I hope to show, matrilineal adat in West Sumatra is far from disappearing. Accommodation is certainly observable, but the Minangkabau matrilineal system has, in my opinion, managed to survive changing times and circumstances. Admittedly, those Minangkabau who stay in West Sumatran cities and outside their own province have a way of life different from that of their counterparts back home—for example, the migrants are more concerned with their conjugal family. Yet it is my observation that in general the migrant Minangkabau are ideologically committed to their matrilineal adat as much as or more than

9. Of 565 societies in G. P. Murdock's World Ethnographic Sample, 15 percent are matrilineal, while 44 percent, 36 percent, and 5 percent are respectively patrilineal, bilateral, and duolineal (Arberle 1961:663).
10. Some exceptions are Evers (1975), Kahn (1976), and Benda-Beckmann (1979).

their compatriots in West Sumatra, and they expect the latter to maintain the tradition in their home territory.

The Minangkabau people are aware of and proud of their unique adat. I was often asked why I, a Japanese, took the trouble to go to America and then to come to West Sumatra in order to study Minangkabau society. They wanted to know why their society seemed so special to me. When I answered that I was intrigued by their "*sistem matriarchat,*" my reply was almost always greeted by understanding nods. The Minangkabau thought it only natural that their tradition should be of great interest to outsiders. Over and over again, people told me about the merits of their matrilineal system: women are well protected, the family tie and spirit are strong, the society is democratic with its communal landholding and communal decision making, and so on. My experiences, though limited, in other parts of Sumatra, lead me to believe that positive identification with adat at the grass-roots level is nowhere stronger (with the possible exception of the Batak in North Sumatra) than in West Sumatra.

The persistence of the Minangkabau adat, above all its matrilineal system, is the major topic of this book. In it, I first describe the traditional family system and the closely related institution of social stratification. Later I retrace and characterize change and continuity in these two aspects of the society. Closely interwoven with this topic is merantau, for change and continuity of the adat are not intelligible without considering the practice of merantau, and the relationship between the darek (the interior) and the rantau (the frontier). I have chosen a historical orientation; and I also try to incorporate sociological insights in analyzing and interpreting the historical processes of the Minangkabau society. In order to make clear the reasons behind this approach, it is necessary at this point to recount my personal encounter with West Sumatra.

Originally I went to Indonesia with the intention of conducting a comparative study in Central Java and West Sumatra. My concern was to investigate the occupational orientations of the Javanese and of the Minangkabau in order to find out why the Javanese tended to become bureaucrats, while the Minangkabau became merchants. The Indonesian bureaucracy had been expanding at an alarming rate since independence, without a parallel development in the industrial and commercial sectors. Part of the problem was that "everybody"—with a few exceptions—wanted to be a *pegawai* (office worker). The Minangkabau were among these few exceptions. According to their own interpretation, the Minangkabau are too independent and not submissive enough in character to work in a bureaucracy. I saw the Minangkabau somewhat in the role of heroes, providing indigenous entrepreneurs in the process of Indonesia's modernization.

My first destination was West Sumatra. I expected to find a very fluid society in West Sumatra, in contrast to Java, which has a long aristocratic tradition. The merantau practice, matrilineage heads as *primus inter pares,* the importance of wealth (inherited or acquired) in the attainment of social status, and the changing matrilineal system, of which I had read prior to my visit—all seemed to warrant such an expectation.

At the beginning, I spent most of the time traveling, talking to people, and making observations in order to get acquainted with the society. I was fortunate enough to own a motor cycle and could visit many villages in a relatively short time. I talked to village heads and village adat experts, asking about their local history, how local customs were practiced, if there had been any change, how popular merantau was among people from the village, and so on. I spent three months traveling through the interior districts of Tanah Datar, Agam, and 50 [Limapuluh] Kota. The experience was rewarding, but hardly encouraging for my original assumptions.

I learned that there were indeed Minangkabau migrants, most of them merchants, in every corner of Indonesia. However, Minangkabau merchants of entrepreneurial quality were the exceptions rather than the rule. A majority of them were *kaki lima* or petty roadside vendors and peddlers. Only a few seemed to complete the leap from itinerant traders to shopowners. The village society was not as fluid as expected, ascription still being an important factor in one's status. I also began to appreciate the persistence of the matrilineal system. Adat itself is perceived as unchanging. After talking to village heads and adat experts, I made it a habit to ask them what were the major changes in adat and *adat-istiadat* (customs) in their village in recent years. Despite the fact that we had been discussing changes in inheritance patterns, marriage arrangements, and father-children relationships, their answer was almost invariably that there had been no change.

As my travel continued and my understanding deepened, I grew increasingly uncomfortable with my misplaced optimism about the Minangkabau entrepreneurial quality and my unsubstantiated ideas about the fluidity of the society, both of which had been important assumptions. On the other hand, I became fascinated by the way a society with such a high migration rate could maintain a seemingly archaic matrilineal tradition. After all, does modernization theory not propound the notion that the trend toward some form of the conjugal nuclear family system is a necessary concomitant of economic development, one of whose essential components is geographical mobility? (cf. Goode 1963).

The persistence of Minangkabau matriliny is all the more remarkable, not only because many scholars have predicted its downfall but because West Sumatra is not a backward area isolated from outside influences. In the middle of the nineteenth century when the Dutch established their political hegemony over the area, the political structure was centralized. Formal education spread rapidly. A money economy permeated the people's life. As the merantau practice intensified, returning migrants brought back new wealth, power, and prestige, together with new ideas and practices, from the outside world to their villages. Yet in the final count, matrilineal adat in West Sumatra has not given in to these disturbing forces, save for occasional accommodations. The resilience of the Minangkabau matriliny begged for an explanation. After spending some more time in the field, I decided to concentrate my subsequent efforts on this question.

The major task I set myself was to understand the nature of change and continuity in the Minangkabau matrilineal system, and the dynamic involved in the historical process of the society. Some conceptual clarifications, above all on the matrilineal system and on merantau, are in order.

In the assessment of change and continuity in the Minangkabau matrilineal system, much confusion has arisen from the failure to differentiate various aspects of matriliny. To treat the matrilineal system as a single entity and to discuss its change and continuity only lead to misunderstanding at best. For change observed in one aspect of the system (for example, inheritance) may not be accompanied by change in another (say, descent). Some aspects of mat-

riliny discussed specifically are the basis of descent group formation, the allocation of authority, the assignment of socioeconomic
obligations, inheritance practices, and residential arrangements.

Another important conceptual clarification is concerned with different meanings attached to the idea of change. An example may
serve to illustrate this point. It has sometimes been argued that the
increasing popularity of the inheritance practice from father to
children underlines the decline of matrilineal inheritance practice.
However, a close examination reveals that the newer practice almost exclusively applies to individually earned property (*harta
pencarian*) and rarely to ancestral property (*harta pusaka*). Change
in this case cannot be understood as the replacement of one practice
with another; it is a modification or accommodation, by which
inheritance practices become more elaborate and types of property
are differentiated, yet essentially without forgoing the matrilineal
principle. This conceptual distinction will become critical when I
later try to assess the continuity of the matrilineal system in contemporary Minangkabau society.

The term *merantau* means "to leave one's home village or home
country." This simple definition belies merantau's complexity as a
social and historical phenomenon. To begin with, we would wish to
know who leaves his or her home village for what reason, for how
long, and for what destination.

I propose that we can distinguish three types of merantau or
geographical mobility in Minangkabau history: village segmentation, circulatory merantau, and *merantau Cino* (Chinese merantau). These merantau types are roughly identified with three historical periods: village segmentation from the legendary period to the
early nineteenth century, circulatory merantau from the late
nineteenth century to the 1930s, and Chinese merantau from the
1950s to the present time. It is important to keep in mind that this
historical identification refers to the dominant pattern of geographical mobility during each period and that merantau types and historical periods are not mutually exclusive. Thus, for example, circulatory merantau and village segmentation still take place today,
although village segmentation is extremely rare.

Merantau for village segmentation is geographical mobility for
the sake of establishing a new settlement. It is generally motivated

by shortages of agricultural land and mounting population pressure. The related occupational pursuits are agricultural. The movement is carried out by a matrilineage or matrilineal sublineage under the leadership of a lineage head. The movement is meant to be permanent. Ties between the old settlement and the new one are sometimes maintained, but they are not an essential feature of village segmentation, particularly after a certain period of time has elapsed.

Circulatory merantau is carried out by individual males, married or unmarried. In addition to land shortage (the so-called push factor), mobility may be motivated by opportunities in the outside (pull factor) and by personal ambition. This type of merantau is directed to cities and towns within a relatively short distance. The occupations pursued are nonagricultural; these people are merchants, office workers, teachers, and artisans. Even if a man is married, his wife and children may be left behind in the village. His contact with his own village is frequent. He goes back home often, once or twice a year, in order to see his conjugal family and his maternal relatives. Geographical mobility is not permanent; the movement forms a circulatory arc between the external destination and one's home village.

Chinese merantau is generally, but not exclusively, associated with nuclear families. Nuclear families may migrate as a unit. A husband on migration may later send for his wife and children from the village. A bachelor on migration may eventually go home to get married in the village and take his bride to the destination of his migration. In either case, Chinese merantau has strong overtones of geographical mobility by nuclear families, already realized or yet to be realized. The movement covers a long distance and it is directed to large urban centers such as Jakarta. Pull as well as push factors are important elements in Chinese merantau, as in circulatory merantau. The typical occupational pursuits are not different from those of circulatory merantau, that is, they are nonagricultural. The psychological proximity of migrants to their home village tends to be close, but their physical contact is not frequent. The circulatory chain of movement between the village and the destination of merantau is weak or already broken. In this form of merantau, people often stay away from the village for a longer duration than in circulatory merantau and they seldom go home to visit. The mobility is semipermanent, not necessarily in intention but in consequence.[11]

These characterizations of merantau pertain to ideal types. In reality, separate aspects of the merantau types may occur in different combinations and permutations. Chinese merantau may involve more than a nuclear family, for example, a husband's or wife's parents. Circulatory merantau may involve migratory rubber tappers. Village segmentation may result in a fishing village instead of an agricultural village. Nevertheless, the merantau types have a certain logic. For instance, the period up to the early nineteenth century was associated with village segmentation, because internal and external circumstances surrounding the Minangkabau society of that time, such as the abundance of unopened land and the scarcity of opportunities for nonagricultural occupations, favored village segmentation as the dominant mode of geographical mobility. This does not mean, however, that circulatory merantau or Chinese merantau did not take place before the middle of the nineteenth century. The same precaution applies to succeeding historical periods.

The distinctions among the three merantau types and their identification with different historical periods is crucial, for the changing patterns of dominant merantau activities have much bearing on the persistence of Minangkabau matriliny. If the theme of the Minangkabau history is construed as the matrilineal system, its dynamic is merantau.

Methodologically, the study combines library research and survey research.[12] Although I tried to incorporate both indigenous Indonesian and Dutch written materials, my meager knowledge of Dutch made it difficult for me to exploit those sources fully. Aside from referring to written materials, I carried out three surveys in the

---

11. Circulatory merantau is occasionally referred to as *merantau pipit* or sparrow merantau. It is not clear when and how the term *"merantau Cino"* was coined. It apparently refers to the traditional pattern of Chinese migration in Indonesia. Although they entertained the idea of eventually going back home, typically they married locally and seldom returned to China.

12. The field research took place in West Sumatra between January 1972 and July 1973. I stayed in Sumatra for ten more months (mainly in Palembang and Bukittinggi) in the capacity of a senior specialist for the Sumatra Regional Planning Study of the Indonesian Ministry of Public Works and Power and the University of Bonn.

field. The first was a questionnaire addressed to 232 village heads in West Sumatra, the second a survey conducted among 395 male household heads in four villages near Bukittinggi, and the third a survey among seventy-five male migrants (household heads) who originally come from two of the four villages but now stay in Padang or in Pekan Baru (central Sumatra). The nature of these surveys will be discussed in more detail in Chapter 4. I also used published as well as unpublished results from previous surveys, for example, agricultural surveys of the West Sumatra Regional Planning Study.[13]

Finally, I should mention, as a warning to the reader, what this book does not seek to achieve. It deals with the Minangkabau from a male perspective. The surveys were conducted by a male researcher, primarily among Minangkabau men. Conspicuously missing is the perspective of women. Of the two most important components of Minangkabau society, adat and Islam, the latter is nowhere adequately treated. The focus is on the cultural dynamics of Minangkabau society; the description of Minangkabau political economy is not a main concern. The interaction between the village and migrants is a major topic, but it is examined from the viewpoint of the village, not from the migrants' perspective.

13. The study was sponsored by the Indonesian Ministry of Public Works and Power and the University of Bonn, and carried out in West Sumatra between 1971 and 1972.

2 / Traditional Minangkabau Society

The precise recording of historical events was by no means the forte of the Minangkabau. The patrilineal Toba Batak in North Sumatra can usually recall epidemics, wars, and village segmentations in terms of generations: ten generations ago, there was an epidemic, and our ancestors moved from the old settlement in the north to a new settlement across the river. This accuracy is rarely possible with the Minangkabau. It is generally believed that the Minangkabau did not have any indigenous writing system before the arrival of Islam (Datuk Maruhun Batuah and Bagindo Tanameh c. 1954:7; Datuk Nagari Basa 1966b:16–17). Arabic writing and calendrical systems must have been introduced to West Sumatra sometime after its Islamization, most probably in the late sixteenth or the early seventeenth century. However, they were seldom used to record history even thereafter.

Even though the Minangkabau developed little predilection for recording history, they have maintained a keen interest in "knowing" the origin of their race and the ideal form of their society. Instead of maintaining dynastic annals and chronicles, the Minangkabau have as a heritage from their past the *tambo* (literally, it seems, stories of old times or traditional historiography). The tambo, originally transmitted orally and later written in Arabic letters, is an assortment of origin stories and adat rules and regulations (*hukum adat*). The tambo describes the genesis of the Alam Minangkabau (the Minangkabau World), demarcates its boundaries, and specifies the relationship between the darek (the interior) and the rantau (the frontier). The tambo further explains the incep-

33

tion of adat, and details rules and regulations concerning the society, interpersonal relationships, and proper conduct.

The society the tambo describes is an ideal world; the rules and regulations it propagates are codes of ideal relations and proper behavior. The world of the tambo is nonhistoric but at the same time panhistoric. It is not grounded at any historical point in time, yet it is a master plan of the Minangkabau society and thus something against which the society at any moment may be judged. As some reports from the mid-nineteenth century to the early twentieth century show, this master plan was not evidently altogether about a dream world.[1]

There are many versions of the tambo which generally corroborate each other. Typically, the tambo starts with a story of the genesis of the Minangkabau World: "In the beginning there was only the Light of Muhammad (*Nur Muhammad*), through which God created this universe, 'the sky and the earth.' From the Light emanated angels and Adam, the first human being. Later God forced Adam and his offspring to live on earth, which was still undergoing the process of perfection" (Abdullah 1972a:183). Adam and Eve had thirty-nine children. Their sons and daughters married each other, except for the youngest son. He was to marry a nymph from paradise, for God willed his descendants to be the rulers of this world. He was named Iskandar Zulkarnain (Iskandar with the Two Horns) because of his golden horns which symbolized the two contrasts of his sovereign land, the East and the West, the North and the South.[2]

Iskandar Zulkarnain sired three sons. The eldest was called Maharaja Alif, the second Maharaja Depang, and the youngest Maharaja Diraja. After the death of their father, the three brothers

1. As Kahn (1976) argues, probably the type of traditional Minangkabau society described here was reinforced by the Dutch colonial government with its policy of forced cultivation of coffee in the middle of the nineteenth century. However, I find it difficult to agree that "the [Minangkabau] 'traditional' system was itself a product of external colonial domination of the Minangkabau social life" (ibid.: 93). In all fairness, it must be admitted that very little is known about Minangkabau society before the nineteenth century, and almost nothing of the period before the first European contact.

2. He was supposed to be Alexander the Great. The following version of the Minangkabau origin story was adapted from Datoek Batoeah Sango (c. 1966:14–23). See also Abdullah (1972a:183–184).

sailed to the east. When they arrived near Langkapuri (Sri Langka), there arose a dispute concerning who was the rightful owner of the royal crown left by Iskandar Zulkarnain. During the dispute the crown slipped from the hands of the three brothers and fell into the ocean. Catik Bilang Pandai, an able follower of Maharaja Diraja, had a replica of the crown made. He advised his master to assert his supremacy by announcing that he had retrieved the crown from the ocean. After the question of supremacy thus had been settled, the three brothers parted and left for separate destinations where they were to become rulers. Maharaja Alif went back to Ruhum (believed to be Turkey), Maharaja Depang went to China, and Maharaja Diraja to the Island of Perca or Andalas (Sumatra).

After visiting many countries, the Maharaja Diraja's party finally arrived at the highest place in the Island of Perca, that is, the summit of Gunung Merapi. There their boat went aground. Maharaja Diraja announced that whoever could repair the ship would be married to his daughter. The ship was restored in due course to its previous condition. In the meantime, four companions of Maharaja Diraja—a cat (*Kucing Siam*), a tigress (*Harimau Campo*), a goat (*Kambing Hutan*), and a dog (*Anjing Mu'lim*)—became pregnant. Later they each bore a daughter. Maharaja Diraja adopted the four daughters. After they matured, the daughters were married to the craftsmen who repaired the wrecked ship, for that was the promise of Maharaja Diraja.[3]

After some time, the sea receded. Gradually the dry land expanded, and Maharaja Diraja and his retinue descended from the summit of Gunung Merapi. At the foot of Merapi they opened a settlement, multiplied, and eventually founded the first *nagari* (village), Pariangan Padang Panjang. Rules and regulations were instituted and leaders elected. Datuk Katumanggungan and Datuk Perpatih nan Sebatang, descendants of Maharaja Diraja, consolidated two types of politico-legal traditions: Koto-Piliang (Chosen Words) and Bodi-Caniago (Valued Character) (Datoek Batoeah Sango:32). Koto Piliang is supposedly more autocratic in carrying out adat, having a hierarchy of authority. For example, matrilineage heads in

3. According to Rasjid Manggis (1971:15), the four animals stand for the names of places the Minangkabau originally came from, that is, Cochin (in mainland Southeast Asia), Champa, Cambay, and "Anjing Mu'lim" probably standing for an area somewhere between South India and Persia.

the Koto-Piliang tradition are hierarchically ranked according to their status and the lineage heads of the highest rank form the final body of deliberation in the village. In contrast, Bodi-Caniago is more democratic; there is no status distinction among lineage heads and final deliberations take place in the council meeting of all the village lineage heads together. As the population grew and multiplied, new settlements were created. Gradually the *alam* (world) was filled and the famous Alam Minangkabau was formed.[4]

Alam Minangkabau

Traditionally, the area under the sphere of Minangkabau influence is called Alam Minangkabau (the Minangkabau World). The Alam Minangkabau is divided into two regions: Luhak nan Tigo (Three Districts) or simply Luhak, and Rantau. The Luhak nan Tigo are the three central areas of West Sumatra, namely Luhak Tanah Datar, Luhak Agam, and Luhak 50 [Limapuluh] Kota.[5] Beyond this Minangkabau heartland is rantau, the frontier settlements later established by people from luhak and sometimes by people from outside the Alam Minangkabau (see Map 3). Rantau is an area which borders the outside world and through which new ideas and practices are introduced to the Alam (Abdullah 1972a:187).

Likened to the eldest brother of the three Luhak, Tanah Datar is historically the most important center of the Alam Minangkabau (Datuk Batuah:16). Pariangan Padang Panjang, the first nagari, is located in Tanah Datar. The area also accommodated the royal court and the seats of other important royal dignitaries: the Daulat Yang Dipertuan Raja Alam (King of the World) in Pagarruyung, the Raja Adat (King of Adat) in Buo, the Raja Ibadat (King of

4. There is an allusion to Noah's Ark in the epic of Maharaja Diraja. Marsden (1966:332) notes a story that Datuk Katumanggungan and Datuk Perpatih nan Sebatang were two of Noah's forty companions in the Ark. They are believed to be half-brothers born from the same mother (Datuk Batuah 1956:21–22). Concerning the process of the creation of the Koto-Piliang and Bodi-Caniago traditions, see Abdullah (1972a:186). These two traditions (*kelarasan*) of Koto-Piliang and Bodi-Caniago stand for the names of four original *suku* (matrilineal clans) in West Sumatra, i.e., Koto, Piliang, Bodi, and Caniago.

5. Luhak corresponds to the darek mentioned in Chapter 1. From now on, luhak and the darek are used interchangeably. The territorial boundaries of these luhak do not correspond to the present administrative boundaries of the districts of the same names, that is, the districts of Tanah Datar, Agam, and 50 Kota.

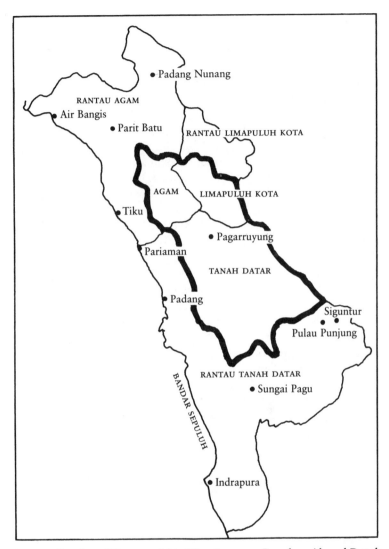

Map 3. Darek and Rantau within West Sumatra. Based on Ahmad Datuk Batuah, *Tambo Minangkabau dan Adatnya* (Jakarta: Balai Pustaka, 1956), p. 187, by permission of the publisher.

37

Religion) in Sumpur Kudus, and Basa nan Empat Balai (the Great Men of the Four Council Halls) (Josselin de Jong 1952:100–104).[6] The circumstances surrounding the inception of the Pagarruyung court are not altogether clear. It is believed that Adityavarman, apparently a Hinduized potentate of the fourteenth century, was most probably the first Minangkabau king and also the first to be associated with the Pagarruyung court (ibid.:96; Datuk Batuah:28; Mansoer et al. 1970:58). Adityavarman, whose surviving inscriptions cover the period between 1347 and 1375, seems to have been related, by birth, to the rulers of the Sumatran kingdom of Dharmasraya (Wolters 1970:58; Josselin de Jong:96; Rasjid Manggis:46).[7] He was raised at the Majapahit court of East Java, but, by the middle of the fourteenth century was back in Sumatra (Josselin de Jong:95–96). By the 1370s, the Minangkabau king, till then under the control of Majapahit, got rid of this Javanese overlordship (Wolters:62). If indeed Adityavarman was the first king at the Pagarruyung court, Minangkabau kingship was to last for about four hundred and fifty years, right up until the beginning of the nineteenth century when the Padri, fanatical Islamic reformists, practically annihilated the royal line.

Despite their long history, the general opinion is that the Minangkabau *raja* (kings) did not possess strong authority or power over the Alam Minangkabau, especially over the interior (Dobbin 1974:320; Loeb 1972:102). The raja seems to have been respected and revered, but nothing more (Raffles 1830:363). G. D. Willinck says the Minangkabau raja was "the poorest pretense of monarchs the world has known" (quoted by Josselin de Jong:22). Apparently, he did not own an extensive amount of land (Datuk Batuah:85; Francis 1860:71–72), did not or could not collect revenues from the villages in the interior (Datuk Batuah:85; Datoe' Sanggoeno Di Radjo 1919:177), and did not control an army (Loeb:102; Datoek Batoeah Sango:75). The main function of the

6. Sumpur Kudus is now located in the district of Sawahlunto/Sijunjung. According to the adat, it belongs to Luhak Tanah Datar. The three kings in theory formed a triumvirate whose head was the Daulat Yang Dipertuan Raja Alam. Basa nan Empat Balai are often likened to ministers of the royal court. Concerning their functions and those of the three kings (*Raja nan Tigo Selo*), see Datuk Batuah (pp. 34–38) and Josselin de Jong (pp. 100–104).

7. Rasjid Manggis (p. 46) associates the location of Dharmasraya with Siguntur in the southeastern part of West Sumatra.

raja vis-à-vis the darek was to act as arbiter in case of disputes and wars between villages (Josselin de Jong:107).[8]

There are indications that the raja may have had some measure of political and financial control over the rantau (the frontiers), particularly the trading ports.[9] Various tambo mention financial obligations of the rantau ports to Pagarruyung, mainly customs duties, harbor fees, and some types of sales tax and house tax (Datuk Batuah:85–86; Datoek Batoeah Sango:77–80; Datoe' Sanggoeno Di Radjo 1919:175–177). Francis (1860:72) also states that the raja received tributes from Siak, Batang Hari, Palembang, Jambi, and Indragiri—all harbor ports in eastern Sumatra.

The Minangkabau raja maintained a special relationship with minor raja who were placed at the ports of entrance to the Alam Minangkabau. The latter were usually members of the royal family sent out by the Pagarruyung court, or they were local chiefs given royal appointments.[10] Some of the notable minor raja were located in Padang Nunang, Parit Batu (both in the north), Air Bangis, Tiku, Pariaman, Bandar Sepuluh, Indrapura (all on the west coast), Sungai Pagu, Pulau Punjung, and Siguntur (all in the south and well-connected to upper tributaries of the Batang Hari)(Datoek Batoeah Sango:93–95; Datoek Madjolelo and Marzoeki 1951:24–25; Parlindungan 1964:525–527) (see Map 3).[11] As representatives of the Pagarruyung court, they were to collect revenues for the raja. Ac-

8. One gets the impression that kingship lasted for a long time precisely because the raja had no strong authority or power, and because there was no external or internal aggression threatening to overthrow kings. Together with its historical inception, the nature and function of Minangkabau kingship ought to be an important topic of historical studies in the future. For a recent attempt of this nature, see Dobbin (1977).

9. From early times, the Minangkabau kings were involved in trade. The capital of the famed maritime kingdom of Srivijaya is supposed to have shifted from Palembang to Malayu-Jambi in the late eleventh century. Under yet unknown circumstances, the latter itself later came under the control of the Minangkabau king—a development which may have taken place towards the end of the fourteenth century, during the reign of Adityavarman (Wolters:90; Hall 1970:30). How long the Minangkabau control of Malayu-Jambi lasted is not certain. Most probably this rather strange situation of maritime trade being under an inland king relatively isolated from major riverine routes did not continue very long (Hall:88).

10. For example, the raja of Pulau Punjung was a local chief appointed by the court, while the raja of Sungai Pagu was related to the royal family (Datoek Batoeah Sango:93).

11. Padang Nunang and Parit Batu were not ports but were situated between the Minangkabau area and the Manda(h)iling area to the north.

cording to Datoek Batoeah Sango (p. 77), the Minangkabau raja or his representatives traveled from one rantau port to another in order to collect these revenues once every three years. However, it seems that in reality actual revenue collection was seldom possible (Datoe' Sanggoeno Di Radjo 1919:177).

While the political and economic significance of the Minangkabau raja is in doubt, his symbolic role as unifier of the Alam Minangkabau is acknowledged by Josselin de Jong. He says: "Jangdipatuan's [raja's] duties were mainly of a sacred nature. He imparted *daulat* [sovereignty] to the country and embodied the unity of the Minangkabau World as the whole" (p. 108). The symbolic role of the raja was often manifested in cases which involved defining the sphere of the Alam Minangkabau.

According to the tambo of Datoek Batoeah Sango (p. 95), ever since the end of the sixteenth century, the Batak were penetrating southward into the Minangkabau area, down to Rao, and sometimes even to Lubuk Sikaping (see Map 1). Yang Dipertuan, the raja, issued an order to the inhabitants of Rao that the Batak be expelled but to no avail. Finally, the representative of Rao came to Pagarruyung to appeal their plight directly to the raja. In response, he sent a member of the royal family (later the Yang Dipertuan of Padang Nunang) to Rao with an appointment as raja of the northern border. Such border areas as Kepenuhan, Tambusai/Rambah, and Rokan IV Koto to the east also received royal kinsmen as raja in response to their requests to the court (Pemerintah Daerah Propinsi Sumatera Tengah c. 1955:see the section on Kampar). In 1677, three Minangkabau settlements in the western Malay peninsula (Rembau, Sungai Ujong, and Naning) appealed to Pagarruyung that a raja be sent to be their ruler. As a result, Raja Ibrahim was sent by the Yang Dipertuan (Andaya 1975:109). (For the locations of some of these places, see Map 2.) These cases underline the role of the Minangkabau raja as definer of the sphere of the Alam Minangkabau.

The rantau ports may well have been important sources of the raja's revenues in the past. Their significance to the Alam Minangkabau, on the other hand, was that the rantau ports were also "border points" which divided Alam from non-Alam. By sending out royal kinsmen and by appointing royal representatives among the local chiefs, the Minangkabau raja bestowed his sovereignty (*daulat*) on the strategic rantau ports of entrance to the Alam Minangkabau. The kingship demarcated, defined, and possibly defended the contour and sphere of the Minangkabau World. In this, "superstitious veneration" of the raja was the major factor, not an organized bureaucracy nor an army.[12]

In whatever way this kingship may have come to existence, it was certainly peculiar in its function in the Malay world. Unlike other Malay kings who usually established their centers near the mouths of large rivers, the Minangkabau raja resided in the interior (Marsden 1966:325). In many respects, the Malay king embodied the state (*negeri*). Not infrequently a Malay king could and did move his center of power from one area to another; in such cases, the state followed the geographical mobility of the king. There is a Malay saying that "Adat is managed by the raja and it is the raja who follows adat. Where there is a raja, there adat exists. When the raja disappears, adat will die too."[13] Such a formulation is alien to the Minangkabau. The Yang Dipertuan was not the Alam Minangkabau, but only a part of it. What he defined was not a kingdom (*kerajaan*) but the Alam Minangkabau. Minangkabau history is not a pedigree of successive raja but the tambo, which incorporates the story of the origin of the Alam and its expansion, the rules and regulations of proper conduct, and the demarcation of the Alam.

The Nagari

Delineated by natural or man-made boundaries (Datuk Batuah:84), the nagari (village) is a territorial unit with its own political and judicial apparatus.[14] It is the highest order of human

12. Marsden (1966:376–377) says "they [Battas in the north] have a superstitious veneration for the sultan of Menangkabau." Concerning the widely shared belief among the Minangkabau and Malays in the supernatural power of the Pagarruyung raja, see Andaya (pp. 109, 274, n. 17), Marsden (1966:345), and Reber (1977:180).

13. In Indonesian, *Adat dipegang oleh radja/dan radjalah jang beradat./Ada radja, adat berdiri,/hilang radja, adatpun mati.* This is an adat saying from island Riau (Kementerian Penerangan c. 1954:1049).

14. This section and the next two (on the matrilineal system and social stratification) refer to the Minangkabau society of the past, extrapolated mainly from the tambo in ideal form. Although the description is sometimes given in the present tense in order to avoid always using the past tense, it should be remembered that some of the description does not apply to contemporary Minangkabau society.

settlement acknowledged by the adat. To be a nagari, a settlement
has to possess facilities such as road communications, a public
bathing place, a council hall, a mosque, and an open field for
amusement and sports (Datoe' Sanggoeno Di Radjo 1919:96).
Supported by wet-rice cultivation, the population of the nagari has
never been of meager size (Raffles:349, 363). In the late seventeenth
century, Tomas Dias, who actually visited the interior, reported a
figure of 8,000 people living at the court of Pagarruyung (An-
daya:111). In another record from the same period, a Dutch official
in Padang listed the following population estimates of five interior
nagari: 1,000 in Menangkabau ("where the emperor lived"), 4,000
in Suruasso, 10,000 in Padang Ganting, and 1,000 in Sungai Tarab
(ibid.).[15] In comparison, the population size of the Southern Batak's
huta, the primary village unit, in the 1840s was around 200 in
Angkola and Sipirok, and 350 to 400 in Mandahiling (Castles
1972:20); these areas are all immediately to the north of West
Sumatra. The average population of the nagari in West Sumatra in
1922 was about 2,400; the range was from 250 to 16,000 (Oki
1977:1). The corresponding figure in present-day West Sumatra is
more than 4,500, ranging between 230 and 39,000 (1971 census).
Rather than being evenly dispersed, the nagari population is usually
concentrated in several settlements within the village.

A concomitant of the lack of centralized political power in the
Alam Minangkabau was the strong autonomy generally attributed
to the nagari, which is often characterized as a village republic
(Abdullah 1972a:185, n. 7). Political and judicial power was indeed
essentially contained within the nagari, and specific adat regulations applied only to a particular village (*adat selingkung nagari*
or adat is [only valid] within a nagari) (Datoek Madjolelo and
Marzoeki:22).[16] An adat aphorism of the Jambi Sultanate (in eastern
central Sumatra) says:

> The world has a raja,
> The outer area has a deputy of a raja,

15. It is not clear if "Menangkabau" refers to the Pagarruyung court or to the
village of Minangkabau near Batu Sangkar.
16. There were (are) sometimes federations of several villages, e.g., IV Koto near
Bukittinggi which includes the four nagari of Kota Gedang, Sianok, Guguk and
Tabek Sarojo. The nagari within one federation often have similar historical origins

> The village has a village head,
> The hamlet has a chief,
> The house has an elder.[17]

A Minangkabau equivalent to this aphorism is:

> The nagari has four suku,
> The suku has a lineage,
> The settlement has a chief,
> The house has an elder.[18]

Presumably the two aphorisms describe the internal organization of society. But one starts with the world and a raja, while the highest level of concern for the other is the nagari.

The self-containment of the nagari has historically produced a high degree of regional variability in customs and traditions within West Sumatra. Interpretation and application of the adat differ from area to area, although "adat that is truly adat," meaning the matrilineal system, the central position of matrilineage heads, and the existence of suku in the nagari (Abdullah 1972a:190), is shared. Adat costumes, house styles, and rituals vary. The languages of different regions have slightly variable inflections, accents, and sometimes vocabulary. This variability is also observed in internal social organization of the nagari.

The nagari consists of different levels and units of matrilineal groupings. There is considerable confusion in identifying and interpreting these levels and units, as Josselin de Jong found after conducting an exhaustive review of the literature on Minangkabau society. Except for general agreement on the highest level and largest unit, the suku (matrilineal clan), and the lowest level and smallest unit, the *samandai* (mother and her children), various

---

and adat. The federation does not have any political or judicial power to interfere in the internal affairs of a member nagari unless it is requested to do so by the nagari concerned.

17. This is a somewhat freely translated version of the aphorism: *Alam mempunjai radja,/Rantau mempunjai djenang,/Negeri mempunjai batin,/Kampung mempunjai penghulu,/Rumah mempunjai tengganai.* See Kementerian Penerangan (p. 1024).

18. This is also somewhat freely translated from the following Minangkabau aphorism: *Nagari nan bakaampé suku,/Suku nan babuah parui,/Kampuang nan batuo,/Sarato rumah nan batungganai.* See Datoe' Sanggoeno Di Radjo (1955:57). *Suku* is a matrilineal clan.

scholars and various regions apply different meanings to such terms as *kampueng* (settlement or clan), *kaum* (group), *jurai* (section), *payung* (umbrella), and *paruik* (belly or womb).[19] Rather than trying to disentangle this probably insoluble terminological confusion, I will discuss three levels and units of matrilineal groupings within the nagari which are essential to the understanding of any nagari in the Minangkabau society, that is, *(sa-)paruik, (sa-)payung,* and *(sa-)suku* in ascending order.[20] In the simplest understanding of these terms, saparuik is a group of related people generally living in one house, sapayung is a group of related houses under the supervision of a lineage head *(penghulu)* and sasuku a group of related lineages who share a common, unknown ancestress (Sutan Mangkuto n.d.:50).

Saparuik (sublineage) literally means people of one womb. It "generally makes the impression of being the most important functional unit" (Josselin de Jong:11). The saparuik is usually associated with a group of people living in one *rumah adat* (adat house) or *rumah gadang* (large house). Supposing that three generations of people are alive and stay in one place, an adat house in theory accommodates the people described in Figure 1. Those who live in the house are all the female house members and the younger boys. Adult male house members belong to the adat house but do not live there. The husbands of the female house members stay at night at the adat house but do not belong to it. The size of one saparuik or one adat house depends on the financial capacity and the proliferation of the group concerned. If an adat house actually accommodates three generations, its size may become very large

---

19. Concerning the different meanings of these and other terms, see Josselin de Jong (pp. 49–55). The meaning of suku can sometimes be complicated (Kahn 1976:66–68).

20. The prefix "sa-" attached to a noun means "people of" or "a group of one . . ." For example, saparuik means people of one womb. The three groupings of *paruik, payung,* and *suku* may be called by different names in different regions. Conversely, these terms may denote different units and levels of groupings in various regions than the ones discussed here. We have to keep it in mind that these particular Minangkabau terms are specifically applied to the levels and units of groupings under discussion in the present context. Since I am mainly concerned with understanding the general organization of matrilineal groupings, I do not refer to exceptions and deviations from my model more than minimally necessary. In the subsequent discussion, the English terms sublineage, lineage, and clan are used for, respectively (sa-)paruik, (sa-)payung, and (sa-)suku.

Figure 1. Members of an adat house: An ideal case

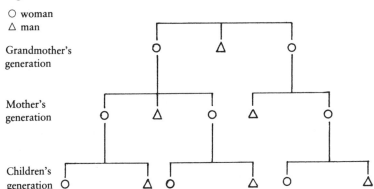

indeed. In the nineteenth century, Verkerk Pistorius (1871:39–40), a Dutch official, found close to sixty people and sometimes eighty people per house around the Kota VII area (Sijunjung). He further reports that one house in Alahan Panjang accommodated more than 100 people. According to Muhamad Radjab's autobiography (1950:4–5), his native house in Sumpur was 16 meters long and 8 meters wide, with the floor 2.5 meters above the ground. At the time of his childhood (around 1910s), the house had seven sleeping quarters (bilik) occupied by seven married female members. Altogether there were about forty people living in the house.[21]

The head of a saparuik is a tungganai or mamak rumah (house elder) who is generally the eldest male member of the house (grandmother's brother in Figure 1) (Josselin de Jong:10). He is responsible for the conduct, welfare, and harmony of his saparuik. Specifically, he is responsible and obliged, both externally (vis-à-vis other saparuik) and internally, to look after and protect all the saparuik properties according to the adat. Together with other male house members, he is also expected to increase the properties of his saparuik and to ensure its prosperity.

As the members of a saparuik multiply, people move from the original adat house to separate houses. A group of related houses

21. The length of his house (16 meters) seems a little short, since it allows only a little over two meters for each bilik.

originating through paruik segmentation is called *sapayung* (Josselin de Jong:11).[22] The meaning of payung is an umbrella and sapayung is a group of people under the protection of a lineage head (*penghulu*). Houses under sapayung are likely to be clustered together within one compound or area of the nagari as long as the necessary land for settlement is available.[23]

The method of accession to penghuluship is not uniform. The position may be occupied by the eldest male member of the original paruik or by a member of each paruik within a sapayung in rotation. In the latter case it means that if, for instance, there are four paruik in a sapayung, the first paruik to occupy the penghulu position will not obtain access to it until the other three paruik have had their chance. Compared to a tungganai (house elder), a penghulu is a position recognized nagari-wide. Installation as penghulu requires an elaborate ceremony; often water buffaloes are slaughtered for the occasion and village notables are invited to witness and sanction the installation (Rasjid Manggis:74). Depending on the region, a penghulu may or may not be replaced before his death.

A penghulu's duties are equivalent to those of a tungganai, only at a higher level. In some nagari, he is assisted in the execution of his duties by three other adat functionaries: *manti,* the secretary of the penghulu; *malim,* an Islamic functionary according to the adat; and *dubalang,* a security guard as well as watchman over the conduct of lineage members (Josselin de Jong:51; Kemal 1964:97–100).[24] But in no sense does the penghulu rule over his payung. Generally, if a problem not solved at the paruik level is referred to him, the penghulu will act as advisor or arbitrator, or sometimes as judge.

22. However, Josselin de Jong uses the term *kampueng* instead of payung.

23. See, for example, the clustering of housing compounds in the present Nagari Kota Gedang (Graves 1971: map on p. 43). Sometimes, a distinction is made between different types of *penghulu,* e.g., *penghulu pucuk* (chief penghulu) and *penghulu andiko* (common penghulu). This distinction is not crucial for the present discussion.

24. Together with the penghulu, these functionaries are called *orang empat jenis* (men of four kinds). This system is usually associated with villages of the Koto-Piliang tradition. Other than *orang empat jenis,* there is, in some villages, a position called *penungkek,* or deputy of penghulu (Rasjid Manggis:74). Villages of the Bodi-Caniago tradition usually have three adat functionaries (*orang tiga jenis* or men of three kinds), namely, *ninik mamak* (penghulu), *cerdik pandai* ("intellectuals"), and *alim ulama* (Islamic sages).

The suku is a matrilineal clan, each with its distinctive name, such as Melayu, Piliang, and Caniago. It is said that suku originally meant a "quarter" and that every nagari must have at least four suku to be complete (Rasjid Manggis:53–54; Datuk Maruhun Batuah and Bagindo Tanameh:20). My own experience in West Sumatra indicates that the number of suku in the nagari varies between two and twenty-five, although it is rare that the nagari has less than four or more than ten suku. The members of a suku are believed to be descendents of a common, unknown ancestress. Ideally, two members of the same suku may not marry either within or outside the nagari (Datuk Batuah:75; Loeb:113). The actual situation, however, shows considerable regional variation. The rule of thumb, in my experience, is that even if two members of one suku marry, suku exogamy within the same payung is strictly upheld. Violation of this prohibition was often penalized by expulsion from the nagari in the past (Sjafnir et al. 1973:15).

According to the Westenenk's count (quoted by Josselin de Jong:67), there are some 100 suku found in West Sumatra. Theoretically, these suku fall into the four major groups of the original suku, Koto, Piliang, Bodi, and Caniago, which in turn are grouped into the previously mentioned two types of political tradition, Koto-Piliang and Bodi-Caniago (Sutan Mangkuto:12–13). That is, if we start from the top, all Minangkabau suku are subsumed under one of the two kelarasan (political traditions) of Koto-Piliang and Bodi-Caniago. The two kelarasan are further subdivided into four major suku, Koto, Piliang, Bodi, and Caniago. Each major suku in turn subsumes its own suku members underneath (for details, see the example of Piliang in Figure 2).[25]

The geographical distribution of various suku is not uniform within West Sumatra. Large suku such as Piliang, Melayu, and Caniago are found in virtually every part of West Sumatra, spreading even beyond the provincial boundary. In contrast, some suku exist only in several nagari and even, in a few cases, in a single nagari. There is no suku chief who presides beyond the confines of the nagari, let alone in all of West Sumatra.

---

25. Strictly speaking, the two major suku groupings are not equivalent to the two kelarasan even though they use the same names. The suku which belong to the major suku group of Koto-Piliang may be found in villages of the Bodi-Caniago political tradition, and vice versa.

Figure 2. Structure of suku affiliation: The example of Piliang

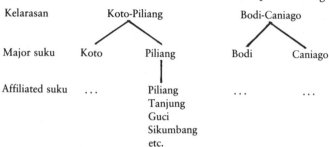

A suku usually consists of more than one payung. The actual number of payung under one suku depends on the proliferation of suku members and on the regulations in the respective nagari. The formation of a new payung depends on how difficult it is to create a new penghulu position; it is more difficult to do so in some nagari than in others. In general, the larger the suku membership, the more payung. In some cases one finds only one penghulu for each suku in the nagari owing to a specific regulation used in the nagari.[26]

In the old days, the members of a suku may have lived in the same vicinity, thus forming a loosely integrated territorial unit within the nagari. However, the growth of suku membership must have militated against maintaining this territorial characteristic. Together with the paruik and the payung, the suku is primarily a genealogical unit. These matrilineal groupings, however, incorporate adopted members who are not related by blood. Adoption, which requires a proper ceremony, usually takes place when an outsider wishes to be a new member of the nagari (Datoek Madjolelo and Marzoeki:5; Bachtiar 1967:373-374). If the outsider's original suku exists in his new nagari, he seeks affiliation with this suku. In case the same suku is not available, he is adopted by a suku in the same suku-group as his own (Rasjid Manggis:54). For instance, if the outsider belongs to suku Sikumbang and if this suku does not exist in his new village, he is more likely to be adopted by another of the Piliang suku group, for example, Piliang or Guci, rather than by

---

26. Even in this case, a suku usually has more than one payung, for other adat functionaries than a penghulu tend to have their own payung under this circumstance. Concerning conditions for the creation of a new penghulu position, see Rasjid Manggis (pp. 71-73), and Datuk Maruhun Batuah and Bagindo Tanameh (p. 22).

suku Koto, and not at all likely to be adopted by suku Bodi or Caniago. Oftentimes, adopted members may use ancestral land but are not entitled to the position of penghulu (Datuk Radjo Penghulu 1972:59). Adoption for the sake of avoiding lineage extinction does not seem to exist (Sihombing 1968:73). (However, see Benda-Beckmann 1979:62, 292–293, for the contrary information.)

Politically and judicially the highest authority resides in the nagari adat council (*kerapatan adat nagari*), attended by the penghulu and other functionaries, the *malim, manti,* and *dubalang* mentioned before (Anwar 1967:38–40). This body arbitrates in disputes (both criminal and civil cases) not resolved at a lower level and decides on matters concerned with the nagari. The nagari adat meeting is held at a special council hall (*balai*), which is modeled like a Minangkabau adat house. The style of the council hall is supposed to reflect the difference between the two Minangkabau political traditions. In the Bodi-Caniago nagari, the council hall has a level floor, signifying that all council participants sit on the same level and that there are no status distinctions among the penghulu. The council hall of the Koto-Piliang nagari has the two ends of the building raised higher than the middle, indicating the status difference between those who sit above and below; penghulu of higher rank sit at the raised ends presiding over common penghulu who sit in the middle (Rasjid Manggis:77–80).[27]

Suku, payung, and paruik (their relationships are summarized in Figure 3) classify nagari members according to a descending order of matrilineal groupings. A nagari consists of multiple suku, a suku consists of multiple payung, and a payung consists of multiple paruik, each unit with its head.[28] These groupings are essentially categories which comprise the microcosm of the nagari, and do not describe what takes place within it. In order to understand how the people interacted and related to each other in the traditional Minangkabau society, it is necessary to review the family system and an institution

27. This correlation between the architecture of council halls and political traditions is not perfect any more, since some nagari shifted from one tradition to another without changing the style of their council hall.
28. The term "head" should be understood as *primus inter pares* in exercising political and judicial power. A raja as the head of a nagari was sometimes found in the rantau, while a penghulu suku as head of a suku existed in some nagari of the Koto-Piliang tradition. In either case, final deliberations usually took place at the nagari adat council or at the suku adat council, which incorporated all the lineage heads within the nagari or suku.

Figure 3. Relation between suku, payung, and paruik in the nagari

Unit   Head of unit

Nagari   (Raja)

Suku   (Penghulu suku)

Payung   Penghulu

Paruik   Tungganai

closely linked to it in traditional society, the system of social stratification.

The Matrilineal System

According to the tambo, the origin of the matrilineal system is explained as follows:[29]

In ancient times, property used to be given to one's children instead of to (sororal) nieces and nephews. One day, Datuk Katumanggungan and Datuk Perpatih nan Sebatang, the two founders of the Minangkabau adat, wished to go to Aceh in North Sumatra. After they sailed out from the port of Tiku/Pariaman on the west coast, the sea suddenly ebbed, for that was the divine decree of God. As a consequence, their ship ran aground on the sand. The two Datuk gathered all of their children, nieces and nephews, and said "Hai, children, nieces and nephews, let us haul this ship because it ran aground on the sand." Their children answered "We are afraid that we will be run over by the ship." Their nieces and nephews replied "If that is the wish of our elders, let us tow the ship. It does not matter even if we might be run over by the ship and killed in the process, for it is the ship of our elders that ran aground." Thus all the nieces and nephews got off on to the sand and pulled the ship. By the assistance of the spirits, the ship floated

29. This version is adopted from Datoe' Sanggoeno Di Radjo (1919:95–96). See also Josselin de Jong (p. 89).

again of itself, and moved to the middle of the sea. Later, following the advice of Cati Bilang Pandai, their able servant, the two Datuk decreed that from that time on all the property be given to the (sororal) nieces and nephews as a reward of their services, instead of to the children.

Other than the fact that the tambo seemingly tries both to reconcile the contradiction between patrilineally-oriented Islam and matriliny and to justify the origin of the matrilineal system, this story is remarkable in the sense that matriliny is explained in terms of inheritance. As Verkerk Pistorius (p. 30) observed more than a hundred years ago, property rights and inheritance law are among the most crucial elements in the Minangkabau matrilineal system.

There are four readily identifiable characteristics of the traditional Minangkabau matrilineal system.

Descent and descent group formation are organized according to the female line. Except for the special case of adoption, one takes after the previously mentioned paruik (sublineage), payung (lineage), and suku (clan) of one's mother, and remains with these groups throughout one's life.

A payung is a corporate descent group with a ceremonially instituted male head, the penghulu. A lineage possesses communally owned properties, including agricultural land, ancestral treasures, and miscellaneous adat titles.[30] In principle, ancestral property (harta pusaka) is inalienable and there is no individually owned property, particularly of an immovable nature. As described before, a sublineage under the payung also has its properly recognized male head, tungganai (house elder). Ancestral properties, or more accurately their usage rights (ganggam bauntuak), are assigned to sublineages for the benefit of their respective members (for more details, see Benda-Beckmann:154–159). Sublineages also control houses and fishponds as their own ancestral properties.

The residential pattern is uxorilocal (matrilocal) or, more strictly speaking, duolocal. After marriage, a husband moves to or near his wife's house and stays there at night. However, he still continues to belong to his mother's house. He frequently goes back there during the daytime.

---

30. All men are supposed to inherit an adat title of their lineage upon their marriage.

Authority within a lineage or a sublineage is in the hands of the *mamak*, not of the father. Mamak literally means "maternal uncle" but it can also refer to classificatory maternal uncles such as a penghulu or a tungganai. The kin term which contrasts with mamak is *kemanakan*: it indicates a male ego's sister's children (sororal nieces and nephews) and classificatory kin of the same order.

These general characterizations will become clearer if we look at how actual family life was organized in traditional Minangkabau society. Because daily family life was centered around an adat house, we start with a description of this communal type of housing.

An adat house is a rectangular wooden structure with a roof curved like buffalo horns (Figure 4).[31] Folk etymology tells us that Minangkabau is derived from *Menang Kerbau*, namely a winning *kerbau* (water buffalo). According to the legend, once, a long time ago, the Minangkabau fended off a Javanese attack by defeating the invaders in a buffalo fight. The Javanese brought in a huge buffalo, while the Minangkabau, unable to match it in size, prepared a hungry, suckling buffalo calf with sharp knives tied to its horns. When put into the fighting arena, the baby buffalo, thinking that his opponent was his mother, ran up to it and put his head under its belly to suck. The Javanese buffalo died of its wounds, the Minangkabau were spared from the Javanese attack, and the shape of the roof of an adat house is supposed to commemorate this legendary feat (Datoe' Sanggoeno Di Radjo 1919:41–42).[32]

The house is supported by numerous pillars made of ironwood (*kayu besi*) "which can stand for one hundred years" (Radjab 1950:4). The proper roof material is palm fiber but corrugated iron plate had already made considerable headway among the villagers by 1907, according to one travel account (Kiyono 1943:283). Facing toward the east (Rasjid Manggis:22), the front side of the house is often decorated with colorful carvings, usually of plant motifs.[33]

---

31. Further descriptions of an adat house are found in Radjab (1969:21–23) and Bachtiar (pp. 357–358).
    32. Another story says that the adat house is modeled after the ship which arrived at the summit of Mount Merapi (Datoek Batoeah Sango:28).
    33. However, Radjab (1969:21) mentions that the house may face either east or west. Concerning some of the motifs, see Sutan Mangkuto (pp. 178–179).

Figure 4. Adat house and granary

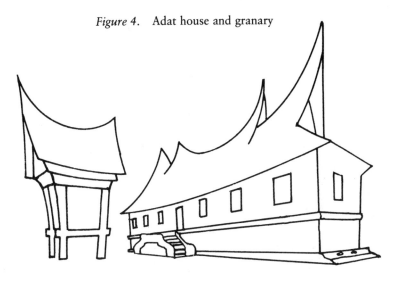

Under the raised house floor chickens, goats, and other domestic animals are kept.

As shown in Figure 5, the adat house has two parts. The front half is an open space (*tangah rumah*). It functions as living room, dining room, sleeping quarters for children, elderly women, and occasional guests, and hall for ceremonies as well as lineage meetings. The back half is partitioned into small compartments. These are the sleeping quarters for the women of the house, especially married or marriageable females, and for their smaller children. The sleeping compartments, called *bilik,* are about three meters wide and four meters long. Depending on the wealth and the size of the paruik, the number of bilik in an adat house varies. The largest adat house still standing in West Sumatra is 120 meters long and 15 meters wide, and contains 20 bilik. However, starting from three, the usual mode seems to be around seven bilik per adat house (Junus 1971:248).[34]

34. The largest adat house in West Sumatra is described in "Rumah Gadang Di Sulit Air," *Aneka Minang,* no. 5 (n.d.), p. 9. Note that the house is exceedingly long considering the number of bilik. As far as I know, a house this large has never existed

Figure 5. Plan of adat house

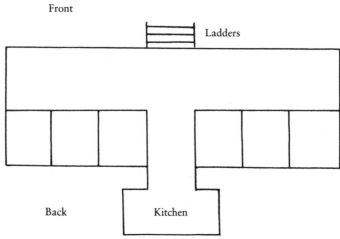

The construction of an adat house is not simply an affair of the individual paruik concerned. In theory, a new adat house implies a segmentation of the paruik. In addition, the physical requirements of construction necessitate cooperation from a wider circle. For example, trees for the central pillars have to be cut down and brought out from the forest—a task which is impossible without the assistance of many people. To secure such cooperation and to legitimize paruik segmentation, proper procedures according to the adat have to be followed. Agreement on the construction should be reached beforehand within the paruik and payung concerned. Notice of the intention to build a house must be given to other payung (Datoek Batoeah Sango:183–184). Even today, in areas such as Nagari Piobang in 50 Kota, a special announcement procession goes through the village before an adat house is built. Accompanied by escorts and traditional muscial instruments, the proces-

---

outside of Nagari Sulit Air. Figure 5 is drawn from the description of Radjab (1969: 22–23). According to Sutan Mangkuto (p. 65), the house in the Koto-Piliang nagari has raised annexes at both ends of the house (much like a council hall of the Koto-Piliang nagari) and the ladder is found at the front center of the house; in the houses of the Bodi-Caniago nagari, the ladder and the kitchen are attached to the side of the house. Concerning the elaborate seating arrangements in the hall during ceremonies and lineage meetings, see Sjafnir et al. (p. 37).

sion is headed by a woman, dressed in bridal costume, for whom the house is built.[35] An adat house was the basic economic unit and the major focus of everyday life in traditional Minangkabau society. In all likelihood, *ganggam bauntuak* (usage rights) were given to each adat house for its members' living (Josselin de Jong:55). Ganggam bauntuak is the right to use ancestral land and to enjoy its produce; it is not a right of ownership and its division is not an ultimate division (there is no right of disposition) (Anwar:89; Rasjid Manggis:57; Datoek Batoeah Sango:135).

Land in the nagari is classified into two types: *hutan tinggi* (unopened land) and *hutan rendah* (cultivated land) (Datuk Maruhun Batuah and Bagindo Tanemeh:41–55). There are four ways to obtain access to *hutan rendah:* by inheritance, by golden spade (gold or money), by iron spade (labor), and by gift (*hibah*) (ibid.:48; Rasjid Manggis:135). The land "obtained" by inheritance is harta pusaka (ancestral property) and it passes through the maternal line. Newly opened land (by iron spade) becomes harta pusaka after one generation (Josselin de Jong:57; Datuk Batuah:82–83). Likewise, land by golden spade (purchased land) turns into harta pusaka at the second generation from its original purchaser (Datuk Maruhun Batuah and Bagindo Tanameh:51). New harta pusaka is called *harta pusaka rendah* (low ancestral property) in contrast to old harta pusaka (*harta pusaka tinggi* or high ancestral property) (Jahja 1968:85).

Hibah generally takes place between a father and his children. If a man wishes to make certain that his individually earned property (property accumulated by his own effort in the form either of money or of labor) is given to his children instead of his kemanakan (sororal nieces and nephews), he may arrange the transference through *hibah* while he is still alive. However, *hibah* requires the agreement of all parties concerned, including one's kemanakan, as well as expensive feasts, and it does not seem to have been very common.[36] To all intents and purposes, harta pusaka was the most important source of livelihood for the members of an adat house in traditional Minangkabau society (Verkerk Pistorius:45).

35. "Batagak Rumah Di Piobang," *Aneka Minang*, no. 4 (n.d.), p. 20.
36. Verkerk Pistorius (pp. 45–46) says that in the Kota VII area (Sijunjung) there had been no case of hibah for the last twenty years (his book was published in 1871).

Although harta pusaka also includes cattle, fishponds, heirlooms, and adat titles (*gala*), agricultural land is the most crucial in economic terms. In principle, harta pusaka is inalienable. However, with the consent of the people concerned, it may be pledged (*gadai* or *sando*) or sometimes sold, provided that there is no other alternative, for a funeral, to marry off a marriageable girl, to repair or to build an adat house, and to inaugurate a newly appointed penghulu (Rasjid Manggis:56). Ideally, the offer of transference should be made to the closest paruik or to the closest payung within the same suku (Datoek Batoeah Sango:134).[37]

Supported by harta pusaka, life in an adat house was highly communal. Most probably, members of the same house cultivated the agricultural land allotted to them together. All produce, mainly rice, was stored in granaries, which were shaped like adat houses and were found in front of the house. A proper adat house should be equipped with three rice granaries: one for the daily use of house members, one for feeding guests and passers-by, and another for ceremonies and special necessities (Sutan Mangkuto:47).[38] The communal and corporate nature of life is reflected in a famous Minangkabau adat aphorism:

> Sharing slights, sharing shames,
> Sharing burial sites, sharing graveyards,
> If going up a hill, climbing together,
> If going down a gully, descending together,
> Jingling clearly like iron,
> Chirping in unison like chickens,
> If there is a good news, relayed from house to house,
> If there is a bad news, immediately coming to help.[39]

After reaching marriageable age or upon marriage, a woman is given bilik (compartment) in the house. If there is not enough room in the house, it is her mamak's responsibility either to enlarge the

37. It is significant three of the four conditions are all concerned with the continuity of a lineage; the marriage of a female member, the maintenance of an adat house, and the installation of a lineage leader are all important for this purpose.

38. As Radjab (1969:23) suggests, women of the same adat house may have cooked and eaten together in times past.

39. In Minangkabau, *Sahino, samalu, sapandam, sapakuburan,/Kok ka bukik samo-samo mandaki,/Kok ka lurah samo-samo manurun,/Sadantjiang bak basi,/ Satjiok bak ajam,/Kaba baiak baimbauan,/Kaba buruak bahambauan.*

house or to build an additional adat house for her (Josselin de
Jong:11; Sutan Mangkuto:206). It is in the bilik that she receives
her husband at night. Marriage is not an individual affair of the two
persons involved. Various mamak, fathers, mothers, and other relatives participate in the process of choosing a proper marriage part-
ner. Proposals may be made either from the bride's side or from the
groom's, depending on the region (Sjafnir et al.:20, 27-33).[40] The
most desirable marriage is between matrilateral cross-cousins, that
is, a man marries his mamak's daughter, and sometimes between
patrilateral cross-cousins, a man marries his father's sister's daughter (Josselin de Jong:61–62).[41]

A husband is called *urang sumando* or *sumando* by his wife's
family. *Sumando* is supposed to originate from the word *sando,*
"to pledge" (Radjab 1969:51). Thus, an urang sumando is a person
pledged by his paruik to that of his wife. He is sometimes likened to a
bull buffalo borrowed for impregnation, and, in many ways, he is
not much more than that to his wife's relatives.[42] Usually he visits
his wife at night and leaves her house in the morning (Josselin de
Jong:10–11; Radjab 1950:5).[43] It is considered to be an acute em-
barassment for both parties if the sumando and his wife's tungganai
(house elder) or other mamak meet each other in the house. When
land was relatively abundant, the sumando most probably worked
on the *sawah* (wet-rice land) of his own adat house, in addition to
cultivating *ladang* (dry fields) and upland. As the population became denser and land scarcer, he may have worked on the land of
his house or that of his wife's house, depending on the availability

40. A class element may also be involved. A man of upper class background is
likely to be proposed to by the prospective bride's family, regardless of her class.

41. My research results in IV Angkat near Bukittinggi show a contemporary
local frequency of cross-cousin marriage as follows: about 17 to 20 percent for 389
male respondents and their fathers (the figures include both patrilateral and matrilateral cross-cousin marriages). This form of marriage is expected to occur more
frequently in one's first marriage than in (possible) subsequent marriages. According
to Naim's research among 157 penghulu from 129 different villages in West Sumatra
(1973a:13), 31 percent married their mamak's daughters in their first marriages. The
figure dropped to 8 percent in the subsequent marriages of those who married more
than once.

42. According to Willinck (1909:525–526), an urang sumando is like a borrowed animal which, during the initial period, tends to run away from a temporary
stable.

43. Verkerk Pistorius even says that the urang sumando only stays at his wife's
bilik until the next day if he is brave enough (pp. 43–44).

of land and on the closeness of his relationship to his wife's family. Except for the occasional gift-giving for such events as the ceremony for the first bathing of a baby (*turun mandi*), circumcision, and marriage, a sumando's economic responsibility toward his wife and children is minimal (Verkerk Pistorius:43; Sjafnir et al.:22).[44] The latter are supported by their harta pusaka (ancestral property) under the supervision of a tungganai. Structurally, the basic building block of the Minangkabau matriliny is a *samandai*, which means people of one mother and includes a mother and her children. The position of the sumando is not recognized in this "block." Upon divorce or the death of the wife, the children remain at the house of their mother and the regular relationship between father and children ceases to be maintained (Junus 1971:253; Sjafnir et al.:18); however, the father, or rather the father's sublineage (*bako*), still continues a ceremonial gift-giving relationship with the children (*anak pisang*) (Josselin de Jong:64; Anwar:78–79).

The precarious position of the husband and father is expressed in a Minangkabau saying: "Urang sumando is like a horse-fly on the tail of a buffalo or like ashes on a hearth. [When a little wind blows, it is gone]" (Hamka 1966:2; Daulay 1960:87). Even after marriage, the husband continues to belong to the house of his mother. His primary allegiance and responsibility are directed to this group. If he becomes seriously ill at his wife's house, he is taken back to the house of his mother for nursing (Radjab 1950:100). If he dies, he is usually buried at the graveyard of his mother's paruik (Loeb:118; Datuk Batuah:148; Sjafnir et al.:63). In retrospect, this rather marginal position of the sumando in his wife's paruik must have been congruent with the communal, extended-family living within the adat house under the authority of the tungganai. As long as the sumando remained marginal, members, particularly women, of the same adat house could maintain harmony and avoid fragmentation.

In contrast to the relatively weak position of sumando vis-à-vis his children, the structurally most important relationship in the

44. This description seems contradictory to the Minangkabau saying "Anak dipangku, kemanakan dibimbing," or "The child is to be embraced [in one's bosom], the kemanakan to be guided [by the hand]." The saying is sometimes interpreted as indicating the father's economic responsibility towards his children (Datuk Nagari Basa 1968:133). Possibly, the saying originally meant a distinction between affective tie (father) and moral responsibility (mamak).

Minangkabau matrilineal system is the one between mamak and kemanakan. After reviewing various Minangkabau kinship terms, Josselin de Jong expressed his surprise by saying, "The most striking fact that emerges from these tables [of kinship terms] is that the kinship terminology so little reflects the very definite matriliny, and almost keeps an even bilateral balance" (p. 44). In other words, maternal kin—presumably more important because of matriliny—are not distinguished terminologically from paternal kin. The major distinctions are found between father (*bapak*) and mother's brother (*mamak*), and child (*anak*) and sister's child (*kemanakan*).[45] Rather than reflecting the lack of "the very definite matriliny" as Josselin de Jong suggests, the existence of this distinction in kinship terminology underlines the central importance of the mamak-kemanakan relation, whether blood-related or classificatory, in the structural arrangement of the Minangkabau matrilineal system.

In addition to the mamak-kemanakan relation, adat recognizes two more distinct interpersonal relations, and their derived social obligations, in traditional Minangkabau society: *bako-anak pisang* and *sumando-pasumandan*. Bako is the father's sublineage, *anak pisang* a brother's children, primarily used by females, *sumando* the in-marrying husband, and *pasumandan* a brother's wife's sublineage, primarily used by females. (See Figure 6.) *Bako-anak pisang* regulates relations and obligations between the paruik of a father and his children. *Sumando-pasumandan* governs the interaction between the paruik of a wife and that of her husband. In both cases, relations and obligations are mainly manifested on ceremonial occasions. For instance, upon the circumcision of an *anak pisang*, the *bako* is expected to present a gift. Likewise, for the wedding ceremony of a *sumando*'s sister, the *pasumandan* is obliged to help the former's paruik.

While the above relationships are essentially ceremony-oriented and female-centered (the fulfilment of obligations being primarily done by females), the mamak-kemanakan relation is diffuse and male-centered. It prescribes a man's relationship and obligations to his kemanakan, inheritors of his lineage, in various aspects of life,

---

45. The latter distinction applies only to a male speaker. For a woman, no terminological distinction is made between her child and her sister's child, for they essentially come from the "same womb": both are called *anak*. A brother's child, however is *anak pisang* to his sister.

Figure 6. Major Minangkabau kinship relations

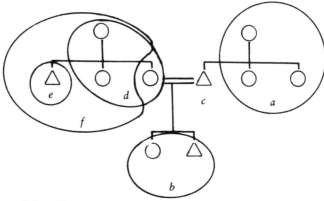

a: Bako of b
b: Anak pisang of a and kemanakan of e
c: Sumando of f
d: Pasumandan of a
e: Mamak of b

as well as the latter's obligations to the former. The mutual obligations and duties of mamak and kemanakan are regulated by the adat (for details, Anwar: 80–85). The mamak is the guardian of the kemanakan and is responsible for the well-being of the kemanakan, who are to continue their lineage. For this, the mamak is endowed with authority as tungganai or penghulu, and is expected to protect and to increase the harta pusaka by means of golden spade (gold or money) or iron spade (labor). The essence of Minangkabau matriliny is above all concentrated in the two-generation relation of mamak and kemanakan.[46]

All in all, the position of a male in traditional Minangkabau

46. This statement needs some qualification. For a long time, almost all students of Minangkabau society have thought that the most crucial human relation in traditional Minangkabau society was that of mamak and kemanakan. I now think that we need to reconsider this assumption, specifically concerning the importance of mothers. There is no doubt that the mamak-kemanakan relation was most important in terms of formal structure. Yet in day-to-day life it must have been the mother who connected her child to his or her mamak and who in fact made sure (by cajoling, pleading, threatening, and so on) that the mamak took good care of her child. The absence of a mother, however, creates little trouble for women. With or without their mothers, women are still incorporated within their extended matrilineal system

society is a strange one in our eyes. He does not own any property, although he may manage and expand it for his sisters and their children. He does not really have a house or a place he can call his own. While still little (probably some time after the age of six or seven), boys sleep in a *surau* (prayer house) where they learn how to recite the Koran at night (Radjab 1950:21; Bachtiar:359). It is considered shameful for a boy to sleep in his mother's house. If he continues to do so, he is ridiculed by his friends, particularly if there is a marriageable or married sister at home (Datuk Batuah:148). Though they go home to their mother's house for meals, boys continue to stay at the surau until they are married. From the day of his departure to a surau, a man ceases to be physically "in" the adat house, even if he still belongs to it. The adat house is referred to by the name of a female house member, not by the name of a mamak (Datuk Nagari Basa 1968:131). It remains to him the house he can point to as his house of origin (*rumah tunjuk*), but the house itself is for his mother and sisters (Hamka 1968:30). In old age, should a man's wife have already died, or if he is divorced, he must, once again, live in a surau (Radjab 1950:21; Hamka 1968:37). After marriage, he is only a visiting guest at his wife's house. Even at the house of his origin, there are many indications that internal, day-to-day affairs are in the hands of the women rather than those of the mamak (Daulay:64–65; Loeb:106; Rasjid Manggis:56, 64; Kemal:42; Bachtiar:368; Benda-Beckmann:83–84; Tanner 1974: 143–144).[47] This relative lack of roots must have been all the more true for those mamak who did not have any function nor position as tungganai, penghulu, or other adat functionaries. The

as perpetuators of blood lines and their identification with their matrilineal group is intact. The situation is different for men. Without a linchpin, a motherless boy was at the mercy of fate. If he was lucky and had a good mamak (and a good maternal aunt), he might still have been incorporated within the circle of his matrilineal family. If not, it is likely that he developed little attachment to his matrilineal family and that he was relatively isolated from the matrilineal system in general. This is all the more likely since Minangkabau boys usually did not stay at their mother's house after the age of six or seven.

47. The study of Minangkabau matriliny from a female perspective is sorely needed. Among other things we want to know how women wield power and influence within and outside the household, how they manipulate matriliny to their advantage and how they perceive matriliny in contrast to the male-centered view of matriliny as basically the mamak-kemanakan relationship.

men's world in traditional Minangkabau society thus consisted of the surau, the mosque, the *lapau* (coffeehouse), the *balai* (council hall) and the *dangau* (small hut built at the edge of a field to guard crops), all of which seem transitory and amorphous compared to the solidity and security of an adat house.

Social Stratification

As Bachtiar once commented, there is a myth about Minangkabau democracy and by implication about the lack of class distinctions within the society (pp. 377–378). The argument goes that all the important properties are communally owned, *musyawarah* (discussion) and *mufakat* (consensus) are two basic principles in every sphere of decision-making, and penghulu and tungganai are each *primus inter pares*. Concerning "social classes" in West Sumatra, Loeb observes: "Unlike the Bataks, the Minangkabau lay but little stress on social classification. Indeed, before the days of Hindu influence, there could have been no other classification between individuals other than an age distinction" (p. 107).

Admittedly, even today there is no such wide cleavage in land-holding in West Sumatra as is evidenced in Java. Nor has Minangkabau society maintained a pan-village aristocracy as in Bali.[48] The term aristocracy (*urang babangso*), although one may occasionally hear or read about it, definitely is not part of the daily vocabulary in the village. Nevertheless, traditional Minangkabau society was hardly free of one of the most pervasive social phenomena—social stratification. In general, one may discern two interrelated criteria for stratification: descendants of original settlers (*urang asa*) versus descendants of latecomers (*urang datang*), and adat functionaries (*pemangku adat*) versus common-ers (*urang kabanya'an*). The two are interrelated, for generally only the descendants of original settlers may become adat functionaries.[49]

48. On the Balinese aristocracy, see Geertz and Geertz (1975). Most probably the Minangkabau king and other royal dignitaries were never part of village life.

49. In a similar vein, Datoe' Sanggoeno Di Radjo (1955:14–15) distinguishes three strata of social stratification: penghulu, *urang patui'* (proper people who were equivalent to *urang asa*), and *kabanya'an*. As mentioned previously, the suku includes blood-related and adopted members; the latter may be equated with the descendants of latecomers.

Many students of Minangkabau society agree that the descendants of those who initially participated in the establishment of a nagari had the highest status within it (Josselin de Jong:50–51; Junus 1971:255; Westenenk 1969:49–50). This principle applies both at the inter-suku and intra-suku levels. Inside each suku, the descendants of the original settlers have higher status than those of latecomers. Between the suku in the nagari, the descendants of the original settlers of the original suku tend to have higher status than the others.

From the viewpoint of *urang asa* (descendants of original settlers), the kemanakan—that is, people defined by matrilineal principles—were divided into three categories.[50] At the top were the *urang asa* themselves, called "kemanakan beneath the chin" (*kemanakan dibawah dagu*), related by blood to the original settlers. Under them were the "kemanakan beneath the navel" (*kemanakan dibawah pusat*), related to the original settlers by the favor (*budi*) of the latter. They were the people who came later from another nagari to settle permanently, who found a suku of affiliation in the nagari (usually the same suku as their native one) and who performed the ceremony necessary for them to be admitted as new members of the suku as well as the nagari. They were given land for agriculture and housing, and seem to have enjoyed the same rights over properties as "kemanakan beneath the chin." However, they were not entitled to the position of lineage head (Bachtiar:373; Datuk Radjo Penghulu 1972:133).[51]

The last category of kemanakan refers to those "beneath the knees" (*kemanakan dibawah lutut*), related to the original settlers by gold or money. In olden times they were either debt bondsmen, prisoners of war, or purchased slaves (Abdullah 1972a:195).[52] They were entitled neither to properties nor to positions as adat functionaries. They were also denied certain privileges such as

50. The following description is drawn from Datuk Maruhun Batuah and Bagindo Tanameh (pp. 16–17). Similar classifications are given in Sutan Mangkuto (pp. 51–53), Datoek Batoeah Sango (p. 133), Bachtiar (p. 373), and Junus (1971:255–256).

51. However, Datoek Batoeah Sango (p. 133) says that in the case where the line of "kemanakan beneath the chin" dies out, the "kemanakan beneath the navel" may inherit the position of penghulu.

52. Slaves were mainly non-Moslems. During the Padri wars, people of non-Padri factions seem to have been made slaves as they were regarded as not being true believers (Graves:70).

building adat houses and wearing special types of clothing, and were not allowed to marry outside their own group (Graves:71). The proportion represented by the three categories of kemanakan is not clear. Most likely, it varied from area to area and also over the course of time. According to one source, in some villages, such as Nagari Silungkang, about one third of the population were descendants of slaves after the Padri wars of the early nineteenth century (ibid.:70). (Slavery itself was abolished by the Dutch in 1860s.) Bachtiar (pp. 378–379) carried out research in Nagari Taram in 1962 and estimated that about 21 percent of some 3,800 population could be classified as "the elite" or "penghulu and their actual [matrilineal] kin." These may be equated with "kemanakan beneath the chin."

The distinction between *urang asa* ("kemanakan beneath the chin") and *urang datang* ("kemanakan beneath the navel" and "kemanakan beneath the knees," although one has to be mindful of a considerable distance between these two groups) is manifested in many spheres of social life, some of which have already been discussed. Since their anscestors established the nagari, the urang asa are likely to control more and better land than the urang datang. The elaborate decorations of wood carving and the annexes attached to both ends of the adat house are often the signs of urang asa (Radjab 1950:22; Junus 1971:249). The wider breadth of the adat house is another indication of urang asa ownership (Verkerk Pistorius:5), for it shows that the house can accommodate ceremonies such as the installation of a penghulu, while the length of a house only shows the number of people living there. Sometimes the residential areas of urang asa and urang datang are separated, the latter living in distinct places, for instance, *tengah sawah*, which literally means "middle of the rice land." Above all, the distinction between the two groups seems to have been made manifest in marriage arrangements. A Minangkabau aphorism says:

> When tested, equally red,
> When weighed, equally heavy,
> When measured, equally long,
> When extended, equally wide.[53]

53. In Minangkabau, *Joko' diuji samo merah,/Joko' dikati samo bare,/Joko' diukue samo panjang,/Joko' dibidang samo laweh.*

For considerations of matching status were crucial in the arrangement of marriages, and, particularly for the daughters of urang asa, lineages were concerned to maintain purity of blood (Sjafnir et al.:16–17).

After generations of proliferation, not every urang asa has the right to elect, or to be elected, penghulu or another adat functionary. This is particularly the case in those nagari where the positions of adat functionaries are monopolized by one paruik (sublineage) within the payung (lineage). The people with such privileges form the elite of the elites within the nagari. The special status enjoyed by these people is most clearly revealed in the greatness (*kagadangan*) of a penghulu. In the traditional Minangkabau nagari, the penghulu was the richest, most knowledgeable, most powerful, both politically and judicially, and most prestigious person.

A penghulu has extra economic resources at his disposal. He may levy taxes, on those who wish to exploit the virgin land or to open new agricultural land in the nagari, to cut trees in the forest, and to pan gold in the river (Datoek Batoeah Sango:138–140; Rasjid Manggis:132–135; Datuk Maruhun Batuah and Bagindo Tanameh:41–42).[54] The penghulu is also often entitled to make use of special *sawah* (wet-rice land), called *sawah kagadangan* (rice land for greatness), which is a portion of ancestral land specifically alloted for the office of penghulu. The rice land is cultivated by his *anak buah* (kemanakan under his leadership). Its produce is put at the penghulu's disposal (Datuk Maruhun Batuah and Bagindo Tanameh:15; Datoek Madjolelo and Marzoeki:18; Rasjid Manggis:76).

Other than Islamic experts (*alim ulama*), the penghulu is the only intellectual in the traditional nagari, monopolizing one of the two most important and respected knowledges, that is, knowledge of adat (the other is Islamic expertise). Supposedly, every suku in every nagari of the Alam Minangkabau possesses its own tambo which details the origin of the suku together with its adat regulations. Except for the due possessor of the tambo, the penghulu, nobody else is allowed to know its contents. The tambo is inherited by the

54. However, it is not clear how far this right of taxation was implemented in reality.

penghulu from his predecessor. Because it is a sacred heirloom (*pusaka keramat*), a special ceremony is required before it is even opened (Datuk Batuah:7).

The penghulu's monopoly of knowledge of adat is in part the basis of his claim to political and judicial power in suku and nagari affairs. It is thus not only his position as penghulu, but also his (presumed) knowledge of adat laws and regulations that make him an authority in settling disputes and in judging suku members' misconduct. He is a member of the highest political and judicial body in the nagari, the nagari adat council (*kerapatan adat nagari*). Other people may observe the council meeting but usually the penghulu are the only ones who participate in the deliberations and in the decision-making process.

Together with Islamic experts, the penghulu are the most respected people in the nagari.[55] Because of their prestige they are often invited (*dijemput*) by a paruik to be a sumando even if they already have more than one wife (Hamka 1966:31). Reflecting his prestige and prominence, a penghulu is distinguished by a special title (*gala*), for example, Datuk Radjo Adie (Sir Kingly-in-Justice), which belongs to and stands for his lineage.[56] To address a penghulu by other than his datuk title is a great offence to him and his lineage members. On ceremonial occasions, he is clad in a special costume of black cloth, a hat (*destar*), and a cane, complete with a *keris* (creese), an heirloom which nobody except a penghulu is allowed to have (Datuk Nagari Basa 1966a:16). The adat house of his paruik is often distinctive with four, six, or eight horns (*gonjong*) attached to the roof, instead of just two (Datoe' Sanggoeno Di Radjo 1919:139–140). Corresponding to his high status, the installation of a newly-appointed penghulu requires a communal feast (*jamuan*), and generally a buffalo and some 1,260 liters of rice (100 *sukat*) are provided for the occasion (Anwar:73).

Such an important position naturally places special constraints

---

55. In coastal areas such as Tiku, Pariaman, and Padang, we find the titles of Marah, Sutan, Sidi, and Bagindo which are outside of the adat structure and inherited in the paternal line. These titles are often more prestigious than penghulu titles in these areas.

56. For more examples of titles and their meanings, see Johns (1958:xxii–xxiv). In rare cases, in some regions, the penghulu may not have the title of Datuk but rather those of Rangkayo, Sutan and so forth.

on its holder (Daulay:76; Rasjid Manggis:70–71; Datuk Maruhun Batuah and Bagindo Tanameh:19). A penghulu may not lose his temper or get angry. He may not roll up his sleeves or trousers. He may not climb trees nor run like a child. He may not even fish in a river, for it might give the impression that he is looking for fish to eat (Westenenk:67).

The stratification system in the traditional Minangkabau nagari shows two characteristics. First, it is mainly based on ascription rather than on achievement. Unless one is an urang asa (and unless a penghulu position is vacant or vacated), it is difficult to become a penghulu. However rich a person may become by means of his individual efforts, and however much pledged land he may acquire, his achievement can hardly be translated into high status unless his paruik possesses ancestral land and its own graveyard (*pandam pakaburan*)—the signs of urang asa (Datuk Maruhun Batuah and Bagindo Tanameh:41).[57] The competition, if any, for the position of penghulu is staged between different paruik of urang asa, not across the line between urang asa and urang datang.

The second characteristic is the extreme local character of the stratification. It is largely specific to the nagari concerned (Junus 1971:255). If urang asa migrate from their original nagari, they have to look for a suku which is willing to accept them as urang datang in the new nagari; they may, however, establish their own penghulu in due course if they are granted the right to do so and if they "fulfil the adat" (*mengisi adat*).[58] The power and authority of a penghulu is essentially confined within the boundaries of his nagari, though his status may be accorded proper respect by people of other nagari.

Some references have already been made to the *alim ulama* (Islamic experts). Due to their special position within the Minangkabau society, some attention should be paid to this group in relation to stratification. It is not clear when Islam was originally

57. However, in some nagari, urang datang may create their own penghulu, if they have stayed long enough in the nagari, obtain permission from the urang asa, and perform the necessary rituals.
58. This practice is called "*gadang manusuak*" (greatness infiltrates) according to Sutan Mangkuto (p. 57). The general impression is that it is impossible to establish a new penghuluship unless newcomers come from a proper family in their old nagari.

introduced to West Sumatra, though it is most probable that it reached the Minangkabau World via the west coast of Sumatra at the beginning of the sixteenth century.[59] By the end of the sixteenth or the beginning of the seventeenth century, Islam had established a secure foothold along the coast of West Sumatra (Abdullah 1967:11–12; Dobbin 1972:5). At that time, the west coast was under the control of the Acehnese from northern Sumatra, people who had already been Islamized. Later the first center of Islamic learning was founded at Ulakan near Padang.

The social process accompanying the Islamization of the whole of West Sumatra is not known. The end result, however, was that Islam was partially incorporated into the existing adat structure. For example, the *malim,* one of the four adat functionaries, represents the religious aspect of adat affairs on occasions such as marriage and divorce. The authority of the *malim* derives more from inherited position, however, than from acquired religious knowledge (Graves:62–63). In this respect, more important are the *tuanku*—of whom we begin to hear so much from the end of the eighteenth century—and the alim ulama in general. They are genuine Islamic experts who gain their fame not by inheriting a position according to adat but by their Islamic learning. They seem to have been much respected in the village, but their exact relation to the adat notables and the penghulu, is not clear. If some of the family histories of alim ulama from the late nineteenth and early twentieth centuries are any indication, it seems that Islamic expertise was often handed down from father to son and that intermarriage between "alim ulama families" and "penghulu families" was not uncommon (Hamka 1966:2; Hamka 1967:50–53, 230–233, 242, 248, 253, 262; Datoek Madjolelo and Marzoeki:47, 63; Dobbin 1972:19; Dobbin 1974:338). These observations may suggest that even within the framework of matriliny the inheritance of Islamic knowledge and position was more likely to be patrilineal, and that the alim ulama and penghulu were not necessarily in an antagonistic relationship.[60]

59. According to some sources, e.g., Hamka, Islam reached the darek much earlier via the east coast of Sumatra (Kathirithamby-Wells 1969:457, n. 25).
    60. Aside from the influence exerted by the tenets of patrilineally-oriented Islam and the personal authority of the alim ulama, closer father-son relations among the alim ulama may have derived from the existence of the surau. In the old times, a

Basically, the alim ulama stood alongside the adat hierarchy. Yet because of their training in various religious schools of differing locations, because of their frequent marriages into different nagari, and because of their contact with students from different areas, the prestige and influence of the alim ulama were not limited to the confines of the nagari where they happened to be born or to reside. It was this group, the alim ulama, who became the instigators of change in the Islamic reformist movement, and later the Padri wars, which rocked Minangkabau society at the end of the eighteenth century.

Summary

According to the ideal conception of the tambo, the Alam Minangkabau, the territorial sphere under Minangkabau cultural influence, was divided into the darek and the rantau. The darek was the heartland from which the Minangkabau drew their origin, principal social institutions, and cultural identity. By contrast, the rantau was an ever-expanding frontier, created by the overflow of population from the darek, where indigenous and foreign elements intermingled. Within this framework, the king of the Pagarruyung court symbolized the unity of the Alam and demarcated its contours. There are many indications that the king did not wield any real political power over much of the area in the Alam Minangkabau, nor over the villages of the darek. Minangkabau society never developed a centralized political power nor institution. Instead, strong autonomy characterized the nagari, a "village republic" where the highest political and judicial power was bestowed on the nagari adat council.

If we ignore regional variations and idiosyncracies, the internal social organization of the nagari can be seen to have consisted of three distinct levels and units of matrilineal groupings: paruik (sublineage), payung (lineage) and suku (matrilineal clan), in ascending

---

surau (prayer-house) also functioned as a school for religious instruction. Alim ulama of any status had their own surau where they could personally train and closely supervise their own sons among the other boys (e.g., Radjab 1950:15, 21–22)—a physical arrangement which was impossible for any other group of fathers in traditional Minangkabau society.

order. These groupings were respectively headed by tungganai, the house elder; penghulu, the lineage head; and suku adat council. A paruik was a group of related people generally living in one adat house, a payung was a group of related houses under the supervision of a penghulu, and a suku a group of related matrilineages who shared a common, unknown ancestress. Among the three groupings, the paruik was probably the most important social and economic unit in everyday life.

The matrilineal system as an organizing principle of nagari social structure was characterized as follows:

(1) Descent and descent-group formation were centered around the maternal line. Except for the special case of adoption, one remained with the descent group one was born to.

(2) The payung and paruik were corporate matrilineal descent-groups with ceremonially instituted male heads (respectively penghulu and tungganai) and communally owned property. The latter (harta pusaka or ancestral property) was in theory inalienable. In essence, material harta pusaka—agricultural land, houses, and fishponds—was for the benefit of the women who were to continue the lineage, while non-material harta pusaka, including adat positions, titles and costumes of adat functionaries (all symbolizing the greatness of a lineage) was for the use of the men, who were to act as guardians of the lineage.

(3) The residential pattern was duolocal. A husband stayed at the house of his wife at night but spent little time there during the day. Even after marriage, he continued to be a constituent member of his mother's house.

(4) Authority within the lineage and sublineage was in the hands of the mamak (maternal uncle), not the father.

Structurally, the mamak-kemanakan tie was the most important connection in Minangkabau matriliny. As long as economic life was principally based on ancestral property, a sumando hardly filled nor could fill a significant role in the nuclear family of procreation. As a sumando a man had few obligations toward his wife and children, but as a mamak he had every responsibility, both economic and moral, toward his kemanakan. He had to ensure that the line be continued, the ancestral property be held intact, and the lineage become more prosperous.

The matrilineal system had an important bearing on another

institution under consideration, namely, the system of social stratification. Generally speaking, two types of stratification were discernible in traditional Minangkabau society: matrilineal descendants of original settlers (urang asa) versus matrilineal descendants of latecomers (urang datang), and adat functionaries (pemangku adat) versus commoners (urang kabanya'an). The two are interrelated, for usually the descendants of original settlers monopolized the right to become adat functionaries. The people who commanded a high status in the village were urang asa and pemangku adat, and, above all, penghulu. Two characteristics of this stratification system were that it was mainly based on descent (ascription) and was specific to the particular nagari.

This traditional Minangkabau society, admittedly rather idealized here, came under attack by alim ulama by the end of the eighteenth century. The alim ulama were not only trained in patrilineally-oriented Islamic tenets but also they stood outside the social stratification originally prescribed by adat. Before proceeding to a discussion of the Islamic reformist movement which culminated in the Padri wars, it is necessary for us to examine how merantau fitted into traditional Minangkabau society.

3 / Migration and Society

As Clifford Geertz has shown in *Agricultural Involution* (1968), the relation between social structure and ecology is not necessarily fortuitous. Take, for example, the practice of the commuting husband in traditional Minangkabau society. The pattern of duolocal residence and the dual nature of a man's position as mamak (maternal uncle) and sumando (husband) had special implications for marriage arrangements. For a man to maintain physical access to the houses of his mother and of his wife, the two residences had to be located close together. It is probable therefore that village endogamy was a general practice in traditional Minangkabau society (Loeb 1972:114; Datoek Batoeah Sango c. 1966:98–99; Josselin de Jong 1952:65–66). One may guess that people frequently married within an even smaller circle, that is, the hamlets.

Other correlates of the commuting husband were permanent settlement and sedentary agriculture. Without them, it would be difficult to keep the female members of a sublineage in one place yet still allow their husbands to visit them regularly. For Minangkabau subsistence farmers, *sawah* (wet-rice cultivation) has long constituted the essential basis of agricultural life. While visiting the darek in the early nineteenth century, Raffles noted: "Throughout the whole of our journey I did not observe a single Ladang, that migratory kind of cultivation so accurately described by Mr. Marsden, and so universal near the southern coast; it had long been superseded by the conversion of the land into regular sawas, and the establishment of fixed property in the soil" (1830:363).

Sedentary agriculture was important to Minangkabau matriliny in another way. The position of the husband is problematic in any

72

matrilineal society. He is needed as a genitor for the continuation of his wife's matrilineage yet he is potentially in a position to compete for authority over his wife and children with the male members of her lineage. The role of the husband remained marginal to the life of his wife and children partly because their sustenance was guaranteed and produced by their sublineage, which controlled ancestral land, the major economic resource. So long as ancestral land could be expanded at a pace consonant with the fecundity of lineage members, the husband continued to be insignificant to his wife and children, at least in economic terms.

There is good reason to believe that population growth may have been relatively faster in West Sumatra than in the rest of Sumatra. The land was generally so fertile that even with poor care a comparatively large rice harvest could usually be expected (van der Veer 1946:91–92). In contrast to much of eastern Sumatra, where marshes and muddy, slow rivers predominated, water-flow in West Sumatra was rapid and clean—an important factor for hygiene.[1] Water was plentiful for irrigation because of abundant rainfall. The matrilineal system itself may have contributed to population growth, for it revolved around the females; their welfare was better attended to than was that of the males. Agricultural land, houses, and other ancestral properties existed for the females who were to continue the lineage line. Children were provided with the guardianship of multiple mamak, and this protection was not affected by the divorce of the parents or the death of a father.[2] When a society protects its female members so carefully, its reproductive capacity is great and the population has the potential to grow. It can hardly be entirely accidental that the Minangkabau are the largest ethnic group among the Sumatrans. According to the census conducted by

1. Comparing eastern Sumatra (lowlands) and western Sumatra (highlands), Fisher (1964:249) once speculated: "In short, since the fourteenth century a complete reversal appears to have taken place in the relative standing of the East Coast Malays on the one hand and the Menangkabaus and Bataks on the other, and it is tempting to seek an explanation in terms of the increasingly unhealthy and enervating conditions of the swamp-ridden lowlands, and the altogether more stimulating climate, as well as the more fertile soils derived from neutral-basic volcanic materials, in the Padang and Toba highlands." Concerning the possible differential effects of virulent malaria between lowland and highland Sumatra, due to ecology and climate, see Fisher (p. 249, n. 28).

2. This observation does not apply as well to boys as to girls; their situation depends more on the presence or absence of their mothers.

the Dutch in 1930, the second largest ethnic group in Sumatra, the Batak, amounted only to some two-thirds of the Minangkabau population (*Volkstelling 1930,* 4:164, 170–171; 5:179).

Despite West Sumatra's fertile soil and its abundance of water and rainfall, agricultural intensification does not seem to have been a common practice.[3] Rare application of fertilizer was compounded by incorrect utilization. Sawah were not properly ploughed. Planting was not done with optimum spacing nor was it carried out at the most suitable time. Agriculture was generally not as labor intensive as it was in Java. Sawah did not receive regular care and attention. It is possible also that communal landholding patterns were not very conducive to intensification. Every measure of improvement, for example, the building of an irrigation channel, had to be agreed upon by the lineage members. It is conceivable that lack of individual return to those who wished to implement intensification—the benefits of an improved harvest, after all, accrued to the lineage as a whole—stifled initiative and innovation. (Admittedly this is a rather ethnocentric interpretation of human nature.) This lack of agricultural intensification may have been partly responsible for the rather curious development, or, perhaps, lack of development, in Minangkabau history. In spite of the practice of sedentary agriculture and the prevalence of sawah, Minangkabau society did not produce corps of soldiers, an urban center, or an aristocracy living off the land. Although it did accommodate a large village population, agriculture in West Sumatra does not seem to have ever reached the point where it could have fed a substantial nonagricultural population.[4]

Thus, an irony develops. The proper functioning of the Minangkabau matrilineal system depended on the availability of agricultural land, while the socioecological conditions of West Sumatra seem to have contributed to rapid population growth. If no measures had been taken to balance the ratio of people to land

3. The description of Minangkabau agriculture is based on van der Veer (pp. 91–92); Graves (1971:101, 229); C. Geertz (1968:117, n. 67); Verkerk Pistorius (1871:19, 24, n. 6). Some of the comments were made in the middle of the nineteenth century, and others in more recent years.

4. Obviously, the lack of strong centralized political power was also closely tied in with this curious development.

as population growth outran the expansion of available land, some sort of internal reorganization of village society would have been inevitable. For example, ancestral property might have disintegrated. The penghulu might have had to forsake the luxury of *sawah kagadangan* (rice field for greatness) and have been stripped of their responsibility for the protection and management of ancestral land. In short, Minangkabau matriliny might have collapsed.

Facing the universal problem of the race between population growth and expansion of agricultural land, the Minangkabau apparently did not look to agricultural intensification as a solution. Instead, the Minangkabau poured out from the ever-expanding frontier. Village segmentation as a form of geographical mobility, admittedly a common practice among many agricultural societies, was nevertheless an essential element of Minangkabau tradition and society. It did not exist simply to permit the maintenance of adequate living standards for the population. Without trying to overstate the case, one might say that geographical mobility or migration was fundamentally related to the survival and vitality of the Minangkabau matrilineal system itself.

Metamorphosis of Settlement

The significance of geographical mobility in traditional Minangkabau society is attested by the tambo, which are full of the imagery of mobility. The conceptual distinction between the darek (land of origin) and the rantau (frontier) is itself a manifestation of this sense of mobility. Also the clear identification of Pariangan Padang Panjang as the first nagari in the Minangkabau World intimates the eventual dispersion of population from one central geographical point to the surrounding areas. We might further recall the story of Maharaja Diraja in relation to the genesis of Minangkabau society. The story conveys a definite sense of geographical mobility from one location on earth to another in its effort to explain the origin of the Minangkabau. Unlike the origin story of the Batak of North Sumatra, the tambo does not see the Minangkabau as having descended from heaven but as having migrated from Ruhum (Turkey) to Mount Merapi.

Another image of geographical mobility is trapped in the very

Minangkabau conception of settlement. The tambo recognizes four
stages of human settlement:

> First, a *taratak* is built,
> Then the *taratak* becomes a *dusun*,
> Then the *dusun* becomes a *koto*,
> Finally the *koto* becomes a nagari.[5]

A *taratak* is a new, small settlement of a few sheds, usually surrounded by forest.[6] Trees are cut down for the settlement and for
some *ladang* (dry fields). Life is not yet settled. At the *dusun* stage,
life becomes more stable. Houses are built more permanently. In
addition to *ladang*, sawah is cultivated. Ancestral property and
lineage heads emerge in embryonic form. In the *koto*, the household (*rumah tangga*) is complete. A *balai* (council hall) is built in
order to secure *sakato* (one word, consensus) among the settlers.
The nagari is the highest order of human settlement; with it, the
settlement's metamorphosis is completed. This transformation is
well described in an account of Nagari Taram by Bachtiar
(1967:360–362).

> Local oral tradition relates that in very early times the ancestors of the
> Taram villagers left their original home, as did the ancestors of many
> other Minangkabau people, to wander through the dense jungle of the
> Padang Highlands until they reached the foot of Sago Mountain,
> where they established a settlement named Tepatan.... This spot on
> the bank of the Sinamar River, which at this point is broad and
> sluggish, was still jungle, but it was thought a favorable place to build
> a small hamlet (taratak).... Since a Minangkabau saying described
> such work as *mantjantjang malateh, manambang manaruko*, mean-
> ing that trees are cut, bushes trimmed, mines exploited, and virgin soil
> upturned, it may safely be assumed that these ancestors, after having
> cleared the site to build their dwellings, went out to explore the sur-
> rounding jungle area and at this time marked trees with a chopping
> knife, thus indicating that they had taken possession of the area....
>   The new settlement soon grew into a dusun called Sawah Tjompo,
> a name indicating that wet rice fields were already in use....
>   As time passed more people from other areas came to join the

---

5. In Minangkabau, *Taratak mulo dibuek,/Sudah taratak manjadi dusun,/
Sudah dusun manjadi koto,/Sudah koto jadi nagari.*
6. The following description is based on: ter Haar (1948:63–64); Datoek
Batoeah Sango (pp. 256–259); Anwar (1967:26–27); Datoe' Sanggoeno Di Radjo
(1919:102–105); Datuk Batuah (1956:87–89).

village settlement, and the original inhabitants themselves also increased in number.... Although each family group built its own house and cultivated its own piece of land, the settlers were very much aware that they could not live without each other's assistance. Various common needs established strong ties between them, and they then wanted a place where meetings could be held to discuss matters of common interest. Thus the first balai or village council hall was built, and with it a koto was born, although not yet a negeri [nagari]....

As the number of inhabitants increased, a political structure had to be created to regulate and coordinate village affairs. The family heads organized themselves by dividing the various rights and duties, creating specialized functionaries, formulating the most essential norms to be adhered to by all villagers, determining the boundaries of village territory, and satisfying all the requirements necessary for the creating of a negeri.

As a nagari became crowded, it spun off any surplus population into virgin territory to form a *taratak*. If the original nagari was close by, the *taratak* maintained a strong relationship with it. As the population of the settlement multiplied, both by internal increase and by the arrival of new settlers, it grew more and more autonomous and self-sufficient. With the passage of time, the taratak became a *dusun*, the *dusun* a *koto*, and the *koto* eventually a nagari. In due course, the new nagari also became a mother nagari to other settlements.[7]

The transformation from one type of settlement to another was not simply a matter of increasing population size. It was also a process of continuing improvement of human existence. A settlement became a nagari, only when communication (roads), government (a council hall), religion (a mosque), sanitation (a public bathing place), and recreation (an open field) were assured. The transformation was an autochthonous development, not the result of any sultan's letter of endorsement (*piagam*), such as usually elevated a settlement to village status in the Sultanate of Jambi in eastern central Sumatra (Pemerintah Daerah Propinsi Sumatera Tengah c. 1955: see the sections on Batang Hari and Merangin). The keen awareness by the Minangkabau of this spontaneous metamorphosis of settlement is ample indication of how important

7. As an example of such a process, see the formation of Lima Kaum/12 Kota (Datoe' Sanggoeno Di Radjo 1919:29–32).

nagari segmentation and geographical mobility must have been in
the history of the Alam Minangkabau. In fact, by elaborating on the
autogenous process involved in the formation of the darek and the
rantau, the tambo essentially relates history in terms of population
growth, village segmentation, and geographical extension of the
contour of ever-expanding Alam Minangkabau.

Early Population Movement

As was mentioned above, the root word "rantau" generally
means "shoreline," "reaches of a river," and "abroad." But in
Minangkabau rantau has a special meaning, namely, the areas immediately outside of the darek—such as rantau Piaman (Pariaman),
rantau Pasaman, and rantau Kuantan (Sutan Pamoentjak 1935),
into which Minangkabau from the darek have been spreading over
the centuries. Whether the movement associated with nagari segmentation may properly be called "merantau" is a moot point. It is
possible that merantau originally meant the movement from the
darek toward the rantau, or the prevalence of a particular mode of
mobility, that is, by water, in times when most of the area was
impassable owing to the thick jungle dominating the landscape.
Today, the Minangkabau do not refer to nagari segmentation as
merantau. Yet to exclude this movement from our consideration is
to miss a crucial historical link which connects the past and the
present of geographical mobility among the Minangkabau.

Other than contrasting the heartland (darek) and the frontier
(rantau), the tambo is very vague about the direction of population
movements in early Minangkabau history. Each luhak in the darek,
however, is roughly identified with a certain general direction:
people in Tanah Datar tended to move to the south and west, those
in Agam to the north and west, and those in 50 Kota to the east (see
Map 3). The migration down to the west coast was probably one of
the earliest movements, given the need to gain access to supplies of
salt. But without detailed studies of each region, a more specific
statement on the course of these movements is impossible.[8]

8. Some preliminary attempts at mapping these migrations have been made by
the Fakultas Pertanian, Universitas Andalas. See Ahmad et al. (1970:5–20); Sjafei et
al. (1971:26–32); Sjafei et al. (1972:1–39). Map 3 shows only the rantau within the
Province of West Sumatra. As will be discussed later, the area to the east of West

In spite of these difficulties, we can obtain some insight into the prevalence of migration in various areas by studying the dispersion of suku (matrilineal clans). As was mentioned above, a suku is not a purely genealogical grouping. In addition to genealogically related members, it also includes adopted members from other areas who may have belonged to the same suku group, to a related suku of the same suku group, or to an unrelated suku. However, one may reasonably assume that the establishment of a new settlement by a group of purely adopted suku members was not common. In order to institute a suku and a penghulu in a new settlement, permission from the mother suku of the original nagari was necessary. It was not likely that such permission would be given freely to a group of adopted suku members. Study of the geographical dispersion of a suku does not necessarily reveal a coterminous distribution of genealogically related suku members. Nevertheless, it should give at least some hints to how extensive the geographical mobility of a particular suku (and of people) may have been in early Minangkabau history.

The materials for this analysis come from two sources. One is my survey of 232 nagari in West Sumatra. In this survey, one question asked of village heads and village adat experts concerned the number of suku in the nagari and their names. Similar information from 103 more nagari was obtained from "Adat Monografi" compiled by the provincial government of Central Sumatra around 1955 (Pemerintah Daerah Propinsi Sumatera Tengah c. 1955). Each of the seventy-three subdistricts (*kecamatan*) in West Sumatra is represented in this total sample of 337 nagari (66 percent of the universe) by at least one nagari, and usually by two or more.

The results of the analysis show that altogether there are ninety-six suku in West Sumatra.[9] If we add up the number of suku in the sample, regardless of whether the same suku recurs in different

---

Sumatra was also traditionally considered rantau territory. Many villages in the northwest (west Pasaman) and in the north of Agam (particularly those near South Tapanuli) claim early connection with the Pagarruyung court (interviews in Kabupaten Pasaman in February 1973). It is possible that people in Agam migrated mainly toward the direction of the west coast.

9. The subdistricts of the municipalities (*kotamadya*) are excluded from this analysis. With suku categories such as Nan Sembilan (Nine Suku) and Nan Enam (Six Suku) (mainly in Tanah Datar and in 50 Kota), only the constituent suku of the suku categories are considered for enumeration.

nagari, the total is 1,914, or on the average, 5.7 suku per nagari. The geographical distribution of the ninety-six suku is extremely uneven. Fifty-six suku (58 percent of 96 suku) are found in only one subdistrict within the whole area of West Sumatra. Forty-seven suku (49 percent) occur only in a single nagari. Only a small number of suku are spread out over a wider geographical area: twenty-one suku are dispersed in more than 5 percent (seventeen) of the total sample nagari, and only twelve suku are spread through more than 10 percent (thirty-three) of the sample nagari. However, these large suku have wide distribution in West Sumatra. The twenty-one largest and the twelve largest suku account respectively for 90 percent and 76 percent of the total number (1,914) of suku in the sample; their names and geographical distribution are shown in Table 3.1.[10] Obviously, despite a large number of small idiosyncratic suku, it is a handful of major suku that lends clan homogeneity to Minangkabau society. It is significant that four of the five largest suku, Caniago, Melayu, Piliang, Tanjung, and Koto, are among the original suku according to adat lore.[11] Particularly, Caniago, Melayu, and Piliang are dispersed widely, reaching even to the western part of the Province of Riau (Pemerintah Daerah Propinsi Sumatera Tengah:see the section on Kampar).

There are a few interesting but unanswerable questions that arise from this survey of suku distribution. Bodi, despite being one of the original suku according to adat lore, does not have widespread geographical dispersion. The distribution of idiosyncratic suku is very uneven. Forty-eight of the fifty-six suku which exist in only one subdistrict are to be found in Luhak Tanah Datar, eight are in Luhak 50 Kota, and there are none in Luhak Agam. According to the basic suku-group classification, the Koto-Piliang suku are more widely distributed than the Bodi-Caniago or Melayu-Mandahiling suku (see Table 3.1). The reasons for these patterns are not clear.

10. That is to say, on the average, 5.1 and 4.3 of the 5.7 suku per nagari are accounted for respectively by the top twenty-one and twelve suku. The classification in Table 3.1 is made by Bagindo A. A. M. Sutan Maninjun of Nagari Ulakan in Padang/Pariaman, according to his father's tambo. The classification might differ slightly depending on sources (cf. Datuk Batuah:74–75). The "Melayu-Mandahiling" suku group is usually subsumed under "Koto-Piling."
11. The four original suku according to adat lore are Bodi, Caniago, Koto, and Piliang. Some sources (Datuk Maruhun Batuah and Bagindo Tanameh c. 1954:34; Rasjid Manggis 1971:53) say, however, that the oldest suku in West Sumatra is Melayu.

Table 3.1. Geographical representation of large suku

Suku name	Nagari represented (N = 337)	Subdistricts represented (N = 73)	Suku group
Caniago	208 (62%)	63 (86%)	Bodi-Caniago
Melayu	201 (60%)	57 (78%)	Melayu-Mandahiling
Piliang	195 (58%)	56 (77%)	Koto-Piliang
Tanjung	150 (45%)	45 (62%)	Koto-Piliang
Koto	140 (42%)	48 (66%)	Koto-Piliang
Jambak	139 (41%)	42 (58%)	Koto-Piliang
Sikumbang	125 (37%)	44 (60%)	Koto-Piliang
Mandahiling	80 (24%)	30 (41%)	Melayu-Mandahiling
Petapang	77 (23%)	22 (30%)	Koto-Piliang
Guci	55 (16%)	20 (27%)	Koto-Piliang
Kutianyir	53 (16%)	24 (33%)	Koto-Piliang
Panai	36 (11%)	17 (23%)	Melayu-Mandahiling
Payobada	32 (10%)	14 (19%)	Koto-Piliang
Kampai	32 (10%)	14 (19%)	Koto-Piliang
Panyalai	31 (9%)	10 (14%)	Bodi-Caniago
Bendang	30 (9%)	17 (23%)	Melayu-Mandahiling
Dalimo	30 (9%)	12 (16%)	Melayu-Mandahiling
Bodi	29 (9%)	10 (14%)	Bodi-Caniago
Pisang	29 (9%)	15 (21%)	Koto-Piliang
Sipanjang	25 (7%)	15 (21%)	Bodi-Caniago
Simabur	24 (7%)	11 (15%)	Koto-Piliang

In general, the distribution of suku strongly suggests continuity between the darek and the rantau. Large suku are evenly distributed in both zones (see, for example, Maps 4, 5, and 6, for the geographical distribution of the three largest suku).[12] But a great divergence exists between the number of suku observed in each of the two regions: ninety-two suku in the darek and thirty-one in the rantau. However, with the exception of only six cases, all of the suku found in the rantau are also observed in the darek. Of the six exceptional cases, two (the Batak and Tambusai clans) fall outside of any pattern, since suku in these cases originated from outside West Sumatra. This general pattern seems to tally with the contention of the tambo that the suku in the rantau came from the darek. Even

12. The maps show the geographical distribution according to subdistricts. Thus, if any sample nagari of a subdistrict includes a suku under consideration (e.g., Caniago), that subdistrict is shaded in the map of this particular suku. There are three noticeable empty pockets in these maps, around Padang Panjang, around Pariaman, and around Batu Sangkar. It is not certain if this is an accidental result due to the sampling process or to some historical factors.

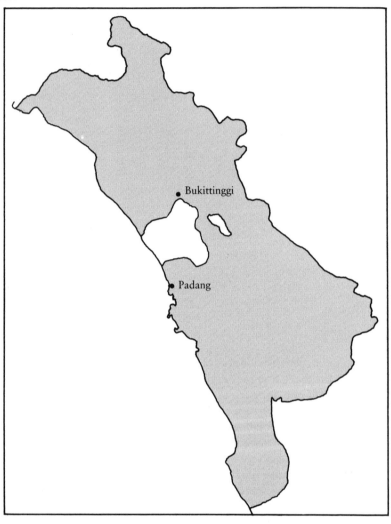

Map 4. Geographical Distribution of Suku Caniago in West Sumatra

Map 5. Geographical Distribution of Suku Melayu in West Sumatra

Map 6. Geographical Distribution of Suku Piliang in West Sumatra

granting that the suku are not purely a genealogical grouping, the widely dispersed geographical distribution of large suku suggests extensive population movement in early Minangkabau history. It is obvious, however, that nagari segmentation, which must have been going on since the legendary time of the tambo, could not continue forever. The old-time rantau was slowly filled up. The gradual closing of the frontier was more consequential to the darek than to the rantau. To begin with, as the frontier of settlement in the rantau was pushed further toward the outer fringes, it became more and more difficult for people in the interior to move. Covering longer distances and increasingly unfamiliar terrain, the later segmentary migration must have been extremely taxing for the people of the darek—physically, economically, and psychologically. Another factor to be considered is status consciousness. Today, darek people, as inhabitants of the Minangkabau heartland, tend to feel superior to rantau people. Though it is impossible to determine when this feeling first arose, it is likely that as the difference between the darek and the rantau became clearly distinguished, some darek people would have been reluctant to migrate because of the loss of status they would face.

Study of nagari segmentation seems to indicate that the darek became increasingly stranded in demographic terms. The pattern of nagari segmentation resembles the expanding concentric circles of ripples in a pool in its mode of movement, though not necessarily in its overall shape. People in the interior moved to the border areas of the darek (*ekor darek, kepala rantau* or tail of the darek, head of the rantau) and into the adjacent rantau. Settlers in these areas later moved further away to more distant parts of the rantau. A famous case in point is the colonization of Pesisir Selatan south of Padang. Originally people moved from Luhak Tanah Datar to Solok (Kubung XIII). From there, some migrated further south to Sungai Pagu. Eventually, the northern part of Pesisir Selatan was colonized by people from Solok, the southern part by those from Sungai Pagu.[13]

It is impossible to pinpoint when the real enclosure of the rantau

13. The information is mainly based on Sjafei et al. (1971:26–30) and my interviews in various nagari in Kabupaten Solok and Kabupaten Pesisir Selatan in May and June, 1973.

began. It must have been experienced as a cumulative effect, felt increasingly acutely by people in the darek. The decisive stroke, however, was the consolidation of Dutch control in West Sumatra after the Padri wars of the early nineteenth century, something which will be discussed further. In any event, when the closing-off of the rantau became conclusive in the middle of the nineteenth century, the Minangkabau were not completely unprepared, and managed to adjust their mode of geographical mobility. For nagari segmentation, albeit of major significance, was not the only pattern of merantau during early Minangkabau history.

The Minangkabau and Trade in Rantau Hilir

Except for legends, scattered inscriptions, and some references in Chinese, Javanese, and Dutch texts, our knowledge of premodern Minangkabau history is still meager. This is particularly true for events in the darek of West Sumatra. A letter sent by Portuguese captives in Malacca in 1510 mentions "Menancabo" to a European audience for the first time (Cortesão 1944:113, n. 2). The letter mentions "the gold that comes to Malacca from a mine in Menancabo on the side of Çamatra"; that there was an abundance of gold in the Minangkabau area was to be widely believed for some time to come. More than one and a half centuries later came Tomas Dias, the first European known to have visited the Minangkabau darek. He reached Buo from the east coast—traveling upstream on the Siak River for part of the way and then proceeding on foot—and met the Minangkabau king in 1684 (Schnitger 1939:55–63). The next European known to have set foot in the highlands was Sir Thomas Stamford Raffles in 1818 (Raffles:341–360). By that time, the Padri movement was at its height and the ensuing Dutch intervention brings us more and more information on conditions in West Sumatra.

Although historical sources are less than complete, we can still try to piece together the available knowledge on the movement of Minangkabau beyond West Sumatra. This movement was considerably different in character than the one inside West Sumatra. While within the Alam Minangkabau the population multiplied, new nagari were established, and nagari segmentation continued, another part of the population was also moving toward the "Rantau Hilir" (Downstream Rantau) to the east (Datuk Batuah:19). This movement involved crossing the Bukit Barisan mountain range, in the general direction of four important rivers in eastern Sumatra: the Siak, the Kampar, the Indragiri, and the Batang Hari, all of which debouch into the Straits of Malacca and lead to the world beyond Sumatra (see Map 2). Initially, the Minangkabau settled in a belt around the eastern side of West Sumatra: from Tambusai in the north down through Rambah, Kepenuhan, Rokan IV Koto, XIII Koto Kampar, V Koto Bangkinang, Kampar Kiri, Kuantan, Indragiri, Muara Kibul, Pangkalan Jambu, Tiang Pumpung, Sungai Tenang, Serampas, Batang Asai, and Limun (Datuk nan III) in the south (Pemerintah Daerah Propinsi Sumatera Tengah: see the section on Kampar; Datoek Batoeah Sango:80–88).[14] At the same time, the Minangkabau must also have been moving still farther east: as early as the fifteenth century, some of them are believed to have been filtering into the Malay peninsula (Kennedy 1962:132; Hall 1970:355; Josselin de Jong:9).

The eastward movement apparently took on a momentum of its own in the late seventeenth century (Andaya 1975:110–112).[15] The Dutch seized Malacca from the Portuguese in 1641—complicating the bitter feud between the sultanates of Johor (on the Malay peninsula and sometimes in the Riau archipelago) and Aceh (in northern Sumatra) over the east coast of Sumatra. Toward the end of the seventeenth century, Acehnese control of eastern Sumatra had already been challenged by the Dutch, and the power of Johor, another claimant to hegemony on the east coast, was in decline. In the early eighteenth century, Raja Kecil, a Minangkabau adventurer, possibly with family connections to the Pagarruyung court, established the sultanate of Siak on the east coast. By that time,

---

14. The information on Jambi was collected from theses written by students at the Akademi Pemerintahan Dalam Negeri of Jambi in October 1973. Muara Kibul down to Limun are situated along upper tributaries of the Batang Tembesi which in turn is the major southernmost tributary of the Batang Hari.

15. Until this time, it appears that the Indragiri and the Batang Hari in the south were more frequented than the other two rivers (Dobbin 1977:16–19, 33; Meilink-Roelofsz 1962:259). Areas of gold and pepper production were better connected to the upper tributaries of these two rivers and control of the Siak and the Kampar to the north had regularly been contested by Aceh and Johor. The pattern changed, however, in the late seventeenth century. The Siak, in particular, became a major route to the east coast.

"many" Minangkabau had already settled in the Malay Peninsula, in the Riau-Lingga archipelago, and along the east coast of Sumatra (Andaya:252, 269–273).

If within the Alam Minangkabau agriculture stimulated internal movement, in the eastward emigration toward the Straits of Malacca, even from relatively early times, commercial activities were an important element. This is not surprising when one remembers the longstanding trading interest of the raja of Pagarruyung in the rantau hilir. Information on the nature, extent, and historical processes associated with early Minangkabau commerce is still fragmentary, but it is clear that three commercial items (gold, pepper, and tin) were significant in the initiation of Minangkabau trading ventures.

Since very early times, the Minangkabau area had been famed for the production of gold, "the metal which God chose" (Cortesão:165). Gold was found in such widely separated areas as Sijunjung, Sungai Pagu, Rao, Salido, Sangir, Sipayang, eastern Tanah Datar, and southwestern Tanah Datar in West Sumatra and in upper Batang Hari, Kuantan, and Kerinci immediately outside of West Sumatra (Hesse 1931:64, 79; Nahuijs 1827:77; Schnitger: 63; Datoek Madjolelo and Marzoeki 1951:20; Kathirithamby-Wells 1976:76; Dobbin 1977:7–10). Not only was West Sumatra favored by gold ("Minangkabau has always been esteemed the richest seat of it [gold]") (Marsden 1966:165), but the Minangkabau seem to have been one of the few local peoples who were skilled in gold-mining and panning. Gold prospecting sometimes motivated migration. Minangkabau settlements in northwestern Jambi (Limun, Batang Asai, Pangkalan Jambu, Serampas, and Sungai Tenang), for example, were the result of gold-prospecting (Datoek Madjolelo and Marzoeki:20; Marsden 1966:165). Invited by "King Regale" and his predecessors, some Minangkabau crossed the Straits of Malacca to Johor (probably in the sixteenth century) to collect gold dust and nuggets for the kings (Hale 1909:163). Gold prospectors were also involved in commercial activities at trade centers in the east and on the west coast of Sumatra, bartering gold for iron, fine Indian cloth, and other commercial goods (Marsden 1966:168–169).

Another valuable mineral, tin, was discovered in the rantau hilir in 1674 (Schnitger:56). This discovery prompted the Dutch East India Company, already established in Malacca, to seek a direct relationship with the Minangkabau "interior." A treaty was signed in 1676 between the Dutch and three tin-producing nagari, Kabon, Kota Rena, and Giti, concerning a trade monopoly of new-found ore (Andaya:106–107). In 1684, Tomas Dias was sent to Buo/ Pagarruyung as an envoy of the Company, "to beg the [Minangkabau] king's help in various trade problems" (Schnitger:58).

The emergence of pepper as a trade commodity in the early seventeenth century broadened the scope of Minangkabau involvement in commerce. With the right ecological conditions and the right pecuniary orientation, many Minangkabau villagers could have been led to the cultivation of this cash crop. It is not clear how much the people in the darek actually participated in pepper production. A considerable amount of pepper was exported from the Minangkabau area to the east coast via Jambi. For instance, 2,000 tons (50,000 bags) were loaded in Jambi in 1623, and it is likely that the pepper came down from the Minangkabau "hinterland" or "back-country" (Meilink-Roelofsz:30, 146, 259). This Minangkabau "hinterland" may have been the darek or it may have been part of the eastern rantau; such areas as Tembesi, Kamang and Tanjung in Upper Jambi, and "the interior of Palembang" were all connected with pepper production to a significant degree (Schrieke 1955a:51, 56; Andaya:134).[16] Other than in the "hinterland," pepper was also cultivated along the west coast. Pepper cultivation may well have started on the west coast sometime in the middle of the sixteenth century (Kathirithamby-Wells 1976:66). In the early seventeenth century, pepper was definitely flourishing in Menjuta near Indrapura (south of Padang), and eventually spread to Bandar Sepuluh and other places along the coast (Kathirithamby-Wells 1976:75; Schrieke 1955a:51–52). The produce from these places, as well as from Barus in the north, was brought down by small boats to coastal towns, particularly Padang, Pariaman, and Tiku, for shipment, since these ports provided better protection for large ships (Hesse:62).

Like gold traders before them, pepper growers were often enmeshed in complex commercial activities themselves. "The pepper growers, hill-folk from Minangkabau, who were not under the sov-

---

16. Kamang and Tanjung are situated along the upper Batang Hari, and Tembesi probably along the Batang Tembesi.

ereignty of the king of Jambi, were accustomed to come down to the coast with their praos laden with pepper. Usually about 100 to 150 of these small ships appeared annually, each carrying a load of some 150 *pikol* [nine tons]. Chinese intermediary traders went to meet them to purchase the pepper. The Minangkabauers bartered it for cloths which they resold in the interior" (Meilink-Roelofsz:259).

As a result of this trade, there developed flourishing commercial centers in the "interior" including Kampar, Petapahan, Kabon, and Indragiri (Andaya:146, 173–174; Cortesão:153; Meilink-Roelofsz:30). When Tomas Dias, on his way to Buo, visitied Air Tiris (V Koto Bangkinang) in the "interior," he estimated its population to be about 10,000, of whom 500 were traders (Andaya:111). While gaining commercial acumen and expertise, these traders must have developed—through their contact with people from the outside—the desire to move further eastward in search of new experiences, more adventures, and larger profits.[17]

Despite these observations, which seem to help explain the mobility of the Minangkabau beyond the Alam, we have little knowledge of the impact this mobility had in West Sumatra, particularly in the darek. It has already been hinted that the major pepper areas seem to have been down on the west coast or over on the eastern fringe of West Sumatra rather than in the darek itself. With only a few exceptions, the gold mines too seem to have been concentrated in the rantau (inside and outside West Sumatra).[18] Tin

17. It is not clear how far people from the outside moved upstream from the east coast toward the "interior" for commercial purposes. Some contact is suggested in the adat monographs of some villages in western inland Riau (Pemerintah Daerah Propinsi Sumatera Tengah: the section on Kampar). In these villages, people from Johor, Malacca, and Perak are counted as part of the original settlers. Within West Sumatra itself, the people of Nagari Sundatar (north of Lubuk Sikaping) claim that some of their ancestors came from Johor (interview in Nagari Sundatar in February 1973).

18. Dobbin (1977:7–9) identifies two important gold-producing areas in Tanah Datar in the darek in the late seventeenth century. Eastern Tanah Datar, and specifically Siluka, Manganti, Sumpur Kudus, and Ungan, was one. The other was south-western Tanah Datar, and in particular Batipuh, the hills around Suruaso, parts of XX Kota, and the area near Lake Singkarak. Situated near the border between the darek and the rantau and adjacent to the Indragiri river, "eastern Tanah Datar" channeled its gold mainly to the east coast of Sumatra. It is not clear how much importance gold from "southwestern Tanah Datar" had in the total gold-export from the west coast.

was discovered in the rantau hilir (the downstream or eastern rantau). The term "interior" as used by the writers quoted above can be highly misleading for it may give the false impression that it is equivalent to the darek. In fact, depending on the direction of orientation, the "interior" may indicate two completely different geographical zones, though both may have been heavily Minangkabau in ethnic composition. Viewed from the west coast, the interior undoubtedly meant the darek; but if the perspective was from the east coast, the "interior" probably meant areas well to the east of the darek, for example, V Koto Bangkinang, Kampar, and Indragiri. Indeed, even today, these are the first densely populated inland areas one comes across if one goes upstream from the east coast. It is likely that the image of an interior (or hinterland) rich in commercial products and active in trading is more appropriately associated with this area than with the darek. These considerations lead us to surmise that the Minangkabau who were active on both sides of the Straits of Malacca during this early period may have been mainly the descendants of early Minangkabau settlers in the rantau hilir, rather than people coming directly from the darek or even from West Sumatra.[19]

Compared with the coastal rantau in West Sumatra, which was sharply circumscribed by the narrow coastal plain, the rantau hilir offered a great sense of expansiveness. This sense of expansiveness was as much a product of sheer geographical spread as it was of the particular mode of merantau there. Nagari segmentation in West Sumatra was constrained by the customs of matriliny, communally-held ancestral property, and penghuluship. In contrast, the rantau hilir offered alternative ways of life (as traders, sailors, and sometimes pirates) where the matrilineal adat could be less binding and where one could even cease strictly to be a Minangkabau.[20] The rantau hilir, with its commercial centers, was

19. A similar movement to the eastward movement took place, on a small scale, via the sea route to Tapak Tuan and Meulaboh in western Aceh. Also probably starting around the seventeenth or eighteenth century, coastal Minangkabau became involved in sea trade and transportation along the western coast. Sailing back and forth between West Sumatran ports and other ports of Sumatra, these traders and sailors were early examples of circulatory merantau. For more details, see Kato (1980).
20. Although the example comes from the west coast, the story of Nakhoda Makuta and his children in the late seventeenth and early eighteenth centuries is

neither entirely Minangkabau nor exactly non-Minangkabau—a
quality which was partly responsible for the sense it gave of expansiveness. It was not an empty space to be Minangkabauized, for the
existence of other ethnic groups, such as Malays and Batak, in the
area was long recognized.

Although the eastward movement was different from village
segmentation in many respects, geographical mobility in both cases
by and large meant no returning to the homeland. Even though ties
between the mother village and the daughter village were sometimes maintained, village segmentation generally meant a permanent separation of the populations in the two settlements. In cases
where it was politically expedient, people in the rantau hilir probably made appeals to the court of Pagarruyung, for example, asking
for a member of the royal family to be their raja. Otherwise, there
seems to have been little regularized communication between West
Sumatra and the rantau to the east.[21] The rantau hilir was a world
the Minangkabau in West Sumatra knew of, but into which, most
probably, they seldom ventured. Even in the realm of fantasy, the
Minangkabau in West Sumatra seem to have had some difficulty
relating to the rantau hilir. The Minangkabau *kaba*, traditional
(originally oral) literature, is strangely silent about any adventurous
exploits by Minangkabau traders-cum-"thieves" on the east
coast.[22] In the few cases where a story refers to the world outside of

suggestive of one migration pattern of this time. Nakhoda Makuta was a native of
Bayang, a nagari south of Padang on the west coast. He first engaged in trading
activities in Java, later moved to Borneo, and finally settled in Piobang (Lampung).
His son, Nakhoda Muda, also eventually settled in Semangka (Lampung), the native
village of his wife. Nakhoda Muda was active in the pepper trade between Semangka
and Bantam. Later, he had to flee from Semangka because of false accusations of
illegal pepper trading brought by the court of Bantam. The whole narrative is remarkable for its lack of any reference to Minangkabau. Nakhoda Makuta and his
descendants seem to have lived as Malays rather than as Minangkabau (Marsden
1830). A possible example from the east coast is the story of Raja Kecil who established the sultanate of Siak. Although he claimed to be a son of a Johor sultan, he
actually seems to have been a Minangkabau adventurer (Andaya:271–272).

21. Most probably the Minangkabau royal court maintained a certain degree of
contact with the rantau hilir before the late seventeenth century (Andaya:109).
There is some indication, however, that the court was not located then at the present
site of Pagarruyung in the center of the darek. Instead it was situated near Kumanis
in "eastern Tanah Datar," close to the rantau hilir. Sometime after 1684, the royal
court moved to the present site near Batu Sangkar (Dobbin 1977:8, n. 28).

22. Concerning "Menancavos" in the Malay peninsula, "great thieves and
Mohametans," see Sheehan (1934:103).

the Alam Minangkabau, the point of departure is Tiku/Pariaman or
Padang, not the ports in the east (for example, Mahkota c. 1962;
Samah 1950). Nevertheless, we should not be blind to the significance of the rantau hilir for the people in West Sumatra. The
Minangkabau of West Sumatra may have left for the rantau hilir
only occasionally; and they may only rarely have dreamed about
adventures awaiting them in the rantau hilir. Yet the rantau hilir
was always there as an alternative, with its promise of new possibilities.[23] After the darek and the rantau pasisir became crowded,
the sense of opportunity which the rantau hilir could provide was
crucial in sustaining the ideal of an ever-expanding Alam
Minangkabau. This became particularly true after the late
eighteenth century; the rantau hilir began to be directly connected
to the darek when gambier (especially in 50 Kota) and coffee began
to be grown in the darek, and the rantau hilir became an outlet of
these cash crops (Dobbin 1977:19–21, 33).[24]

I am not maintaining that there was no commercial merantau
within West Sumatra or that there was no nagari segmentation in
the rantau hilir during this time. Traders were certainly already
active in West Sumatra, particularly on the west coast. It may well
have been the case that nagari segmentation was more frequent
than commercial merantau in the rantau hilir. However, the relative
importance of commercial merantau in the rantau hilir, together
with its marginal position in the Alam Minangkabau, clearly set it

23. Even though the information comes from the latter half of the nineteenth
century, the following story is instructive in this connection. In the autobiography of
Moehammad Saleh, a Minangkabau merchant from Pariaman, is recounted a story
of a certain rich merchant who failed in business, lost his fortune, and moreover
incurred many debts. He could not stay in Pariaman and one day "went to the land
located in the eastern side" (*pergi kenegeri yang terletak sebelah timur*). The expression meant that he secretly fled to the eastern part of Sumatra. Because of the
disgrace, he could never come back to Pariaman nor to the western coast of Sumatra.
He died in "other people's land" (*rantau orang*) (Saleh 1965:166–167). The rantau
hilir indeed seems to have been an alternative to West Sumatra, though not a very
honorable one in this case.
24. The traffic between the darek and the rantau hilir, however, was shortlived.
After the middle of the nineteenth century, the Dutch cut off communication between the two areas in order to stop the flow of commodities from the darek across
the Straits of Malacca (Schrieke 1955b:96–97). West Sumatra was connected again
to the rantau hilir, for a while, during the economic boom of the 1920s. Since 1960,
as Pekan Baru has grown into an important urban center in eastern Sumatra, the
rantau hilir has remained one of the major destinations of Minangkabau migration.

apart from the darek and even from the rantau pasisir. "Passing" as a Malay merchant was an alternative open to a Minangkabau trader on the east coast, but it was hardly possible for one living in West Sumatra.

Commercial activities in West Sumatra itself, especially in the darek, experienced a great leap forward in the early nineteenth century with the introduction of coffee. This was also the time when the Padri wars were being waged in the interior. Under the impact of these wars and subsequent Dutch control, trading in West Sumatra came to develop its own special pattern of commercial merantau.

Toward the Padri Wars

If the eastern frontier of the Alam Minangkabau remained open for a relatively long time, that to the north, west, and south soon encountered obstacles. The Batak had been pushing southward toward the Minangkabau from a comparatively early date. The shoreline of the west coast quickly cut off any further advance in that direction. To the south, the inhospitable mountainous landscape thwarted extensive movement—even today the transportation network between West Sumatra and Kerinci and western Jambi is one of the worst in Sumatra. Among these three directions, the west deserves our special attention. In contrast to the expanding rantau hilir, it was this cul-de-sac, the rantau pasisir which first attracted foreign power, for the west coast provided excellent ports for exporting gold and pepper. These ports became points of contention among the Acehnese, the British, and the Dutch.

The first to arrive on the west coast were the Acehnese from the northern tip of Sumatra. An Acehnese royal representative (a sultan's son) was already found in Pariaman in the middle of the sixteenth century (Kathirithamby-Wells 1969:457). By 1612, Tiku and Pariaman were largely under their control, and Acehnese governors (*panglima*) were stationed there.[25] The Dutch and the British appeared very soon thereafter. A Dutch ship arrived in Tiku in

25. Apparently their control was less than complete. For example, they had to send a naval expedition in 1621 in order to suppress a rebellion in Tiku (Dasgupta 1962:92).

1602, and a British ship came to Pariaman in 1605 (Dasgupta:69, 91, 120). They engaged in the pepper trade on the west coast, with the permission of the Acehnese king, during most of the early seventeenth century. Eventually, however, the desire for larger profits and less restricted trading activities induced them to seek direct relationships with local chiefs. In this struggle, the Dutch eventually emerged as the winning party. In 1663, they concluded the Painan Contract with coastal chiefs in rebellion against the Acehnese. By the terms of this contract the Dutch gained a monopoly on the pepper trade, and in return they guaranteed the protection of the coastal areas against Acehnese aggression (Vlekke 1942:171). In 1666, the Dutch quickly suppressed a revolt by Acehnese agents, and the latter's influence on the west coast came to an end (Hall:321). By this time, the Dutch had begun to focus their activities in Padang, which was to remain the administrative center of West Sumatra all through the Dutch period and even until today.

The establishment of Dutch hegemony was not always a smooth business. Coastal chiefs were often at war with each other in the late seventeenth and early eighteenth centuries (Abdullah 1967:12, 15; Kathirithamby-Wells 1977:172, n. 102). Rebellions against the Dutch were not infrequent on the coast during the same period (Mansoer et al. 1970:99; Datuk Madjolelo and Marzoeki:44). Although Dutch activities were concentrated on the coast, their presence was also felt in the darek. The salt monopoly they imposed raised the price of this commodity drastically; Dutch salt was sold at a price 200 percent higher than that coming from Natal or Tapanuli to the north. The darek, which had traditionally relied on salt produced on the coast (Dobbin 1977:19), must have suffered greatly under this policy. Opium and arak (rice wine), sales of which were controlled by the Dutch, spread widely.[26] Their increasing popularity, together with the prevalence of gambling and crimes for money, caused great alarm among concerned Islamic teachers as early as the eighteenth century (Schrieke 1973:12–13; Dobbin 1974:328).

The coastal rantau was not only under foreign domination but

26. Both opium and arak may have been known in West Sumatra before the Dutch arrived. However, the systematic commercialization by the Dutch, by importation and the leasing of monopolistic sales rights, must have greatly encouraged their consumption.

was also in turmoil because of frequent feuds between local chiefs. The society was undergoing economic suffering and "moral decay." Against the onslaught first of the Acehnese and later the Dutch, the Minangkabau kingship proved to be powerless. Worse, the opportunistic Raja Alam (Minangkabau king) together with some coastal raja sometimes even collaborated with foreign powers. After a treaty with the Raja Alam in 1668, the Dutch representative in Padang became the Raja's stadholder with the titles of *mentri raja* (king's minister) and *wakil mutlak* (sole agent) (Kathirithamby-Wells 1969:478). Between the early 1750s and the early 1770s, the Minangkabau royal court, now disfavoring the Dutch, repeatedly but vainly courted the British in Fort Marlborough near Bengkulu for an alliance whereby the British were to oust the Dutch and to gain control over the coast between Pariaman and Natal (Kathirithamby-Wells 1977:160, 164). When the British temporarily captured Padang from the Dutch in 1781, royal envoys arrived at the coastal town with a message of congratulations upon the British military success. The British recipient noted that it was a message "which will be repeated with equal sincerity to those who may chance to succeed us" (Marsden 1966:335). Under these circumstances, the Padri movement seems to have been more than merely a doctrinal dispute between different religious schools or a conflict between adat and *agama* (religion). Facing the crisis of an eroding Alam Minangkabau, the Padri movement was also an attempt to find an alternative way to unify and strengthen the Alam, which, in this case, turned out to be Islam—the world religion that transcended differences among the nagari.

The origin of the term "Padri" is not clear. Folk etymology suggests that it comes either from *padre* (priest in Portuguese) or Pedir, a religious educational center in Aceh and a port of departure for Mecca (Graves:105). The Padri movement initially started as a kind of moderate Islamic reformism in the late eighteenth century. The most notable proponent of the movement during the initial stages was Tuanku nan Tuo of Koto Tuo, IV Angkat in Agam. He was particularly concerned with the prevalence of social vices such as murder, robbery, gambling, drinking and opium smoking. He hoped to change this situation by teaching the conduct proper for true Moslems. The movement, however, became radicalized after three *haji* (pilgrims) came back from Mecca in 1803, and especially after Tuanku nan Rinceh took over the leadership.[27] Tuanku nan Rinceh was of the opinion that all Minangkabau customs contrary to the Koran had to be abolished, and that any infringement of the Koran's instructions should be punished by death (Dobbin 1974). His new tenets were "faith, circumcision, abstinence and prayer five times a day"; "tobbacco, opium, *sirih* [for betel chewing], cockfighting, gambling and strong drinks" were prohibited (ibid.:336). Persons or villages that did not follow these tenets were punished or attacked. Given the nature of these tenets, the most common targets of these attacks were the adat notables, who were more likely to have the resources to indulge in these vices than ordinary people.

In the meantime, the coast of West Sumatra was directly subjected to the influence—no doubt, unintelligible and arbitrary to the Minangkabau—of international power politics. In 1781, the British occupied the west coast in opposition to the Dutch who supported the independence struggle of the United States. This occupation lasted until 1785. They retook the same area in 1793, this time in response to the Napoleonic wars in Europe; they intended "to counter the power of Napoleon on the Continent by denying him access to the colonies of the occupied countries" (Graves:125). It was not until 1819 that the Dutch returned to the area. Direct Dutch intervention in the Padri movement started in 1821, under the terms of an agreement between the Dutch administration in Padang and fourteen penghulu from the darek who claimed to represent the Minangkabau raja. According to the agreement, the Dutch were to fight against the aggression of the Padri and in return were to be ceded the "Minangkabau Kingdom" (Graves:138). However, effective military intervention did not take place until 1830 when the Diponegoro war in Java ended and extra troops could be deployed (Dobbin 1972:16; Hall:545). By 1833, the Padri wars began to take on the appearance of a war against the intruding foreign power. The fighting ended in victory for the Dutch, rather than for either the Padri or the anti-Padri factions (Abdullah

27. It is generally believed that these three haji were influenced by the Wahhabist movement in Mecca during this time (Dobbin 1974:332–333).

1967:26–27). In 1837, Bonjol, the last stronghold of the reformists, fell under the Dutch onslaught, and its leader, Tuanku Imam Bonjol, surrendered.

It has been customary to view the Padri movement as merely a local Islamic reformist movement. But if it is viewed in a different context, namely, as an attempt to reexamine the existing conception of the Alam Minangkabau and to create a new basis of solidarity, some of its features become more intelligible. First of all, in this framework the purely religious nature of the movement cannot be taken for granted any more. We will have to explain why religious teachers were promotors of the movement and why the movement's idiom was Islamic reformism.

With the possible exception of the royalty, Islamic teachers were the only group in Minangkabau society who possessed supranagari influence and concerns. This characteristic is reflected in their titles. The title of a tuanku generally included the name of his nagari of origin or residence (Hamka 1967:43, n. 1), for example, Tuanku Imam Bonjol (of Bonjol) and Tuanku nan Saleh of Talawi. This style contrasts strongly with purely adat titles, both for penghulu and for nagari Islamic functionaries according to adat, as, for example, Datuk Bandaro Kuning and Malim Marajo. Adat titles stand for particular lineages, not for individuals who currently happen to hold them; the successor of a Datuk Bandaro Kuning will himself be a Datuk Bandaro Kuning, and the same will be true for his successors. Nor are adat titles modified by nagari name, for they are only relevant to a specific nagari, and presumably most people in the nagari understand which title stands for which suku and lineage. By contrast, a tuanku title was applicable only to a specific person. There was only one Tuanku Iman Bonjol but there must have been dozens of Datuk Bandaro Kuning in the history of a lineage. The tuanku title was personal because it stood outside of the adat hierarchy, or, conversely, it stood outside the adat hierarchy because it was personal. Furthermore, a nagari name was affixed precisely because the tuanku's audience came from a wider area than a single nagari—the nagari name was a convenient way to identify a tuanku within the whole extent of Minangkabau society. Even today, if two Minangkabau, strangers to each other, meet, the first identity to be established is the nagari of origin.

In accordance with an adat saying which related that "*Syarak*

(Islam) ascended [from the coast], while adat descended [from Mount Merapi]" (*Syarak mendaki, adat menurun*), it is generally believed that Islam was introduced from the west coast to the darek. Also the first center of Islamic learning was founded in the coastal village of Ulakan in the latter half of the seventeenth century. Eventually it came to be considered the sole authority in religious matters in West Sumatra; "Until the rise of the Padri movement it was still anathema to the religious teachers in Minangkabau to question the religious authority of Ulakan" (Abdullah 1966:8–9). So it is significant that the reformist movement was launched in the late eighteenth century, not on the coast but in the darek. This makes it seem probable that reformism found fertile ground in the relatively newly Islamized darek, rather than in the Islamic conservative stronghold of the coastal rantau.

Many of the Islamic teachers of later fame in the Padri movement studied in Ulakan (Datoek Madjolelo and Marzoeki:40–41), which was, geographically speaking, sandwiched by the two most important centers of Dutch commercial activity in West Sumatra, namely Padang and Pariaman (see Map 1). Among them were some from the darek. As *urang darek* (darek people), and thus as true offspring of the Minangkabau World, these future Islamic teachers must have been deeply troubled by the turmoil, the moral decay, and the presence of foreign intruders on the coast. It was these people who later initiated the reformist movement on their return to the darek. Notable examples of those who embodied this pattern were the two chief instigators of the movement, namely, Tuanku nan Tuo of Koto Tuo and Tuanku Mansiangan of Koto Lawas (ibid.:40–41; Dobbin 1974:328, 335).[28]

There are some indications that the Padri movement was not necessarily directed against adat. Along with the Islamic teachers, there were many penghulu who later joined the movement (Abdullah 1967:20, 23–24; Graves:113; Dobbin 1972:10–12; Dobbin 1974:333). Although some reformists seem to have initially opposed the system of matrilineal inheritance (Dobbin 1974:330), this opposition never became the main thrust of the movement

28. Tuanku Mansiangan, one of the most influential Islamic figures of the time, was a son of Tuanku nan Tuo's teacher. After Tuanku nan Tuo separated himself from the radicalized Padri movement, he became its figurehead (Dobbin 1974:335).

(Graves:109–111). Despite the violent commotion the Padri movement caused in West Sumatra, it is believed that the substance of Minangkabau adat remained relatively unaltered (Abdullah 1972a:199–200; Graves:114). The most significant impact of the Padri movement on adat was that henceforward Islam and adat became one in a new idea of the Alam Minangkabau.

Compared to the secure buffer zones to the east and south (the expansive rantau hilir and the inhospitable south), the northern and western borders of the Alam Minangkabau had been subjected to increasing foreign invasions from the seventeenth century on.

The movement of some Batak, for example, the Lubis and Siregar clans, seems to have reached Upper Mandailing in the sixteenth century or by about 1600, and they were moving further southward from there (Castles 1975:70, n. 17; Datoek Batoeah Sango:95). In the meantime the west coast was occupied first by the Acehnese and later by the Dutch. It seems to have been important that both the Batak and the Dutch were *kafir* (infidels). Before the Padri movement, the Minangkabau had by no means been strong Moslems. An observation about the Minangkabau of the darek in the middle of the eighteenth century, cited by Dobbin, reads: [they are] "mostly pagan, or rather without religion, with the exception of the notables, who consider themselves Mahometans." Dobbin comments, "Islamic obligations such as the five daily prayers and the *puasa* fasting were laxly observed and mosques were poorly attended" (1974:327). In the face of external aggression by groups who could be defined as infidels, Islam, in addition to distinct adat, offered a means to secure identity and cohesion for Minangkabau society. Tuanku nan Tuo, an instigator of the Padri movement, once "impressed upon his pupils how essential it was for the Minangkabau to be welded into a community which based its actions on the will of God" (Dobbin 1977:29).

As a consequence of the Padri wars, a new sense of the relationship between Islam and adat appeared that is most vividly reflected in changing adat aphorisms. It is said that before Islam arrived in West Sumatra, "adat was based on appropriateness and propriety" (*adat bersendi alur dan patut*).[29] The aphorism underlines the flexibility and variability of Minangkabau adat. After the introduction

29. Concerning these changing aphorisms, see Nuzhadi (1971:v), Abdullah (1972a:200), and Datuk Nagari Basa (1968:129–130).

of Islam, it was replaced by a new formulation, "adat is based on Islam, Islam is based on adat" (*adat bersendi syarak, syarak bersendi adat*). The new aphorism in a sense indicated the interdependency of adat and Islam, but in another sense merely suggested a noncommittal parallel relationship. The aphorism was further reformulated during the Padri wars as follows: "Adat is based on Islam, Islam is based on the Holy Text" (*adat bersendi syarak, syarak bersendi Kitabullah*). This version, which had been generally accepted since that era, clearly insisted on the supremacy of Islam over adat. By its terms every violator of adat in theory became directly accountable to God Almighty. The aphorism also offered a framework which transcended the local variability of adat. According to Nasroen (1957:28–30), transient and specific adat was perfected by transcendental and universal Islam. It was thus only after the Padri wars that the curious but inseparable Minangkabau connection between matrilineal adat and patrilineally-oriented Islam developed. In the new understanding of this relation, a good Moslem should be a good adherent of adat, and a good adherent of adat should be a good Moslem.[30]

Minangkabau Society in Transition

The economic background of the Padri wars still remains largely to be described.[31] By comparison to the meager state of our knowledge of eighteenth century West Sumatra, we begin to obtain in-

---

30. Manifestations of this idea can be clearly observed in two instructive historical incidents. One is the existence of two purely Batak yet matrilineal nagari (Simpang Tonang and Cubadak) near the border of the Minangkabau and the Southern Batak. According to my interview with a village head of Simpang Tonang (February 1973), the Batak migrated from Pidoli-Penyabungan in South Tapanuli about 400 years ago. See also Datuk Batuah (pp. 166–171). Apparently, these originally patrilineal villages became matrilineal after conversion to Islam during the Padri wars. The other is the conversion of the Rejang people to Islam by Minangkabau and Kerinci migrants and their subsequent shift from patriliny to matriliny. According to Jaspan (1964), this took place around the 1920s and 1930s when the Kaum Muda (Young Group), Islamic reformists from West Sumatra and Kerinci, were active in the Rejang area. Despite these examples, we should be aware that the relation between adat and Islam has not always been void of tension.

31. A notable recent attempt is Dobbin (1977). However, her study does not deal with the economic activities of the Padri factions. Considering the fact that the Padri factions needed much arms and ammunition to fight the Dutch, it is important to know how they secured economic means to purchase military supplies and from whom they purchased them.

creasingly more information on Minangkabau society in the
nineteenth century, as the Dutch involvement in and later political
control over West Sumatra progressed. A noted economic reality of
the early nineteenth century was the expansion of coffee cultivation, above all in the darek.

Coffee was originally introduced to Java by the Dutch East India
Company toward the end of the seventeenth century (Graves:192).
It was soon to become one of the most important colonial commercial products; by the middle of the eighteenth century, coffee and
tea were, after textiles, the most important commodities sold by the
company in Amsterdam (Andaya:196).

Coffee was probably already cultivated in West Sumatra in the
late eighteenth century. However, coffee exports from Padang in
1800 amounted to only 2,000 *pikol*. In 1820, the figure rose to
17,000 *pikol*, and in 1833, to 81,000 *pikol* (Huitema 1935:46).[32]

In view of its ecological requirements (cool weather, good rainfall, relatively high altitude and so forth), coffee was mainly cultivated in the darek, for example, Maninjau, Singkarak, Solok, IV
Kota, Bukit Kamang, Air Terbit, Rao-Rao, and Candung
(Graves:184; Dobbin 1977:30–36; Nahuijs:173). Coffee cultivation must have greatly stimulated the commercial activities of the
darek. Coffee had to be bought in the production area, transported to collection points in the darek, and then brought down to
Padang for export. Areas of coffee cultivation presented profitable
markets for itinerant traders and artisans. Even the Padri wars of
the early nineteenth century may have ultimately encouraged commerce. Troops, both Dutch and Padri, had to be mobilized and
moved from one area to another. Supplies had to be procured in the
villages and had to be transported by the villagers. During the initial
stage of the Padri wars, Minangkabau merchants in the darek made
a considerable profit by selling rice to the Dutch troops
(Oki 1977:39). Traffic of goods and people became more frequent
than ever. The export of coffee itself actually increased while the
Padri wars were raging (Graves:194).

The Padri wars and the intensification of coffee cultivation were

32. This increase does not necessarily reflect solely gains in production; it probably also includes the increase in the amount of coffee exported from Padang rather
than from some other port.

the prelude to a profound transformation of Minangkabau society. The end of the fighting and the consolidation of Dutch power led to change in many aspects of the Minangkabau life. These changes may be summarized under four headings: the development of the transportation system; the spread of a money economy; the establishment of an overall administrative structure; and educational progress.

In their prosecution of the war, the deployment of soldiers, military equipment, and supplies was a matter of grave concern to the Dutch. Their central position was on the coast, in Padang, while the strongholds of the Islamic reformists were far off in the darek. Supplies and soldiers sent from Batavia (now Jakarta) had therefore to be transported from Padang to battlegrounds in the interior. The main obstacle to this effort was the Bukit Barisan mountain range. One of the major pathways connecting the darek and the rantau in olden times was the route taken by Raffles in 1818, that is, from Padang to Kubung XIII, then across Lake Singkarak by boat. It took Raffles and his company one week to reach Pagarruyung from Padang, a distance of not more than eighty miles. (See the map inserted between pages 344 and 345 of Raffles 1830.) Partly from military considerations and partly for the transporation of coffee, a new path, the Anei Pass, was built in 1833 (Travellers' Official Bureau of Netherlands India n.d.:31). The pass, which links Kayu Tanam in the rantau and Padang Panjang in the darek, is only ten miles long, but it climbs up more than 2,000 feet. It still remains the major route between the two regions of West Sumatra. The problems of coffee transportation gave further impetus to extending the road network. By the end of the 1850s, three more routes were created from the coast to the interior: Air Bangis to Rao, Tiku to Maninjau, and Pariaman to Padang Panjang (Graves:222).

The discovery of coal in Sawahlunto in 1867 brought about the introduction of another type of transportation, the railway. For the exploitation of coal, railways were opened between Padang and Sawahlunto via Padang Panjang in 1894, seven years after the construction was ordered. The line was later extended from Padang Panjang to Bukittinggi and Payakumbuh. The discovery of coal was also responsible for the improvement of sea transportation. An order was issued in 1886 for building a new port at Padang to accommodate the larger ships that were expected to stop over for supplies of coal. In 1892 a contract was signed for a regular shipping connection between Java, Bengkulu, and Padang (Travellers' Official Information Bureau of Netherlands India:27, 31).

In step with the development of the transportation system, urbanization progressed. As is exemplified by Fort de Kock (now Bukittinggi) and Fort van der Capellen (now Batu Sangkar), both of which were built in the 1820s, urban centers were mainly of Dutch creation. Initially serving military purposes, these towns and cities rapidly developed into commercial, administrative, and educational centers. Urbanization began to create a corps of urbanites, lower government officials, merchants, artisans, and non-Minangkabau, who were not strongly bound by the adat of the nagari.

The second development, the spread of a money economy, was closely related to coffee cultivation. Although coffee deliveries to the Dutch were not substantial until 1820, coffee production was not necessarily inconsequential before that time. In addition to home consumption, coffee could have been sold to other buyers than the Dutch for better prices. Most notably, coffee may have been channeled to the eastern coast of Sumatra. This possibility is particularly likely considering the contemporary expansion of the British, fierce trading competitors of the Dutch, to the Malay peninsula. They had established a settlement in Penang in 1786, occupied Malacca in 1795, and purchased Singapore in 1819.

Coffee cultivation above all meant an increased flow of cash. Traditionally, the medium of commodity exchange in West Sumatra was either barter or gold dust (Verkerk Pistorius:34, n. 29). Spanish dollars were already in circulation, though limited, by the middle of the seventeenth century, for the tolls on pepper exports on the coast were measured in this currency (Kathirithamby-Wells 1976:70, n. 29). The circulation of this coinage jumped tremendously in the early nineteenth century in response to coffee exports and to the appearance of American buyers, who tended to use Spanish dollars in their transactions (Dobbin 1977:24–25).

Coffee cultivation not only meant cash incomes for the producers; it also presented economic opportunities to coffee purchasers, transporters, other traders, and artisans. Handicrafts, most probably hitherto mainly for home consumption, became commercial enterprises in the darek, for example, weaving in Agam and Nagari Silungkang and gold and silver smithies around Bukittinggi (Verkerk Pistorius:36–37, n. 30; Bickmore 1868:432). Markets also prospered. In 1825, thirty-four and fifteen markets were counted respectively in Tanah Datar and in Agam as subjects of market taxation (Graves:190). By the end of the nineteenth century, a weekly rotating market system was established in all of West Sumatra by which a nagari in each subdistrict took a turn to hold its own market once or twice every week and attracted people from neighboring villages (Abdullah 1971:9). Some of these weekly markets were already attracting up to 3,000 to 4,000 people in the 1830s (Dobbin 1977:27). In 1879, 15,000 persons visited Bukittinggi for an "ordinary market day"; the comparable figure in 1904 was 29,000. One hundred twenty-five *bendi* (a horse-drawn, two-wheeled carriage for transporting passengers and commodities) were registered in Bukittinggi in 1892 and 531 in 1904. Likewise in Payakumbuh, 33 *bendi* were counted in 1885, 969 in 1903, and 1,200 in 1904 (Oki:38).

From the beginning, Minangkabau merchants and middlemen were deeply involved in the process of coffee collection. Coffee, unlike gold, is a bulky commodity for its value and had to go through many hands before it reached its destination on the coast. Petty merchants purchased coffee from local producers and resold it in the new urban centers of the darek such as Bukittinggi and Batu Sangkar. Depending on the location of a coffee production area, more than one merchant could be involved before the coffee reached a local urban center. From there, it had to be brought down by bearers to the west coast. By the end of the 1830s Minangkabau middlemen were so entrenched in coffee collection that "Michiels [a governor of West Sumatra] dismissed [them] as unnecessary 'parasites' and 'swindlers,' whose only contribution was to raise the ultimate cost of goods" and who "should be 'forced to return to agriculture'." Michiels came to the conclusion that forced cultivation and delivery of coffee was the only solution to this problem. To this end and to hinder the drain of coffee to the east coast and to Singapore, the Coffee Cultivation System was introduced to West Sumatra in 1847 (Graves:196–197, 204, 206–207).[33]

---

33. The traffic to the east coast was definitely active in the 1830s, partly because cheaper commodities were available in Singapore (Graves: 195–199, 202–203). By shipping their produce via the east coast, coffee cultivators could avoid the heavy export duties imposed by the Dutch on the west coast (Oki:35).

Its economic implications aside, the Coffee Cultivation System brought about the systematization of the administrative structure, for the efficient implementation of forced cultivation and delivery was not possible without a well-organized administrative apparatus.[34] Under Dutch control, the Province of Sumatra's West Coast was divided into two residencies, the Padangsche Bovenlanden (Padang Highlands) and the Padangsche Benedenlanden (Padang Lowlands). Assistant residents and *controleurs* (both regional administrative heads) were assigned under a resident in descending order of territorial jurisdiction.[35] The governor down to the *controleurs* were all Dutchmen. Among the native officials, the *tuanku laras (larashoofd)* administered a federation of several nagari, while the *penghulu kepala (nagarihoofd)* acted as head of the nagari.[36] Within the nagari itself, *penghulu suku rodi* took charge of their lineage members. These Dutch-appointed native officials were held responsible for the implementation of the corvée services, coffee cultivations, and coffee deliveries under their respective jurisdictions. They received commissions for successful execution of their duties.

Another important development within the new administrative structure was the emergence of supranagari native officials who were not tied by adat. Although the offices of tuanku laras, *penghulu kepala,* and *penghulu suku rodi* were new, their holders were all from the traditional nagari penghulu elite. In spite of their new titles, their power was still limited to their area of origin and was generally not transferable elsewhere. From the 1840s on, however, a new breed of native officials appeared. These were the *jaksa* (prosecuting magistrates in the Dutch court system), the coffee-warehouse masters, the *koffee mantri* (coffee-crop inspectors), and other lower

34. By forcing the peasants to maintain rice cultivation for subsistence and not for export, and by suppressing coffee prices, the Coffee Cultivation System (officially called the Forced Delivery System) considerably dampened the desire of the indigenous population to pursue commercial agriculture (Oki:29–31, 34, 38; Schrieke 1955b:96–99). Not until the last quarter of the nineteenth century, when non-coffee cash crops (such as cassia, cinnamon, gutta percha, nutmeg, and tobacco) emerged, did the Minangkabau again begin to be actively involved in commercial agriculture (Oki:30, 36).

35. The following account is based on Graves (pp. 157–158, 169–176, 214, 233–237) and Abdullah (1967:35–38).

36. The nagari federation was sometimes according to local adat and sometimes fabricated by the Dutch.

officials, such as the clerks and secretaries who worked for various government offices. They were relatively well educated, and many of them could be and actually were appointed anywhere in West Sumatra. They were to form a nucleus of an oftentimes self-perpetuating intellectual elite who sent their children and relatives to the new institutions of higher education through their connections with Dutch officials.

Concurrent with the emergence of an embryonic professional and official class was the spread of secular education. In 1846 there were eleven autonomous nagari schools in the Padang Highlands. In the 1850s nagari schools expanded to the Lowlands; seven schools were established along the coast and three more were added to the Highlands (Graves:259, 275-276). With the intention of improving teaching capabilities, a Normal School (Kweekschool), the first in Sumatra and one of only three teachers' training schools in the Outer Islands, was founded in Bukittinggi in 1856 (Abdullah 1967:62; Graves:266). This expansion of secular education is reflected in student enrollments. There were 233 students in nagari schools in 1855. The numbers grew to 629 in 1860 and to 1,128 in 1864 (the highest number reached before 1870) (Graves:275-276).

Initially the government did not pay much attention to indigenous educational development save for the establishment of the Normal School. However, by a royal decree of 1871, the colonial government was formally committed to native education. Government schools were built, some of the former nagari schools were subsidized, and school curricula were standardized. The operation of schools came to be closely supervised. In order to qualify as a government school, a school had to have a graduate of the Normal School on its teaching staff. The Sekolah Raja or Princes' School (a nickname for the Normal School) was expanded as well as upgraded. The way was also opened for Minangkabau students to pursue higher education in other areas, for example, at the Batavia Normal School. In 1877 for the first time a student from the Sekolah Raja left for further study in Holland (ibid.:346-354).

Change in all the above spheres was to continue all through the latter part of the nineteenth century. In the twentieth century, however, there was a significant shift in the direction of change. In the nineteenth century it had been largely self-contained, its social dynamics mainly operating within the confines of West Sumatra.

But after 1900, the Minangkabau were more and more drawn into the larger framework of the Dutch East Indies, and the social dynamics of their transformation began to take effect beyond the provincial boundaries of Sumatra's West Coast.

In the early twentieth century, West Sumatra began to be linked directly to other parts of Sumatra. Automotive public transportation was opened between Bukittinggi and Medan in the mid-1910s. By 1920, the road to Pekan Baru in the east had been improved a great deal (see the map attached to Encyclopaedisch Bureau 1920). As the sole port connecting West Sumatra to Batavia, Padang assumed greater importance during the same period. The city became more cosmopolitan in character and its population grew. The first permanent American Christian mission arrived in Padang in 1900 (Gould 1961:118–119). The population of Padang had fluctuated between 9,000 and 15,000 during the period of 1770 and 1865. There are no figures available for the remainder of the nineteenth century. But by 1905, Padang was already a city of respectable size—47,000, of which 39,000 were natives and the rest foreigners (Dutch, Chinese, Arabs, and others) (Evers and Thalib 1970:15; Encyclopaedie van Nederlandsch-Indië 3, 1919:235).

The year 1908 was the opening of a new era in the economic life of West Sumatra. Because of decreasing returns on coffee production, which were already apparent as early as 1870s, the government abandoned the Coffee Cultivation System in 1908. It hoped to increase its revenues by stimulating local economic activities and imposing monetary taxation on them (Schrieke 1955b:95–99; Abdullah 1967:57–58). (The initial levies ignited a series of brief, unsuccessful rebellions, primarily in the darek. For more information, see Oki:68–82.) Various restrictions on indigenous agriculture were abolished. The ban on rice exports, which had been instituted to maintain the subsistence basis of native society, was lifted. The route to the east coast ports, which had been closed to cut off trade with Singapore, was reopened. The People's Credit System was instituted; it was enthusiastically welcomed and gave much impetus to the subsequent development of economic activities in West Sumatra (Oki:47–57).

Not only in West Sumatra but also in other parts of Sumatra economic opportunities were increasingly abundant. Tobacco plantations in Deli near Medan were in operation by the late nineteenth century. Rubber plantations in northern Sumatra rapidly expanded from the early twentieth century. Likewise, smallholder rubber cultivation spread swiftly in inland Riau, Jambi, and South Sumatra. Oil exploitation progressed in northern and east central Sumatra. Tin production on the islands of Bangka, Belitung, and Singkep off the east coast of South Sumatra continued to grow. Toward the end of the nineteenth century more intensive coal mining was initiated in West Sumatra, and another mine was opened in South Sumatra later.[37] These boom areas presented profitable markets and commercial opportunities not only to large merchants, who were likely to be Chinese, but also to middlemen and itinerant traders. The purchasing power of these new markets is demonstrated, albeit in extreme dimension, by the case of rubber in Jambi. "In 1925 a Chevrolet agent reported 156 American cars in Jambi although there were only three miles of roads" (Gould:100).

The administrative structure also witnessed significant changes in the early twentieth century. In 1914, the laras system was replaced by the demang system. In contrast to the tuanku laras, who functioned as both the administrative and the adat head of a nagari federation, a demang (subdistrict head) was a purely administrative official (Abdullah 1967:58). He did not have any adat or pseudo-adat role. He did not need to be a penghulu, and his appointment was not restricted to the area of his origin. The demang was a full-fledged bureaucrat, in theory owing his position to merit and training. He could serve anywhere in West Sumatra as well as in other Malay-speaking areas, including East Sumatra, Riau, and Kalimantan (Graves:369–370).

Around the turn of the century, many areas of Indonesia were directly incorporated into the Dutch East Indies (Vlekke:327–329; Legge 1964:79–80). This meant an inevitable expansion of bureaucracy. Since the beginning of the twentieth century, the center of Dutch colonial economic interests had shifted away from Java to the Outer Islands, particularly to Sumatra. As described above, plantations and other enterprises started to operate in many parts of Sumatra. In each case, more and more literate and semiliterate native personnel were needed to fill low-level administrative

37. Concerning these economic activities, see Gould (pp. 100–101); Bartlett et al. (1972:43–51); Allen and Donnithorne (1957:97–98, 103, 169–172, 175–178).

positions. It was often the Alam Minangkabau that provided the needed educated and mobile personnel. "Minangkabau *perantau* [migrant] civil servants, who had a relative headstart in education, came along in the baggage of the Dutch colonial offices and took positions in the indigenous ranks of the new administrations" (Graves:341). According to a report of 1915, 165 men from Nagari Kota Gedang, a village long famous for producing Dutch-educated intellectuals, were estimated to be government officials; seventy-nine of them were already serving outside West Sumatra (ibid.:391).

The Ethical Policy, inaugurated in 1901 and oriented to the welfare of the natives, greatly contributed to the expansion of vernacular schools and the development of Western education (Furnivall 1967:229–236). In 1913, there were 111 *volksscholen* (people's schools), or reorganized elementary schools, in West Sumatra. By 1915, the number had arisen to 358, and then to 548 by 1925 (Abdullah 1971). The diffusion of secular education to practically every village was also significant in symbolic terms. *Guru mengaji,* traditional Islamic teachers who taught the recitation of the Koran in the villages, were clad in the Chinese-style shirt (*baju Cina*) and striped sarong without any sandals. School teachers, by contrast, strode along in high-collared jackets (*jas tutup*), trousers, and shoes (Radjab 1950:16). They personified something new, Western, and modern to the villagers. Whether this "something new" was accepted by the villagers or not, the wide diffusion of village schools brought the villagers face to face with the distant, or maybe not so distant, shock waves of what we might call modernization.

The reform of Islamic education and the expansion of modern religious schools also began to take place in the 1910s, after Islamic reformists in the Kaum Muda (Young Group) movement returned from Mecca. Adopting the government schools as their model, they introduced the grade system to the religious schools. Secular subjects were incorporated in the curriculum, new texts were prepared, and girls admitted for the first time (Abdullah 1971:13, 54–59).

Dutch-language instruction, which had previously been available only rarely to the natives, took new strides in the early twentieth century. HIS, Dutch-native seven-year primary schools, were established in Bukittinggi and Padang in 1914. In the late 1910s, the government also founded a MULO (More Extended Primary Education), a junior high school (ibid.:61–62). Knowledge of Dutch was an essential condition for higher education, which was then available mainly in Java and Holland. An increasing number of Minangkabau students were involved in this overseas education. Between 1874 and 1900, seven of the 183 students enrolled at the STOVIA (the School for Training Native Doctors) in Batavia were originally from West Sumatra. For the 1900-1914 period, more than thirty-six of a total of 200 students were Minangkabau (Graves:367).[38]

Obviously, it is absurd to think that pre–nineteenth-century Minangkabau was an idyllic unchanging society. Though we can only speculate on their impact, the incorporation of kingship and the introduction of Islam, just to mention two developments, must have meant considerable adjustment on the part of the existing society. Whether we talk of the Minangkabau society of the fifteenth or of the nineteenth century, that society is still a process as well as a state. Nevertheless, the foregoing description makes it clear that for the Minangkabau of West Sumatra, the nineteenth and twentieth centuries were quite distinct from previous centuries in terms of the scope, rate, and intensity of change to which their society was subjected.

Summary

Though the Minangkabau tendency to merantau is well recognized in contemporary Indonesia, the connection with its historical antecedent, geographical mobility in the form of village segmentation, has been seldom pointed out. To begin with, some features of the Minangkabau matrilineal system suggest a pattern of sedentary agriculture and periodic village segmentation in the early history of this society. Above all, the institution of the commuting husband implied permanent settlements and sedentary agriculture. Correlated to the economic insignificance of the husband vis-à-vis his wife and children was the existence of sufficient ancestral land to support the members of the matrilineage. Considering that agricultural intensification was not the general practice and that

38. HIS stands for Hollandsch-inlandsch school, MULO for Meer Uitgebreide Lagere Onderwijs, and STOVIA for School tot Opleiding van Inlandsche Artsen.

Minangkabau population growth may have been fast in comparison to other Sumatran ethnic groups, village segmentation must have been a regular feature of the societal process in West Sumatra. Indeed, the study of the proliferation of suku (matrilineal clans) in West Sumatra strongly suggests an extensive movement of suku and thus the frequent occurence of village segmentation in times past.

The tambo (traditional historiography) suggests that the Minangkabau were well aware of their own geographical mobility in terms of seeking new areas of settlement. The origin story of the Minangkabau does not relate their ancestors' descent from heaven but their migration from Ruhum (Turkey) to Mount Merapi when all the land was still under the sea and thus when nobody inhabited the area which subsequently emerged. Eventually, the Alam Minangkabau itself was gradually filled up, first in the darek (the land of origin) and then in the rantau (the frontier), by the expansion of population and by village segmentation. By the same token, the Minangkabau's four-stage concept of settlement projects the nonstatic nature of their habitation patterns. Like a human being, the settlement grows up, in size and complexity, from *taratak* (a collection of huts), to *dusun* (small settlement), to *koto* (large settlement), and to *nagari* (village). And like a human being, the settlement produces offspring upon reaching maturity. This conception of autochthonous metamorphosis is a tacit indication of the importance accorded to village segmentation in the formation of the Alam Minangkabau.

While village segmentation proceeded in West Sumatra, part of the population was also moving to the Rantau Hilir (Downstream Rantau), crossing the Bukit Barisan mountain range in the general direction of four important rivers in eastern Sumatra: the Siak, the Kampar, the Indragiri, and the Batang Hari. Although there are some indications that the Minangkabau were moving in this direction as early as the fifteenth century, the movement picked up momentum mainly from the seventeenth century. This migration was partly due to changing political configurations along the Straits of Malacca, the decline of Aceh and Johor, and the rise of the Dutch.

Different from village segmentation within West Sumatra, the movement in the rantau hilir was often commercial in nature, that is, people migrated individually as merchants, transporters, and sailors. Three commodities, gold, pepper, and tin, invited Minangkabau commercial involvement in the rantau hilir. A review of trading centers and production areas associated with these commercial items shows that they were mainly located outside the darek. The Minangkabau who were active trading on both sides of the Straits of Malacca before the nineteenth century may well have mainly originated from the rantau hilir rather than directly coming from across the Bukit Barisan mountain range.

Whether the rantau hilir was demographically consequential to West Sumatra or not, its ideological importance for the concept of an ever expanding Alam Minangkabau is apparent. Compared with the rantau pasisir, which was sharply circumscribed by the narrow coastal stretch, the rantau hilir exhuded a sense of expansiveness—a reflection of geographical spread as well as a commercial merantau less constrained by the customs of matrilineal system than village segmentation. This sense of expansiveness which the rantau hilir could offer gained significance particularly after the rantau in West Sumatra became crowded and the west coast fell under foreign domination, first of the Acehnese and later of the Dutch.

The closing years of the eighteenth century witnessed two important developments in Minangkabau society. The eruption of the Padri movement—which I view as a social movement attempting to restructure and revitalize the existing concept of the Alam Minangkabau—eventually invited Dutch intervention and the establishment of Dutch political hegemony in West Sumatra. Another key development during this time was the cultivation of coffee. The economic prospects of coffee cultivation were no doubt partly responsible for Dutch intervention in the Padri wars. But, more importantly, coffee cultivation decisively involved West Sumatra, and above all the darek, in the money economy and the rapid spread of commercialization.

The middle of the nineteenth century marked the beginning of a new era for Minangkabau society. The Padri movement was pacified by the Dutch. Dutch political control was securely established from the coast (the Padang Lowlands) to the darek (the Padang Highlands). The Coffee Cultivation System was introduced to maximize the profits of the colonial government. Subsequently the transportation network was elaborated, urbanization stimulated, the money economy extended, the administrative structure systematized, and native education advanced. Development in these areas was to continue through and after the end of the nineteenth century. Only in the twentieth century, however, was Minangkabau society more and more drawn into the larger framework of the Dutch East Indies.

After reviewing these social developments, we may ask ourselves at this point what implications they have on the Minangkabau practice of merantau. As was mentioned already, village segmentation was a regular feature of the societal process in West Sumatra. The notion of geographical mobility and village segmentation is deeply embedded in the world of the tambo. The tambo essentially views the Alam Minangkabau as ever-expanding in correspondence to the growth and movement of the population. In demographic terms, too, we have seen that this notion of mobility was largely replicated as the Alam was settled, from the foot of Merapi to the darek, and then to the rantau, including the rantau pasisir and the rantau hilir. Since the seventeenth century, however, actual demographic mobility had been increasingly curtailed by the invasion of foreign elements: the Batak from the north, and the Acehnese and the Dutch from the west. It is in this context that the existence of the expansive rantau hilir was ideologically important for sustaining the notion of an ever-expanding Alam Minangkabau. Although I doubt that there was frequent traffic between the rantau hilir and West Sumatra, above all the darek, before the end of the eighteenth century, steady movement between the two regions was a significant demographic phenomenon between the late 1700s and the middle of the nineteenth century. Dutch economic power, centered in Padang in the west coast of Sumatra, was counterbalanced by the British, who began to establish strongholds along the Straits of Malacca. Attracted by the cheapness of commodities such as Indian cloths and Siamese salt available at the British free ports of Penang and Singapore, the Minangkabau increasingly exported gambier and coffee, the main commercial products of the darek, via the east coast (Graves:195–199, 202–203; Dobbin 1977:33). Active traffic between the darek and the east coast is also suggested by the prosperity of markets around Payakumbuh—the main starting point for the eastward route out of the darek—during this time: in 1833, a Dutch traveler was strongly impressed by such a market which he described as filled by a great variety of goods and swarming with buyers and sellers (Dobbin 1974:342).

The middle of the nineteenth century marked a radical change in the notion of the Alam's expansion. After the consolidation of their political power and the implementation of the Coffee Cultivation System, the Dutch closed the traffic between the darek and rantau hilir in order to check the coffee drain to the east coast (Schrieke 1955b:97). Furthermore, the systematization of the administrative structure by the Dutch led to the creation of a "Minangkabau land" on the west side of the island; the tight administrative boundary contained and restrained the Alam Minangkabau within the Dutch-created Province of Sumatra's West Coast. Thus physically limited, the notion of an ever-expanding Alam Minangkabau lost some of its ideological vitality.[39] Significantly, the Minangkabau social process between 1850 and 1900 was, as pointed out already, contained within West Sumatra. It was almost as if internal social forces were germinating, biding the time till they could start to pour out again from West Sumatra in the new century.

The Dutch presence in West Sumatra after the middle of the nineteenth century had three vital consequences for Minangkabau society. As in Java, the population in West Sumatra grew rapidly under the Pax Nederlandica. Although reliable figures are difficult to come by for the nineteenth century, one estimate indicates that the population of West Sumatra nearly tripled between 1852 and 1930: from 690,000 to 1,900,000 (Graves:24; *Volkstelling 1930*, 4:114).[40] Second, the entrenchment of the Dutch administrative

39. Disregarding Tapanuli, which was initially under the supervision of the governor in Padang, this administrative boundary roughly corresponds to the present Province of West Sumatra. The major difference is that the present province does not include Bangkinang to the east and Kerinci to the south. One important consequence of this administrative demarcation was that by making Padang the provincial capital, the Dutch disturbed the traditional balance between the darek and the rantau. Henceforth politically strong Padang often dominated the cultural heartland of the darek. The idea of the darek flanked by the two rantau, that is, the rantau pasisir and the rantau hilir, became insignificant. As the connection between Padang and Batavia (the capital of the Dutch East Indies) became closer, Padang (or the west coast) was no longer an end point but a gateway to opportunities in Java, and thereby overshadowing the rantau hilir with a great sense of expansiveness. Though this tendency has been mitigated since the flourishing of Pekan Baru after the late 1950s, it is still perceptible even now.

40. The figures are rounded. During the same period, the native population of Java more than quadrupled (Nitisastro 1970:5, 75). Probably improved sanitary conditions were a major reason for the increase in West Sumatra.

apparatus and its omnivorous incorporation of every nagari into
the Province of Sumatra's West Coast meant that village segmentation ceased to be an autogenetic process and became an administrative concern.

If these two trends aggravated the population problem and made
village segmentation less easy, the third consequence of Dutch co-
lonialism, the proliferation of the money economy, opened up new
avenues for geographical mobility. The Dutch encouraged coffee
cultivation. The introduction of various spices and rubber, and the
commercial production of copra soon followed. The transportation
network between the darek and the rantau was facilitated by the
opening of the Anei Pass. Together with the ongoing systematization of the administrative structure, the resultant flourishing of
commercial activities provided new possibilities for population
movement. The Minangkabau matrilineal system itself probably
encouraged men to take advantage of these possibilities for migration. The men's position in the Minangkabau village was more
insecure, and in a sense freer, than that of women, owing to their
relative lack of physical and material roots in the matrilineal system; both house and land were largely for the benefit of women.
Traditionally men were expected to play an enterprising role outside the household, in opening new agricultural land and increasing the harta pusaka of their sublineage. For, after *hutan
tinggi* or unopened land was divided between suku at the initial
stage of opening and settling a new village, the subsequent expansion of ancestral land in correspondence with population growth
primarily rested on the initiative and efforts of male members of
each paruik. Men were not strongly tied down to land as small
landholders since land essentially belonged to women. Yet
communally-held land provided merantau-aspirants with security
to fall back on and sometimes financial resources for business or the
advancement of education. And the matrilineal kinship network
could help the recruitment and placement of new migrants.

Starting from the middle of the nineteenth century, historical
forces at work in society continued steadily to enlarge the context
of Minangkabau life: from the nagari to the supranagari domain,
and from West Sumatra to the Dutch East Indies and even to Holland. The response to this opportunity was increasing mobility
among the Minangkabau people. What is today celebrated as typi-

cal Minangkabau merantau practice began to take form and to pick up momentum—merantau not as village segmentation but as an individualized flow of merchants, artisans, students, clerks, government officials, political activists, professionals, and religious teachers. If one may paraphrase Graves's description of Minangkabau educational development, the newer merantau practice, which may have started as a small trickle in the 1840s and 1850s, had grown to a modest flood by the 1920s (Graves:107). This upsurge of merantau temporarily slowed in the Great Depression which first hit Sumatra in 1929 with the crash of rubber prices (Gould:102). The Japanese invasion of the archipelago in 1942 came before the Indies had fully recovered from the Depression. It was followed by eight years of war (World War II and the subsequent war of independence against the Dutch). By that time, the practice of the new merantau had become imbedded in the society and culture of the Minangkabau people.[41]

41. Migration similar to village segmentation, however, was not unheard of even in the late nineteenth and the early twentieth centuries. For example, a number of people moved from more populated villages in Agam (the present subdistrict of Tanjung Raya) to more sparsely populated, preexisting villages in the same region (the present subdistrict of Lubuk Basung) in the late nineteenth century. Evidently this type of migration was more commonly observed in such outer areas as Pasaman and Indrapura (Oki:132–135).

4 / Changing Patterns
of Merantau

The Minangkabau men's tendency to merantau, in the general sense of leaving one's home village in search of wealth, knowledge, and fame, was noticed in the early twentieth century. Lekkerkerker speculated on its causes in his book of 1916. His opinion was that "emigration-sickness" was closely related to the Minangkabau man's place in the society. As he saw it, merantau was a way to escape from the bondage of "matriarchy"; "a Minangkabau man, consciously or not, is always looking for a place where he can find his 'freedom' and 'personality'."[1]

A famous, presumably age-old, adat aphorism commends:

> Karatau and madang [grown] far upstream,
> No fruit, no flowers yet,
> Go merantau, young man, first,
> At home, no use yet.[2]

Despite the importance of Minangkabau migration, long recognized by Lekkerkerker and by the aphorism, it is extremely difficult to ascertain the actual scope and magnitude, let alone such characteristics as destinations, of merantau. By the 1920s there may indeed have been many Minangkabau perantau (migrants) active in many parts of Sumatra. On the other hand, it could be that these

---

1. This passage is Abdullah's rephrasing of Lekkerkerker's opinions (1967:66). Also see Lekkerkerker (1916:207–212).

2. In Minangkabau, *Karatau madang dihulu,/Babuah babungo balun,/ Marantau bujang dahulu,/Dirumah baguno balun. Karatau* is a species of mulberry, while *madang* is often used in the making of pillars for houses.

118

perantau were mainly government officials, merchants, office clerks, and artisans, and that they simply were more noticeable to Dutch administrators and scholars than other less conspicuous migrants (for example, Banjarese peasants and fishermen from Borneo moving to eastern Sumatra) would have been.[3] The aphorism itself could have been more a statement of an ideal than a real practice.

In order to assess the social significance of the famed Minangkabau practice of merantau, it is essential to obtain a clear understanding of its magnitude and nature, in addition to its ideological underpinnings. Yet factual information on the merantau practice is meager. The first and only systematic source of information on migration during the Dutch colonial era comes from the 1930 census. The census results do not necessarily provide fully detailed or accurate information on migration—Minangkabau or otherwise. Nevertheless, the census is a valuable source and any attempt to comprehend the merantau phenomenon in the colonial period must rely on and extrapolate from it.

The situation after independence is no better in terms of data; it is in many ways worse than during the Dutch period, for there is no nationwide information available. The censuses of 1961 and 1971 are of little use in the present context, because neither of them provides information about the ethnic background of the population. Yet, though understandably on a far more modest scale than the census, there have been a few surveys conducted on the subject of Minangkabau migration in recent years.[4] These surveys were

3. Governor Harun Zain of West Sumatra (1966–1977) makes a similar observation about the high visibility of Minangkabau perantau, which is due to their occupations in contemporary Indonesia: "Minangkabau, if they go to the rantau, open restaurants. Or they become *tukang jahit* or peddlers, or there are also many who become civil servants. In either case, what is clear is that their places [destinations of merantau] are always where they easily meet many people. Thus it is not surprising if their [Minangkabau perantau's] number looks as if very many because they are indeed everywhere" ("Harun Zain: Fondasi, Menjelang Isi," *Tempo*, 8 October 1977, p. 26). *Tukang jahit* are tailors who, with their own or rented sewing machines, sew practically anything in a short time at a roadside or at a shop.

4. For example, Thamrin (1972), Fritz (c. 1972), and Naim (1973b). Undoubtedly, there are many geographically mobil ethnic groups in Indonesia. As far as I am aware, however, the Minangkabau are extremely self-conscious about the practice of merantau even in comparison to other migration-oriented ethnic groups. In addition to those surveys on merantau which were carried out by Minangkabau, Thamrin (1972) and Naim (1973b), we often encounter articles on merantau in the regional newspapers (*Haluan* and *Singgalang*). Together with numerous books on the Minangkabau adat by Minangkabau authors, these writings suggest that geograph-

carried out within many financial and time restrictions, under different assumptions, and for various purposes. They are often plagued by internal methodological problems as well as those of comparability. Despite these shortcomings, they can not be written off; they do furnish indispensable data which would otherwise be unobtainable. In addition to these data, the results of my own survey in West Sumatra will be incorporated into the subsequent analysis. The results of my survey are often mentioned in the remaining chapters; some explanation of its methodology is therefore in order here.

Methodology

Between January 1972 and June 1973, I conducted five types of surveys in West Sumatra, some of which dealt with the question of merantau to a great extent. The five surveys were: a nagari survey in 232 nagari in West Sumatra; a household survey among 395 male respondents (household heads) in four villages near Bukittinggi; a household survey among 75 male perantau (household heads) in Padang and Pekan Baru (Province of Riau), who originally came from two of the four nagari in the second survey; a survey on family history among 132 of the 395 respondents in the second survey; a survey on merantau history among the same sample of 132 respondents in the fourth survey. These surveys were carried out roughly in this chronological order. They grew out of questions which I came to form through my experiences in the field.

Initially I visited ninety-two nagari in the three interior districts of Tanah Datar, Agam, and 50 Kota from January to April 1972. The selection of the nagari I visited was not totally random. On the basis of information supplied at the subdistrict office, I tried to choose at least two contrasting nagari in each subdistrict—contrasting, for example, in strength of adat, economic life, merantau rates, and educational development. These criteria could not always be upheld, for inaccessible villages had often to be dropped from consideration.[5]

---

ical mobility and the matrilineal adat occupy a very prominent place in the Minangkabau consciousness.

5. Seventy percent of 516 villages in West Sumatra are accessible by normal vehicles, but 15 percent can be reached only by footpath (Fritz:29–30).

The purpose of the trip was to get acquainted with the society and with variations of adat by visiting different villages in the cultural heartland. In each nagari, I held an interview with the village head and village adat experts. The contact was made through letters of introduction from the governor, the district head (*bupati*), and the subdistrict head (*camat*) to the village head (*wali nagari*). The interview usually lasted for about one and a half hours to two hours. The interview was structured but no formal questionnaire was used at this stage of the initiation to the society. In the interview, I asked questions about general economic and social conditions in the village, adat (that is, marriage customs, number and names of suku, number of penghulu or lineage heads, and so on), educational development among the villagers, estimated merantau rate from the village, estimated occupational composition of perantau, popular destinations for merantau, and so forth. For the remaining five districts in West Sumatra, a similar survey, encompassing 140 more nagari, was carried out between December 1972 and June 1973. The standardized questionnaire was used in the interview. In order to make the most of the limited amount of time available to me, the questionnaire was mailed to most of the nagari in three districts (Solok, Sawahlunto/Sijunjung, and Pesisir Selatan) through the district and subdistrict offices, and later I collected the returned questionnaires at each subdistrict office.

While visiting the central districts, I began to appreciate that, contrary to my expectations, the matrilineal system was still very much part of village life. I became curious to know why this was the case. In order to understand how the system actually operated in contemporary society, I decided to select a subdistrict for more detailed study. To this end, the subdistrict of IV [Empat] Angkat Candung was chosen. IV Angkat Candung is located about four miles to the east of Bukittinggi, along the road to Payakumbuh. It consists of two former adat federations, IV Angkat and Candung. My research site was IV Angkat.

The area is located near Bukittinggi, the most important urban center in the darek, and is thus susceptible to influences emanating from this city. Most of the seven villages in IV Angkat have well-developed home industries such as embroidery and tailoring, and their economy is not solely dependent on agriculture. The area has experienced rapid progress in education and in the practice of merantau, especially for the last three generations. Theoretically, these factors should have brought about change in the way the matrilineal system is practiced. It was anticipated that accommodations observed in this area would offer indications of what might happen to the system in less developed areas in the future. In addition, IV Angkat has been relatively untouched by scholars. I hoped that its study would provide useful materials for comparison with the previous studies carried out in other villages of West Sumatra.

In the household survey, ten percent of the male household heads (a total sample of 395) were randomly sampled from the registers of four village offices in IV Angkat.[6] The interview, which lasted for about two hours and used the questionnaire, was normally held at the respondent's house. He was asked about his demographic background (age, education, occupation, and merantau experience), the demographic background of his family (namely, of his spouse, children, parents, and spouse's parents), family relationships (for example, how often he rendered financial help to his kemanakan), and some attitudinal questions. The same questionnaire was later applied to seventy-five male perantau who originally had come from two of the four villages, but who were then residing in Padang or in Pekan Baru. The intention of this research was to compare the demographic and other characteristics of village residents and perantau. Padang and Pekan Baru were chosen as merantau sites because of financial and time considerations in administering the survey; they are the two most important merantau destinations within a relatively short distance from Bukittinggi, my place of residence. Only two of the four villages were considered for this part of the research, for the information obtained in the villages suggested that the perantau from these two villages were much more active in Padang and Pekan Baru. Names of the perantau from these two villages were supplied by the perantau associations of IV Angkat Candung in the cities. It often turned out to be difficult to contact the perantau; especially the merchants, who seldom kept regular working hours. As a result, only seventy-five perantau respondents (household heads) were reached for interviews.

6. Male household heads here were the urang sumando, not the mamak of the house. The choice was based on the impression I gained during my trip through the central districts that husbands are now the main providers for the households rather than the mamak. Fortunately for my sampling purpose, detailed registers and maps of the villages were kept as a result of the 1971 census.

After completing the survey in the villages and in the cities, I felt the need to add a historical perspective to my research. This was the result of my increasing desire to understand what aspects of matriliny had undergone modification and what aspects had not. In an attempt to incorporate a historical dimension, 132 randomly selected respondents (30 percent) of the sample of 395 males in the village household survey were revisited for further interviews. Depending on the depth of their respective genealogical knowledge, either the male respondent or his wife was questioned about his or her sublineage (paruik). For the survey on family history, questions were asked mainly about house segmentation for the last three generations within the sublineage, and the mode of usage of ancestral land. For the survey on merantau history, the same respondent was asked to enumerate his or her immediate matrilineal kin, going up two generations and down one: the grandmother and her siblings, the mother and her siblings, and the respondent's own siblings and children.[7] For each of these sets of kin, information was obtained on the (approximate) year of birth, the (approximate) year of death (if applicable), level of education, occupation, marriage and divorce, merantau experiences, year(s) of departure for merantau, and so forth.For the oldest generation (the grandmother and her siblings), it was not always easy to secure complete information, for often neither the respondents nor the other members of the household knew the life histories of these people.

In addition to these primary survey results, the previously mentioned studies by other researchers will be incorporated in the discussion. Because of the general paucity of data, only two time-periods will, in the main, be used in the subsequent attempt to analyze the magnitude and nature of merantau activities—the Dutch period and the post-Dutch period (including the Japanese occupation lasting from 1942 to 1945). Where data are available, the post-Dutch period will be further subdivided. Let us first try to grasp the characteristics of merantau practice in the colonial era by means of the 1930 census.

---

7. If a respondent is a male, his children do not, of course belong to his matrilineage. Yet even in this case, I chose to ask about his children rather than about his kemanakan on the assumption that he would know more about the former than about the latter; the assumption was again based on my impression that fathers nowadays spend most of their time at their wives' houses rather than at their mothers' homes.

Overview: The 1930 Dutch Census

The 1930 census supplies two types of information which give clues to the migration rates of different ethnic groups in Indonesia. One is information on the ethnic background of the population, while the other is data on place of birth and place of present domicile. If the main habitation of an ethnic group can be identified geographically with a census unit, the first kind of information should indicate the ratio between those who stay in their native area and those who live outside it. Strictly speaking, however, this ratio is not equivalent to a rate of migration. It may, for example, cover the offspring of migrants, born outside the native area and residing there at the time of the census enumeration. Such people obviously did not experience any migration. The second type of information should obviate this difficulty. Differences between place of birth and domicile must be contingent on the geographical mobility of each adult individual, or, in case of children, of their families. Yet such data suffer from a different kind of disadvantage. The people born in a particular area do not necessarily all belong to the ethnic group with which that area is identified. For instance, not all people born in West Sumatra are Minangkabau. Nevertheless, if the over-whelming majority of the population in the area belong to this ethnic group, one may assume that changes from birthplace to domicile give some approximation of geographical mobility among its members. In both cases, we must be aware that any figures derived by these means can suggest only rough estimates of population movements. It should be also noted that both kinds of information provide only on-the-spot indications of geographical mobility. Past migration experiences and a good part of seasonal migration activity can not be extrapolated from our calculations.[8]

With these reservations in mind, let us look at the data on four ethnic groups noted for their geographical mobility, namely, the Minangkabau, the "Tapanuli Batak," the Buginese, and the Banjarese.[9] The following residencies are identified as the main areas of

8. Specifically, there are people who migrated seasonally but happened to stay in their villages at the time of the census enumeration. For a more general discussion of these problems, see Nitisastro (1970:86–91).

9. In reality, there is no ethnic group called "Tapanuli Batak." According to the 1930 census (*Volkstelling 1930*, 4:15), the Batak in the residencies of Tapanuli and

Table 4.1. Geographical distribution of selected ethnic groups in 1930

Ethnic groups	Native area	Outside	Total	Percentage outside	In British Malaya
Minangkabau	1,717,031	99,404	1,816,435	5.5%	13,790
Tapanuli Batak	758,262	163,880	922,142	17.8%	51
Buginese	1,380,334	152,701	1,533,035	10.0%	4,961
Banjarese	809,842	89,042	898,884	9.9%	20,339

SOURCE: *Volkstelling 1930*, 4:20, 164, 170–171; 5:19–20, 161, 166, 179–180; 8:13.

habitation of these four ethnic groups: Sumatra's West Coast with the Minangkabau, Tapanuli with the Tapanuli Batak, Southern Celebes (Celebes en Onderhoorigheden) with the Buginese, and Southeastern Borneo (Zuider- en Ooster-afdeeling van Borneo) with the Banjarese. The representation of each ethnic group in the population of its respective residency was 91 percent Minangkabau for Sumatra's West Coast, 73 percent Tapanuli Batak for Tapanuli, 45 percent Buginese for Southern Celebes, and 61 percent Banjarese for Southeastern Borneo (*Volkstelling 1930*, 4:164, 167, 170; 5:161, 166). This only roughly approximate correspondence of the latter three ethnic groups with demarcated provincial territories is unfortunate but unavoidable; the results of the 1930 census were often analyzed only at the residency level. However, this does not present a serious problem for our discussion, as will become apparent shortly. Table 4.1 shows the geographical distribution of the four selected ethnic groups; Table 4.2 shows the relation between

---

Sumatra's East Coast were divided into seven distinct groups: Angkola, Mandailing, Padanglawas, Toba, Karo, Timoer, and Pak-Pak. Of these, the first four Batak groups, whose homelands are located in Tapanuli, are more noted for geographical mobility than the others. Since among these four "Tapanuli Batak" groups, the Toba Batak are the most famous for migration, ideally we should concentrate on them for comparison. Unfortunately this is not possible, because the Batak were not subdivided into the above seven groups in the census enumeration outside the residencies of Tapanuli and Sumatra's East Coast. In order to minimize the chance of obtaining an inflated migration rate, the category Tapanuli Batak was adopted here for consideration instead of Toba Batak; my assumption is that those Batak who were found outside Tapanuli and the East Coast in 1930 were more likely to be either Angkola, Mandailing, Padanglawas, or Toba, rather than Karo, Timoer, or Pak-Pak. Concerning the mobility of the Buginese, Banjarese, and Batak, see *Volkstelling 1930*, 8 (p. 45) and Cunningham (1958).

Table 4.2. Relation between birthplace and domicile of people born in the four residencies

Place of birth	Still in same district	Moved within residency	Moved from residency	Total
Sumatra's West Coast	1,734,589 (91.9%)	100,748 (5.3%)	53,200 (2.8%)	1,888,537
Tapanuli	943,714 (87.4%)	63,920 (5.9%)	71,964 (6.7%)	1,079,598
Southern Celebes	2,839,935 (91.4%)	203,437 (6.5%)	65,131 (2.1%)	3,108,503
Southeastern Borneo	1,165,740 (89.6%)	90,035 (6.9%)	44,768 (3.5%)	1,300,543

SOURCE: *Volkstelling 1930,* 8:94–95.

birthplace and domicile of those people who were born in the residencies identified as the homelands of the four ethnic groups.

The figures for those in British Malaya in Table 4.1 are not included in the total. The figures for Minangkabau in the same table refer to "Minangkabau in a narrower sense." Kerincinese, Kuantanners, Batins, and Penghulus, who were categorized as "Minangkabau in a broader sense" (*Volkstelling 1930,* 4:15), are not included in this calculation.[10] These people, especially the Kuantanners, Penghulus, and part of the Kerincinese, may have been descendants of ancient Minangkabau migrants, possibly several centuries back. However, their native regions were already in 1930 long identified with areas outside of West Sumatra, and thus they should not be considered as Minangkabau in the present context.

The well-known Minangkabau propensity to merantau notwithstanding, the two tables indicate that the Minangkabau (and West Sumatrans) did not rank high in migration rates by comparison with the other ethnic groups and areas under consideration. The results in Table 4.1 are all the more remarkable because ethnic-

10. These ethnic groups are identified with the following regions: Kuantanners with the east of West Sumatra (inland Riau), Kerincinese with the south of West Sumatra, and Batins and Penghulus with the southeast of West Sumatra.

ity and residency as its homeland correspond only roughly among non-Minangkabau ethnics; this fact should considerably deflate the figure of mobility by overlooking internal movement within the residency. For example, the homeland of the Banjarese should ideally be identified with the district of Hulu Sungai in the residency of Southeastern Borneo; this identification was not possible because the results of the 1930 census were often analyzed only at the residency level. Because the residency of Southeastern Borneo as a whole was regarded as the Banjarese homeland in the present consideration, Table 4.1 does not take into account the mobility of those Banjarese who moved out of Hulu Sungai yet still remained in Southeastern Borneo.

The results in Table 4.1 and Table 4.2 may mean that the Minangkabau practice of merantau was not yet pervasive in 1930 and that the Minangkabau migrants were disproportionately visible to Dutch administrators and scholars because of their educational advancement and nonagricultural occupations. On the other hand, these rather unexpected results may be in part an artifact of the particular methods adopted in the census making. In the Outer Islands, "domiciled residents" were counted, that is, "all persons resident in the census area" were enumerated "even though they happened to be temporarily absent at the time of the census" (*Volkstelling 1930*, 1:93; 8:36). There are indications that the most popular Minangkabau merantau pattern at this time was circulatory, by which men left on short-term migrations, thus "temporarily absenting" themselves from their homes. Possibly many Minangkabau circulatory migrants were counted as absent "domiciled residents" in their home villages, not at the destinations of merantau. (Or it may be that a large number of Minangkabau circulatory migrants returned to their villages anyway, soon after the Great Depression in 1929.) In addition, some Minangkabau seem to have been mistakenly counted as Malays rather than as Minangkabau (ibid., 1:93). Unfortunately, there is no way to know how important these factors may have been in lowering the estimates of Minangkabau migration rates. Despite these obvious limitations, a few other traits of Minangkabau merantau patterns may be derived from the census.

The geographical distribution of the some 99,000 Minangkabau

Table 4.3. Geographical distribution of Minangkabau emigrants in 1930

Aceh	8.6%	Bengkulu	6.7%
Tapanuli	9.9%	Lampung	0.8%
East Sumatra	51.0%	Bangka	0.3%
Riau	6.1%	West Java	4.3%
Jambi	7.0%	C. & E. Java	0.9%
Palembang	2.4%	Other in D.E.I.	2.0%

SOURCE: Volkstelling 1930, 1:183; 2:177, 179, 181; 3:152; 4:162, 164, 167, 171, 173, 174, 176; 5:161, 170, 172, 175, 177.

residing outside West Sumatra was heavily concentrated on Sumatra (Table 4.3).[11] Ninety-three percent of them resided on this island, with East Sumatra alone accounting for half. The explanation for this pattern lies in the great economic prosperity and the resulting opportunities available in East Sumatra during 1920s. Large tobacco and rubber plantations were in operation. Palm oil, pepper, coffee, and tea plantations, though on a less extensive scale than tobacco or rubber, also prospered there. These plantations offered both clerical jobs and captive markets (a huge corps of indentured plantation workers) to the educated, mobile, and commercially ambitious Minangkabau. In this context, we should be also mindful of the 14,000 Minangkabau counted in British Malaya (see Table 4.1). Hamka (1967:51, 84–85) says that people left for Malaya in order to evade taxes after 1908. Apparently, many more Minangkabau were also attracted to Malaya because of its rubber boom. "Pai Kolang" (go to Kelang, or go to Malaya in general) seems to have been a popular slogan during this time (Lekkerkerker:207–208). From Table 4.3, it is evident that Java had not yet assumed much importance as a destination of migration in 1930; and indeed, according to Hamka's autobiography (1966:42), "Java was still far away at this time."

Another noteworthy observation can be made about the urban-rural characteristics of the Minangkabau emigrants' destinations. The 1930 census enumerates populations for two types of urban centers: municipalities (gemeenten) and towns (kota). These places were primarily administrative centers of the colonial government.

11. The figures in Table 4.3, strictly speaking, do not solely refer to emigrants. "C. & E. Java" refers to Central and East Java, and "Other in D.E.I." to other places in the Dutch East Indies.

The list of the place names (Medan, Padang, Bukittinggi, Palembang, and Pematang Siantar) also indicates that in many cases they were commercial, educational, and Western cultural centers as well. Out of some 92,000 Minangkabau emigrants in Sumatra, 16.8 percent were counted in municipalities and towns (*Volkstelling 1930* 4:25).[12] Although this figure is higher than the share of the Minangkabau urban population in West Sumatra's total population (4.1 percent), it may be still regarded as low considering the urban roles (as government officials, merchants, and artisans) generally associated with Minangkabau perantau.

The final implication we may draw from the census derives from the sex ratio among the emigrants. In this regard, we may again study two sets of figures: those based on ethnic background and those based on the relationship between birthplace and domicile. The first set of figures was calculated for the emigrants of each ethnic group residing outside their homeland residency as previously identified. The resulting numbers of females per 1,000 males among the emigrants of the four ethnic groups are: Minangkabau, 705; Tapanuli Batak, 858; Buginese, 848; and Banjarese, 933 (*Volkstelling 1930*, 3:153; 4:162, 164, 167, 170–171, 173–174, 176–177; 5:161, 166, 170, 172, 175, 177). The second set of figures was calculated only for those who were staying somewhere else than their native residency at the time of the census enumeration, for example, people who were born in West Sumatra but were staying outside West Sumatra at census time. The numbers of females per 1,000 males thus obtained are: those of West Sumatra origin, 486; Toba Region origin, 867; South Celebes origin, 569; and Hulu Sungai origin, 901 (*Volkstelling 1930*, 4:37; 5:47, 49).[13] From these results, it is apparent that the Minangkabau

12. No figure is available for the whole of the Netherlands Indies. Excluding Sumatra's West Coast, there were altogether thirty municipalities and towns in Sumatra. The census lists only sixteen of them in its tabulation of the Minangkabau urban emigrant population in Sumatra. We may assume that the number of Minangkabau emigrants in the other fourteen municipalities and towns was insignificant and thus omitted.

13. Because of the way the data are presented in the census results, the residency category here does not match that in Table 4.2; except for West Sumatra, the present geographical categories are more narrowly defined. Toba Region, South Celebes, and Hulu Sungai are respectively more closely identified with the Toba Batak, Buginese, and Banjarese than the zones listed in Table 4.2. Toba Region refers to the subdistricts (*onderafdeelingen*) of Toba Plateau, Toba, Silindung, and Samosir. The

and West Sumatran emigrants were disproportionately male, compared with other mobile ethnic groups in Indonesia. Even granted
that the female-male ratio among emigrants is generally low, the
results for the Minangkabau are extreme. Among those who migrated from around Bukittinggi (Oud-Agam—one of the most famous areas for merantau in West Sumatra), the sex ratio was as low
as 379 females per 1,000 males (*Volkstelling 1930*, 4:37).

In sum, the 1930 census shows that the migration rates of the
Minangkabau were not then as high as those of the three other
mobile ethnic groups ("Tapanuli Batak," Buginese, and Banjarese);
that the destinations of merantau were almost exclusively in
Sumatra, above all East Sumatra, and were mainly nonurban areas;
and that, even by comparison with the other mobile ethnic groups
the proportion of female to male migrants was very low.

Overview: The Contemporary Scene

For the period between 1930 and 1970, there is no systematic
information available on Minangkabau migration.[14] Since 1970,
however, there have been a number of attempts to estimate
Minangkabau migration rates and to capture some of the characteristics of merantau practice. The estimates of migration rates
given in these studies diverge considerably. The most conservative
figure lists 616,000 Minangkabau currently (1971) residing outside
West Sumatra (Thamrin 1972:11), while the highest estimate gives
2.2 million Minangkabau perantau outside their native province
(Naim 1973b:57).[15] A realistic estimate probably lies somewhere
between these two extremes, for reasons explained below.

---

figures for Toba Region include migration between these subdistricts. The results for
West Sumatra indicate only those people who moved within Sumatra, excluding
West Sumatra, Palembang, and Bangka, while those for the other areas refer to the
whole of the Dutch East Indies.
    14. A possible exception is the 1961 sample census. While it does not have any
information on ethnic backgrounds, it does give information on the places of birth
and domicile. For more details, see McNicoll (1968).
    15. Thamrin's research was conducted in conjunction with the 1971 "10 percent
sample census"; in this census, some portion of the larger census population was
revisited for more detailed interviewing. Based on the instruction of the governor's
office of West Sumatra, questions on merantau were included in these interviews.
Despite this large-scale effort, however, the research results are not very reliable, as

The population in Indonesia almost doubled from 1930 to 1971 (1.96 times to be precise). If we assume that the Minangkabau population increased at this rate for the last forty years, the total Minangkabau population in Indonesia in 1971 would be 3,560,212, that is, 1,816,435 times 1.96. Further, supposing that 91 percent of the population in West Sumatra in 1971 was ethnically Minangkabau, as it was in 1930, we get 2,538,738 as the number of Minangkabau residing in West Sumatra (2,789,822 times .91) (Kantor Sensus dan Statistik Propinsi Sumatera Barat 1971:96). If these assumptions are accepted, then we may propose a figure of some 1,021,000 as the estimated number of Minangkabau perantau staying outside West Sumatra in 1971. This would constitute roughly 30 percent of the total Minangkabau population in Indonesia. According to another study conducted in West Sumatra, it has been estimated that approximately 180,000 to 200,000 Minangkabau left West Sumatra between 1958 and 1972, with an annual emigration rate of 12,000 to 15,000 (Fritz:75).[16] Thus, whatever the reality of Minangkabau merantau may have been in 1930, there is no doubt that it has achieved extraordinary proportions since that time.

There are four studies which show vividly the acceleration of Minangkabau merantau activities since the colonial period. Two of these studies were conducted among Minangkabau perantau in the

the report itself admits. The inclusion of the merantau questions was decided only two weeks beforehand, resulting in poorly thought-out questions and inadequate coaching of census enumerators. Naim's estimate was derived by the same method as the one to be described shortly below. The figure is very high because Naim counted the "Minangkabau in a broader sense" and also included the Minangkabau in Malaya. The figure is probably further inflated in that he adopted a population increase factor of 2.52 for Sumatra between 1930 and 1971. Since this rate is influenced by the large number of emigrants from Java to Sumatra over the last forty years, it is not appropriate to use it for projections of the total Minangkabau population.

16. These estimates are based on a survey conducted among 315 urban households in Padang and 910 rural households in other parts of West Sumatra. Information was supplied by household members concerning those who were away from the village at the time of the interviews. It is not clear from the description who were considered to be absent household members. Also the report does not specify how the above estimates were arrived at. In any case, since the estimates were based only on the number of people who were away at the time, the real emigration rate (encompassing those who had once migrated but had since returned home) would be considerably higher.

rantau (destinations of migration): one in provincial and district capitals of four southern Sumatran provinces (Jambi, South Sumatra, Bengkulu, and Lampung), and the other mainly in Jakarta (Naim:1973b).[17] The other two were carried out in West Sumatra, the information given by respondents concerning those family members who were away from home at the time of the research.[18] Unlike the first two, these latter two studies covered movement within as well as outside West Sumatra. In all four cases, however, the perantau enumerated refer only to those people actually away from home at the time the research was carried out.

The results of the four studies are given in Table 4.4. The years referred to in the table indicate distinct historical events of approximately ten-year intervals. The Dutch colonial era ended in 1942 as the Japanese army invaded the Dutch East Indies. By 1951, both the Japanese occupation and the independence war against the returning Dutch were over. The year of 1958 saw the eruption of a regional rebellion in West Sumatra which lasted in some areas for a few years but was effectively ended by 1961.[19] Although the results of the West Sumatra Regional Planning Study (W.S.R.P.S.) differ considerably from the other three studies, the general pattern is clear. Over 80 percent of the perantau currently in the rantau (migration sites) left their village after the Dutch period, and about half of them did so after 1962. Obviously, this overrepresentation of post-Dutch period migration is partly due to the research method employed. The population increase after the colonial period inflates the absolute number of perantau even if the proportion of people migrating remained the same as during the period of Dutch control. Also many people who went away from the village before 1942

17. The first study was done by the Sumatra Regional Planning Study of the Indonesian Ministry of Public Works and Power and the University of Bonn between 1972 and 1973. The urban population (household heads) of these four provinces was randomly sampled for interviews. From this sample, I selected only Minangkabau migrants for consideration here. The materials were made available to me by K. H. Junghans, J. Fritz, and Risman Maris. The sample for Naim's study (carried out in 1971–1972) was in no way random.

18. These are: the research conducted by the West Sumatra Regional Planning Study and the one by Thamrin, both in 1971. Materials from the former were supplied to me by K. H. Junghans and J. Fritz.

19. The breakdown of periods in Table 4.4 is different in Thamrin than in the others. "During the Dutch period" and "Before 1962" in Thamrin refer respectively to "before 1945" and "before 1958." A dash means there is no information.

Table 4.4. Time of departure for merantau (cumulative percentage)

Research identification	During Dutch period	Before 1952	Before 1962	Total sample size	Sex of sample
S.R.P.S.	15%	22%	64%	161	males
Naim	14%	23%	55%	427	males
W.S.R.P.S.	—	—	26%	409	males
W.S.R.P.S.	—	—	23%	285	females
Thamrin	12%	—	45%	18,001	males & females

SOURCE: Infrastructure survey of the Sumatra Regional Planning Study (S.R.P.S.); Naim (1973b:58); Infrastructure survey of the West Sumatra Regional Planning Study (W.S.R.P.S.); Thamrin (1972:Appendix III).

must either have died or come back since then to spend their old age at home. Nevertheless, the huge discrepancy between the pre-1942 and post-1942 data seems to indicate that more and more people have been leaving for the rantau since the Dutch collapse, especially after 1961.

As noticeable as the increasing rate of migration after 1942 is the change in destinations. From Table 4.3 we learned that 93 percent of the Minangkabau living outside West Sumatra in 1930 were found in Sumatra. If the places of birth and of domicile are compared, 83 percent of those who were born in West Sumatra, yet moved out of this province, were still located in Sumatra (*Volkstelling 1930* 8:94–95). If we consider those West Sumatrans (people born in West Sumatra) who had experienced interdistrict or wider mobility—that is, those who had moved from their district of birth to another district in West Sumatra, as well as those who had moved outside West Sumatra altogether—65 percent had moved only within the province of Sumatra's West Coast, 29 percent had gone to other areas of Sumatra, and a mere 6 percent had left for the rest of the Dutch East Indies.

Two of the four studies described above give clues to the geographical distribution of Minangkabau perantau in 1971. From Table 4.5 it is clear that the geographical distribution of Minangkabau perantau changed dramatically between 1930 and the early 1970s. Intraprovincial mobility shrank from 65 percent of all

migration to about 25 percent. Migration to other areas in Sumatra
and outside Sumatra, however, increased a great deal.
A particularly significant finding in Table 4.5 is the concentration
of perantau in two cities. According to the W.S.R.P.S., Pekan Baru
and Jakarta account for close to 50 percent of all perantau who left
West Sumatra. This finding may need interpreting in a broader
perspective. In 1930, only 17 percent of all Minangkabau emigrants
to other parts of Sumatra resided in urban areas (municipalities and
towns). A comparable figure is not available for the situation in
recent years. However, the W.S.R.P.S. survey indicates that today a
far greater proportion of Minangkabau perantau leave for urban
centers. Ninety-two percent of some 700 perantau it enumerated
(both males and females) were located in towns, and only 8 percent
in villages.[20] This increase, of course, is partly due to the rapid
growth of urban centers in Indonesia after independence. There
were only three Sumatran cities (Palembang, Medan, and Padang)
with populations of over 50,000 in 1930; and the total population
of these three cities was only 236,783 (*Volkstelling 1930*, 4:142–
143). In 1971, however, there were twelve cities (*kotamadya*) of
comparable size, with a total population of 2,361,472 (Biro Pusat
Statistik 1972:13–73). In correspondence with the increasing number of true cities and the disproportionately rapid growth of urban
populations, the Minangkabau migrants seem indeed to be now
mainly attracted to urban centers.

In this regard, there seems to have been a convergence of Minangkabau perantau in several cities in Indonesia. The 1961 and 1971
censuses do not provide any information on ethnic background and
the inference to be drawn below therefore remains conjectural.
But on the basis of his interviews with local government officials
and Minangkabau perantau leaders, Mochtar Naim estimated that
up to 760,000 Minangkabau perantau may live in five cities outside
West Sumatra: Jakarta, Bandung, Medan, Pekan Baru, and Palembang.[21] There is no way to verify how accurate this estimate is. A

20. Calculation made from the original data tabulation. Unfortunately, no formal definition of "town" and "village" is given in this tabulation. Considering that
about 30 percent of the perantau in the survey were in Pekan Baru or Jakarta and
another 10 percent in Padang (all unquestionably urban centers), a substantial portion of the towns may be construed as cities.
21. His estimates for the individual cities were as follows (Naim 1973b:145,
152, 161, 169–170, 191): Jakarta: 500,000; Bandung: 50,000; Medan: 100,000;
Pekan Baru: 70,000; and Palembang: 40,000.

Table 4.5. Destinations of merantau in 1971 (in percent)

Research identification	Within West Sumatra	Pekan Baru	Other Sumatra	Jakarta	Outside Sumatra & Jakarta	Sex of sample
W.S.R.P.S.	26%	15%	32%	21%	6%	male
W.S.R.P.S.	26%	17%	36%	16%	5%	female
Thamrin	25%	—	—	—	—	male & female

sizable divergence between these off-hand figures and a more studied estimate is evidenced in the case of Jakarta. Naim surmised that a maximum of 500,000 Minangkabau might be living in Jakarta as of the early 1970s. According to another calculation, however, there were only about 60,000 Minangkabau residing in Jakarta in 1961 (Castles 1967:185). As Naim himself acknowledges (1973b:170), it is hard to imagine an increase from 60,000 to 500,000 within the ten years between 1961 and 1971.[22] Yet despite its unreliable, exaggerated character, Naim's estimate at least conveys a sense of perantau convergence on several key cities as perceived by a native Minangkabau.

Among the five cities, Pekan Baru and Jakarta are especially noteworthy in terms of the rapid increase of Minangkabau perantau after the colonial period. In 1930, Pekan Baru was still a village of 2,990 souls.[23] By 1954, its population had grown to 28,314 and to 70,821 by 1961 (Suleman 1973:14). The population figure given by the 1971 census was 145,030 (Biro Pusat Statistik 1972:47). This swift urban growth was due mainly to two factors. Large reserves of oil were found by Caltex near Pekan Baru in 1939

22. The Castles' estimate is essentially based on information on ethnic backgrounds in the 1930 census and on the birthplace of Jakarta's population in the 1961 census. Because it does not count those Minangkabau who were born outside West Sumatra, it is bound to be low. Minangkabau migration is believed to have increased considerably after the regional rebellion of 1958. Even allowing for these factors, Naim's figure for the Minangkabau population of Jakarta appears too high. However, it is undeniable that the Minangkabau population of Jakarta has grown very rapidly. If the estimates of the W.S.R.P.S. can be trusted, some 54,000 to 60,000 Minangkabau moved from West Sumatra to Jakarta between 1958 and 1971 (calculated from Table 4.5 and Fritz:75); this figure does not include perantau who moved from other parts of Indonesia to Jakarta.

23. "Memorie van Overgave" of H. J. Dorenbosch, *controleur* of Kampar Kiri, February 15, 1938, found in the collection of the Tropical Institute, Amsterdam, p. 16. The figure is most likely from the 1930 census. Information supplied by William O'Malley.

(Bartlett et al. 1972:51). Their exploitation, which did not really take place until after the Second World War, made Pekan Baru a sprawling commercial center. The transfer of the provincial capital from Tanjung Pinang to Pekan Baru in the early 1960s further stimulated the latter's development as an administrative center. No accurate figure is obtainable concerning the number of Minangkabau perantau presently in Pekan Baru. In view of its geographical proximity (about 160 miles east of Bukittinggi) and easy access, Minangkabau must have been increasingly attracted by the occupational opportunities available in this rapidly growing city. If Naim's estimate is anywhere near the truth, the Minangkabau may have constituted close to half the population of Pekan Baru in 1971.

The development of Jakarta as a destination of Minangkabau migration is no less impressive than that of Pekan Baru. For 1930, Castles estimated that there were some 3,200 Minangkabau within the boundary of the Jakarta Raya (Greater Jakarta) of 1961. As mentioned before, his estimate for 1961 was 60,100. During these thirty years, the Minangkabau population in Jakarta thus increased by 18.8 times, while the population of Jakarta itself multiplied by a factor of only 3.7 (Castles 1967:166, 185). It is probable that the rate of increment in recent years is much higher than that in the period 1930–1961. Undoubtedly the attractions of the national capital—economic, political and educational opportunities, and the perception thereof—were powerful pull factors in this trend.

With respect to occupation, it is commercial activity that is most often associated with Minangkabau perantau. In particular, *pedagang kaki lima* (roadside peddlers) are sometimes taken as synonymous with Minangkabau perantau.[24] There are no data available concerning perantau occupations during the Dutch period. Research in recent years, however, seems to confirm this popular image to some extent (Table 4.6). "Merchant" is the most prevalent occupation of perantau, followed by "white collar" and "artisan," all of which may be called urban occupations. Evidently "agriculture" is not at all common: only 5 percent and 7 percent respectively of the respondents in S.R.P.S. and Fritz give this as their occupation.

24. "Djakarta Rantau Bertuah," *Tempo*, 15 January 1972, p. 41. Also see "Si Padang dan Kaki Limo," *Aneka Minang*, no. 13 (n.d.), pp. 6–11, 15, 35–36.

Table 4.6. Occupations of Minangkabau perantau

Research identification	Agri./ Manual	Artisan	Merchant	White collar	Other	None	Sample size
S.R.P.S.	9%	21%	47%	20%	3%	0%	235 males
Fritz (p. 76)	10%	10%	35%	27%	14%	4%	409 males

Reviewing migration trends after the Dutch period, we may draw several conclusions. Migration rates have increased dramatically, particularly after 1961. Migration is now predominantly directed to areas outside West Sumatra. Many more people leave for urban areas than before. And there seems to be convergence of Minangkabau perantau in several major cities in Indonesia, notably Jakarta and Pekan Baru. Their most prevalent occupations are commercial, but white collar jobs and artisanry are also significant.

A Survey on Merantau History: A Case Study

The comparison of the 1930 Dutch census and the recent studies discussed above suggests the strong possibility that the Minangkabau merantau pattern has undergone substantial change in recent years. Yet both the census and the later studies have their limitations in helping us pursue implications of this comparison. For example, they only refer to current perantau. Are their findings applicable to returned migrants (those who once migrated but later returned to their villages) as well as to those long dead? Are their findings actually comparable? What are the other possible changes in merantau patterns between the two time periods under consideration? In order to answer these questions, a survey on merantau history was conducted in IV Angkat.

IV Angkat is a loosely integrated adat federation of seven villages which share similar historical origins and adat. Initially, there were only four villages in the federation. As a result of village fission "a long time ago," these four villages multiplied to the present seven.[25] IV Angkat is one of the four original areas settled by people who moved from the first nagari in the Alam Minangkabau, Pariangan

25. The adat federation of IV Angkat is nominal today. The seventh nagari was actually recognized officially after the Second World War.

Padang Panjang, to Luhak Agam. These areas are IV Angkat, Sungai Puar, IV Koto, and Kamang, all near Bukittinggi. Each area originally consisted of four villages, and these sixteen villages are supposedly the only nagari of the Koto-Piliang tradition within the predominantly Bodi-Caniago region of Luhak Agam (Datoek Batoeah Sango c. 1966:42).[26]

Situated along the road between Bukittinggi and Payakumbuh to the east, all the villages in IV Angkat have a relatively easy access to the *Kota Sejuk* ("cool city," that is, Bukittinggi) only a few miles away. The area occupies about 3,300 hectares of generally flat land around Mount Merapi—roughly 40 percent of the land area in the subdistrict of IV Angkat Candung. There is a total population of 26,800 in IV Angkat (1971), with an average population of 3,800 per village. The area was previously known for some of the best rice in West Sumatra and as the rice-basket of Luhak Agam (Datuk Pamuntjak 1961:18). Despite this fertile soil IV Angkat now suffers from an acute land shortage due to population pressure. The average holdings of agricultural land and sawah amount respectively to only 0.48 hectares and 0.34 hectares per household. Currently, close to 90 percent of the village land is utilized for agricultural purposes. The remaining 10 percent is used either for settlement or else is too poor or too far away to be agriculturally exploited. Out of the total cultivation area, 70 percent is sawah, 56 percent of which are irrigated; the rest are rain fed. The sawah are often also planted with *palawija*, or secondary crops. There is no significant upland crop in the area. Besides timber and bamboo, the uplands are used for plants of secondary importance such as chilis, bananas, and corn.[27]

Economic activities in IV Angkat are not limited to agriculture. The area is particularly famous for two types of home industry, embroidery (*sulam*) and the making of readymade clothes (*konveksi*). These activities, however, are not universal in IV Angkat; they are mainly undertaken in five of the seven villages. Embroidery, according to one village elder, was introduced to the area from

26. However, according to Datuk Nagari Basa (1966b:24–25), the four original areas in Luhak Agam are IV Angkat, Sungai Puar, IV Koto, and Kurai-Banuhampu.
27. Agricultural data were supplied by the West Sumatra Regional Planning Study.

Egypt in the late 1910s and was quickly taken up by many households thereafter. It is today more or less exclusively the work of women. By contrast, sewing is more frequently done by men. It is not clear when *konveksi* first made headway in IV Angkat. The four villages, which must remain anonymous, exhibit four somewhat different types of economic activity. In one village, *konveksi* is widespread. In another, the manufacture of wooden sandals and large paper parasols (used by roadside vendors as shelters from the sun) used to flourish. However, the demand for these goods has declined in recent years, because of the importation of cheap Japanese rubber sandals and the increase in roofed markets. Consequently *konveksi* has become more popular. Both places have sent many merchant perantau to different areas of Indonesia.

Embroidery was originally introduced in the third village discussed here, and it continues to be pursued more vigorously here than in all the other villages of IV Angkat. Probably because of the independent income that its females thus obtained, many of them have achieved higher education and become teachers. As a consequence, many of their children have been sent to institutions of higher education. In recent years, this village seems to have sent large numbers off as white collar workers. The last nagari is the most agricultural of the four. This village does not have any history of active home industry, either for men or women. But its agricultural life is more intense than that of the other three. Its sawah is extensively used for secondary crops as well as for rice cultivation. About eighty percent of the sawah, which itself occupies eighty-five percent of the total agricultural land, is planted with chilis, cabbages, corn, and other secondary crops once the rice is harvested. The produce is sent to Bukittinggi's markets, whence some is even transshipped to Singapore via Pekan Baru. Lacking commercial activities (until exportable secondary crops were introduced), the village is a latecomer to the practice of merantau. But since 1950, people in the village have become more and more merantau-minded. Today, their orientation to merantau is as strong as that of the other three villages.

How far these four villages have come in terms of social change, say, since the turn of the century, is reflected in an intergenerational comparison of three phenomena—educational level, occupational structure, and rate of merantau—made possible by my survey on merantau history. This survey was carried out among 132 respondent, his(her) children and siblings, his(her) mother and her siblings, and his(her) grandmother and her siblings. In evaluating the survey results, obviously we may not put the mother of a twenty-five-year-old and the mother of a seventy-five-year-old respondent in the same category, even if both are "mothers"; in generational terms, the former may well be equivalent to the latter's daughter. On the other hand, to maintain the two categories of respondent's age and respondent's kin relations in the presentation of the research results would seriously complicate matters, for we would need a three-dimensional table showing age categories, kin categories, and whatever categories are used in classifying responses to a particular question. In the end, I decided to collapse the age and kin classifications into one generational category. It is extremely difficult to create generational categories which can place the different kin of respondents quite dissimilar in age in a comparable generational framework. The solution proposed below is at best an approximation, used only as a heuristic device. In Table 4.7, four generational categories are put forward; groups indicated by the same Roman numeral belong to one generational category. In order not to give a false impression, no designation such as "mother's generation" is applied in the following discussion.[28]

The extent of educational progress over the generations is shown in Table 4.8, which, like the rest of the tables in this chapter, is based on my survey on merantau history. ("No answer" is not included in the calculation; this is true for the other tables that follow.) In Generation I, on the average only eight percent of the sample had received any formal education. In Generational IV, not only had practically everybody been to school, but they had at-

28. The male sample size for each generational category is: Generation I, 88; Generation II, 128; Generation III, 195; and Generation IV, 131, with the total sample size of 542. The female sample size is: Generation I, 138; Generation II, 246; Generation III, 237; and Generation IV, 118, with the total sample size of 739. The discrepancy between the size of the male and the female samples is partly because "father" and "grandfather" are not included in the survey and partly because female kin were better remembered than male kin, particularly for older generations. Why this tendency is reversed for Generation IV (which has more males than females) is not clear. This generational category includes children of fifteen years and up.

Table 4.7.   Generational categories in the case study

Age of respondent	Children	Relation to respondent		
		Self & siblings	Mother & siblings	Grandmother & siblings
Below 36	IV	IV	III	II
36 to 55	IV	III	II	I
Above 55	III	II	I	I

tended for longer periods; about 30 percent had even gone beyond junior high school.[29]

No less dramatic than the educational progress demonstrated is the change in the occupational composition of the population (Table 4.9). In Generation I, three quarters of the men were farmers, and a majority of the women (60 percent) were engaged in agriculture. By Generation IV, the agricultural proportion of the population had decreased to 15 percent for men and a mere 7 percent for women.[30] (The table enumerates current perantau, and so the low agricultural figures for Generations III and IV are influenced by merantau practice.)

The changes in educational level and occupational composition are closely related to the increasing rate of merantau. As education progresses, urban merantau orientations grow, for advanced education is mainly available in cities and towns. Better-educated people tend to seek nonagricultural occupations which match their educational attainments. As occupational orientations become less agricultural, people tend to merantau because no suitable occupa-

29. "*Mengaji*" (learning the recitation of the Koran) was not defined as formal education. In the tabulation, to be classified under "grade school," a person had to have received a minimum of three years elementary education. One year of attendance was a minimum condition for inclusion for the other educational categories (except "no school"). The distribution of educational achievements in Generation IV is rather unusual, in the sense that the proportion of those with "higher education" (senior high school and college) is large compared to those with "lower education." The reason for this rather top-heavy distribution is not clear.

30. The table refers only to main occupations. As will be discussed in Chapter 7, it is very common for the rural population in West Sumatra to have more than one occupation. If additional occupations had been asked about in the questionnaire, the agricultural population would have been much higher. Most of the "Other" among Generation IV are students.

Table 4.8. Educational progress through four generations

	Male generations				Female generations			
	I	II	III	IV	I	II	III	IV
No school	87%	55%	10%	5%	95%	70%	13%	0%
Grade school	10%	40%	64%	36%	3%	27%	64%	37%
Junior high	3%	4%	18%	26%	2%	2%	20%	34%
Senior high	—	1%	6%	22%	—	1%	2%	15%
College	—	—	2%	11%	—	—	1%	14%
Sample size	77	116	154	129	126	238	209	118

tions are available in the village. As people leave the village for merantau, educational aspirations for themselves and for their children are raised in hopes of attaining better, usually urban, occupations and higher incomes. Once on the rantau, occupations are more likely to be nonagricultural because of the occupational structure in the cities to which most Minangkabau are attracted. Table 4.10 shows the percentage of people who have had any merantau experience over the generations. About a quarter of the men and only a handful of the women in Generation I had merantau experiences. By Generation IV, an overwhelming majority of the men (89 percent) have been on the rantau and more than 60 percent of the women have shared that experience.[31] Whether we look at educational levels, occupations or merantau rates, the stepped-up pace of change has been truly remarkable in IV Angkat.[32] This, however, should not delude us into thinking that transformations have been equally dramatic in the rest of West Sumatra. Areas such as western Pasaman, southern Sawahlunto/Sijunjung, southern Solok, and eastern 50 Kota are less advanced in education, more predominantly agricultural and less oriented to merantau. An example of this regional variability can be seen in merantau rates. In my nagari

31. People between the ages of fifteen and nineteen at the time of the research were excluded from these calculations; they were less likely to merantau because of their youth. If they were included, the merantau rates for Generation IV would be 75 percent for the men and 51 percent for the women.
32. The pace of change may have been still more remarkable than the data show, for many "no answers" in Generation I probably inflated this generation's results; I suspect that most of the "no answer" group in fact belonged to the categories "no school," "agricultural," and "no merantau experience."

CHANGING PATTERNS OF MERANTAU   143

Table 4.9. Change in occupational composition through four generations

	Male generations				Female generations			
	I	II	III	IV	I	II	III	IV
Agricultural/Manual	74%	40%	25%	15%	61%	58%	27%	7%
Artisanry	9%	16%	19%	21%	3%	7%	27%	26%
Commercial	10%	22%	37%	27%	9%	5%	11%	3%
White collar	0%	10%	15%	15%	0%	1%	4%	10%
Other	3%	8%	1%	15%	0%	0%	1%	21%
None	4%	4%	3%	7%	27%	29%	30%	33%
Sample size	77	115	159	131	124	240	211	118

survey, 232 village heads were asked to give an estimate of what percent of the population of their village were on merantau at the time of the research. The average merantau rates per nagari in the eight districts (*kabupaten*) of West Sumatra are: Tanah Datar, 17%; Agam, 34%; 50 Kota, 6%; Solok, 13%; Padang Pariaman, 21%; Sawahlunto/Sijunjung, 8%; Pasaman, 12%; and Pesisir Selatan, 15%. The site for my case study was chosen in order to observe changes in family system and social stratification. In all respects, if there are areas in West Sumatra where such change must be expected, IV Angkat would be certainly one, considering the rapid social development it has experienced for the last three or four generations.

In the discussion of changing merantau patterns that follows, a comparison is made between the Dutch and post-Dutch period. The two time periods are demarcated by the Japanese invasion of 1942 rather than by the declaration of independence of 1945. Despite restrictions imposed by the Japanese authorities, the fluidity of the society greatly increased by comparison with the Dutch period. After the detention of Dutch and Eurasians, many bureaucratic

Table 4.10. Change in merantau rates through four generations

	Male generations				Female generations			
	I	II	III	IV	I	II	III	IV
Merantau experience	27%	52%	67%	89%	5%	27%	50%	62%
Sample size	82	118	159	99	126	239	213	89

posts and business opportunities were taken up by Indonesians (Kahin 1952:102–103). Trading became more active despite the decrease in the supply of goods (Sutter 1959:257–258). Geertz makes the following observation about commercial activities in Java during the Japanese occupation:

> The Japanese restriction of larger-scale trading activities aided, somewhat paradoxically, the same development. The Chinese being almost entirely forbidden to travel, a Javanese who could wheedle a travel permit and a requisition to transport a certain amount of trade goods was in a relatively good position. . . . Thus, though the Japanese reduced trade to a minimum, they still curiously enough increased the spread of the trading spirit, of the concept of making a profit through commerce, through the whole urban society. All townsmen, their standard of living much depressed, seem to have spent most of their time thinking of how they might get hold of a few bolts of cloth or a trade permit by means of which they could improve their lot (1965:105).

Likewise, in West Sumatra local trading probably became more active both in volume and intensity, though long-distance trade may have declined.[33] Small industries, such as textiles, were encouraged for the sake of self-sufficiency, when the importing of consumer goods proved increasingly difficult (Sutter:196–197, 224; Oki 1977:232–234). The population grew mobile under such local manpower programs as the recuitment of *Heihō* (auxiliary military forces) and *Rōmusha* (forced labor) (Sutter:269).[34] Indonesian society itself was in rapid transition after the Japanese invasion, and merantau patterns were involved in this change.

The post-Dutch era will be further divided into two phases: 1942–1961 and after 1961. For during the PRRI rebellion and after its termination in 1961, many Minangkabau left West Sumatra in order to escape the military rule imposed by the central govern-

33. Apparently many small businesses were launched in West Sumatra during the Japanese occupation. Out of 805 merchants surveyed by Ahrens (c. 1972:152) in West Sumatra in 1971–1972, about 12 percent started up between 1941 and 1945—a rate higher than during the preceding twenty to thirty years of Dutch rule combined. This rate of initiation into trading is surpassed only in the 1951–1955 period (about 15 percent).

34. The *Heihō* were sent off to various places depending on the interests of the Japanese army; laborers under the *Rōmusha* program were also sent to work on military construction projects both within and outside Indonesia (Anderson 1972a:13, 25).

Table 4.11.   Changes in destination of merantau over time

	Males			Females		
	Dutch period	1942– 1961	After 1961	Dutch period	1942– 1961	After 1961
West Sumatra	35%	25%	17%	45%	29%	25%
Other Sumatra	42%	52%	37%	47%	54%	33%
Java	12%	21%	43%	4%	17%	39%
Other	11%	2%	3%	4%	0%	3%
Sample size	134	164	168	84	114	117

ment. (PRRI stands for Pemerintah Revolusioner Republik Indonesia or Revolutionary Government of the Republic of Indonesia.) During the initial stage of the rebellion, there was a rumor that the central government army was killing civilians and raping women in eastern central Sumatra, which they attacked first, and that they would do the same once they occupied West Sumatra (Mossman 1961:166). Together with unmarried girls whose chastity was (imagined to be) in danger, some rebels were "packeted" (dipaketkan) to their families and relatives who had already been in the rantau.[35] After the rebellion was over, a number of ex-rebels and their families left West Sumatra, fearful of possible reprisals by the occupation army. Changing village-level political alignments also must have made some ex-rebel villagers reluctant to stay on in the village. Deteriotating economic conditions and demoralizing atmosphere under the military rule in West Sumatra further induced many Minangkabau to try their fate elsewhere.

Some results of the survey clearly replicate shifts already discussed in previous sections of this chapter. In terms of the destination of merantau, West Sumatra steadily declined in importance, while other areas, above all Java, gained in popularity (Table 4.11).[36] Within Sumatra, North Sumatra and Riau, whose capital is Pekan Baru, more or less changed places. During the Dutch period, 28

35. "Harun Zain: Fondasi, Menjelang Isi," Tempo, 8 October 1977, p. 19.
36. "Sample size" in Table 4.11 is sometimes larger than the actual sample size because some people changed their destination over the years. Migrants of the "Dutch period" who moved to a different place after 1941 were counted twice, in both the Dutch period and the post-Dutch period.

percent of merantau activities (of males and females combined) are directed to North Sumatra; this figure declined to 15 percent for the 1942–1961 period and to 11 percent after 1961. The comparable set of figures for Riau is: 8 percent, 19 percent, and 21 percent. Other than the increasing attraction of Pekan Baru after the 1950s, this change was certainly due to the decreasing lure of North Sumatra itself after 1941. The once flourishing plantations of the former East Coast largely ceased to function, and the Province of North Sumatra, including its provincial capital Medan, came under the political and military control of the Batak, not necessarily amiable neighbors of the Minangkabau.

The orientation to urban areas, above all to Pekan Baru and to Jakarta, is also prominent after 1942. During the Dutch period, only 10 percent of merantau activities (men and women combined) were directed to these two places. The comparable figures for 1942–1961 and after 1961 are respectively 22 percent and 44 percent. Between the two cities, Jakarta is clearly the biggest gainer. During the Dutch period, Jakarta (then Batavia) attracted only 5 percent of the perantau (both men and women). The percentage went up to 13 in 1942–1961, and to 34 after 1961. As pointed out in the previous chapter, Jakarta's increasing importance has contributed to the transformation of Padang from a port of entry for the foreign power (the Dutch) to a port of departure for Minangkabau heading for the outside world in search of opportunities, imagined or real.

With respect to perantau occupations, commercial activities have maintained their predominance among the men over the three periods even though their share has declined (Table 4.12). In line with the general educational progress of the population, more men now leave as white-collar workers than in the Dutch period. One finding, which is suggestive of possible future trends, is the emergence of unemployed older male and female perantau after 1961 (about seven percent for both men and women). These are retired fathers and mothers who have followed their children to the rantau. There is little significant change for the occupations of female perantau except that, since 1961, the proportion of "none" has declined and that of students (here categorized in "other") has increased.

It has been said that "the trip abroad, merantau, became very nearly required for every young bachelor in traditional Minangkabau

Table 4.12.   Changes in occupation of perantau over time

	Males			Females		
	Dutch period	1942–1961	After 1961	Dutch period	1942–1961	After 1961
Agricultural/Manual	8%	3%	1%	6%	1%	0%
Artisanry	19%	20%	17%	7%	3%	6%
Commercial	57%	44%	39%	16%	9%	11%
White collar	7%	23%	22%	0%	6%	6%
Other	5%	8%	9%	0%	5%	14%
None	4%	2%	12%	71%	76%	63%
Sample size	103	93	117	73	87	83

society," for by proving his worth in the rantau, a bachelor "was more likely to be successful in customary ways [marriage, respect, lineage position, and so on]" (H. Geertz 1967:84). A previously mentioned adat aphorism says "Go merantau, bachelor, first," for "at home there is no use yet." My survey in IV Angkat shows that this bachelor-perantau image was not entirely realistic until after 1961. Beginning in the Dutch period and up until that time the marital status of male perantau on their departure was more or less evenly divided between "single" and "married." Only after 1961 did the bachelor perantau come to overshadow the married in the ratio of eight to two. This proportion was exactly reversed for the female perantau up until 1961. That is to say, the married female perantau outnumbered the unmarried in the ratio of eight to two. However, an increasing number of single women now leave for merantau; the post-1961 ratio is four to six.

One of the most significant trends in recent merantau practice has been the participation of women. We saw earlier that according to the 1930 census the female-to-male ratio among Minangkabau emigrants was low by comparison with the other three mobile ethnic groups. However, more and more women are involved in merantau today. In 1930, the number of women per 100 men among the Minangkabau in Batavia was 52 (*Volkstelling 1930*, 1:149). In 1961, ratio of women to men among those who migrated from West Sumatra to Jakarta was 78 to 100 (Castles 1967:190). Similarly, in 1930 the number of native women per 1,000 native men in Padang was 757; by 1971 it had increased to 957 (*Volkstel-*

ling 1930, 4:142; Kantor Sensus dan Statistik Propinsi Sumatera Barat:90).

The increase of female perantau is mainly due to two factors. First, more and more married men take their wives and children with them onto the rantau. During the Dutch period, only 17 percent of the married male perantau took their wives (and children) to the rantau at the time of their departure; for the post-Dutch period the figure is 48 percent. Even though there is no difference in this respect between the periods 1942–1961 and after 1961, the number of married men who stay in the rantau with their nuclear families is increasing. During the Dutch period, 23 percent of the married male perantau stayed with their nuclear families in the rantau, 66 percent without, and 11 percent married in the rantau. The same sets of figures for the post-Dutch period are respectively 52 percent, 40 percent, and 8 percent for the 1942–1961 period, and 73 percent, 18 percent, and 9 percent for the period after 1961.[37] The married male perantau now usually call for their wives and children from the village once they have established themselves in the rantau.

A second factor contributing to the rise in female migration is that the justifications for it are more diverse now than hitherto. Women used to merantau primarily to accompany their husbands: 75 percent of the cases did so during the Dutch period. Although a majority of the female perantau still accompany their husbands (50 percent of the cases), the practices of unaccompanied merantau and merantau with child are increasing among women. Only 3 percent of the female perantau left the village unaccompanied during the Dutch period; the figure was 12 percent for the 1942–1961 period and 26 percent for the period after 1961. (In contrast, most males, about 70 percent of the cases, left for merantau by themselves in all the three periods.) The increase in the child-accompanied female merantau over the same three periods is 5 percent, 6 percent, and 13 percent respectively. The results reflect two new trends in recent years: young women, usually unaccompanied, leave the village in pursuit of higher education (they are likely to stay on in the rantau

37. The results include both those who were married at the time of departure and those who married later. Also included are cases where wives and children were later summoned from the village.

even after finishing school) and older women, frequently widows, merantau in the company of their children.

In general, then, the results of the survey on merantau history confirm the impression we formed from the 1930 census and other studies. The merantau rate has increased substantially since the Dutch period. The destinations of merantau tend now to be further away from West Sumatra than before. The concentration of perantau in Jakarta and Pekan Baru is noticeable. In terms of perantau occupations, commercial activities are still prevalent among men; but white-collar jobs are on the rise by comparison with the Dutch period. Both among men and women, the migration of young unmarrieds is increasing. This factor, coupled with the popularity of nuclear family merantau, explains the growing participation of women in migration.

Summary

In traditional Minangkabau society, village segmentation, the predominant mode of geographical mobility, was mainly stimulated by population pressure and land shortage. It could be characterized as agricultural, rural, permanent, and collective. People of the same lineage or sublineage migrated in search of new agricultural land with the intention of creating permanent settlements. As the frontier for new settlements diminished and as new economic opportunities arose, the pattern of this movement began increasingly to give way to what I call circulatory merantau. This shift, as explained in the last chapter, seems to have taken place after the middle of the nineteenth century. Circulatory merantau was primarily nonagricultural in occupational orientation. It was mainly carried out by individual males, and was most probably directed to small urban centers.

During the Dutch period perantau were mainly individual merchants and artisans, although there were also some office workers. They were mostly active within West Sumatra and in other parts of Sumatra. As Sumatra did not have many population centers at this time, and as economic prosperity was widespread in the rural areas, for example, among smallholder coffee and rubber growers, and in plantation zones, these people seem to have been constantly on the move seeking profitable markets. As their counterparts had already started doing in the nineteenth century within West Sumatra (Graves 1971:184–185; Verkerk Pistorius 1871:15), these merchants and artisans traveled from one market town to another following the weekly market circuit. Timing their arrival with the payday of plantation workers, they also visited one plantation after another in East Sumatra, carrying their commodities on their backs or on bicycles (Hamka 1962:10; Naim 1972:11). Minangkabau petty traders, sometimes even peddling with pushcarts, were frequently noticed in Asahan and Langkat in the early 1930s.[38] This constant traveling must have been partly responsible for the decision not to take their nuclear families with them on the rantau.

Merantau was basically circulatory during the Dutch period; perantau often came back to visit their villages (Naim 1972:35). Men sometimes left home after the planting of the rice, tried their fate in the rantau, and came back before the harvest (Schrieke 1955b:140–141). In some cases, they came back for the Lebaran, an Islamic celebration marking the end of the fasting month, once a year or every two years, bringing back the fruits of their labors in the rantau (Radjab 1950:170). The destination of merantau was still not so far from home, so "circulation" was not a great expense. Usually unencumbered by their nuclear families, married men too had great freedom of movement to go where they wished, including their home villages. And in these villages most of their families, matrilineal and nuclear, were still resident. These were all contributing factors to the circulatory nature of merantau at that time.

Circulatory merantau was not without precedent even before the Dutch period. It is said that one of the traditional reasons for a man to leave the village was to acquire knowledge, wealth, and fame, and eventually come back home to enrich his lineage, his village, and even the Alam (for more details, see Abdullah 1971:18–22). According to the tambo, the suku system was introduced by Datuk Perpatih nan Sebatang who traveled to China and observed the clan system there (Abdullah 1972a:107). The Padri movement was invigorated by three haji who came back from Mecca. Likewise, the Kaum Muda movement of the early twentieth century was started

<hr/>

38. See the article of Hassan Nur Arifin on conditions in Asahan in *Sinar Deli*, 28 May 1932, and page 11 of the "Bestuurs Memorie" of W. Ph. Coolhaas, *controleur* of Langkat, 11 May 1933. Both pieces of information were supplied to me by William O'Malley.

by Islamic teachers who returned from study in the Holy City. As the last two instances show, the person who best embodied the traditional ideology of circulatory migration was the *urang siak*, a religious student. *Urang siak* often traveled from one religious school to another in order to study under different teachers. After acquiring sufficient knowledge, they were expected to come back to their villages and give religious guidance to their fellow villagers. Nevertheless, we have to remember that the model of the *urang siak* was hardly typical of everyday social practice. People did study religion (that is, recitation of Koran) at the local surau. But how many men would have actually spent their youth traveling from school to school? I suspect it must have been a tiny segment of society.[39]

There were also many migration situations where the circulatory ideology did not apply. Even though ties between mother and daughter nagari were sometimes maintained (Josselin de Jong 1952:107), the idea of returning to one's native nagari was not crucial to the notions behind village segmentation. As far as I am aware, there is no story (*kaba*) relating the homecoming of those Minangkabau merchants who were active in the eastern rantau in the seventeenth and eighteenth centuries. Though they retain some elements of cultural identity with the mother country, the Minangkabau of Negri Sembilan, on the Malay peninsula, do not seem to have developed any yearning to return home to stay. Their traditional relations with Minangkabau society, specifically with the court of Pagarruyung, were mainly based on political expediency. That the ideology of returning home may be an old one is seen in this traditional aphorism:

> Rain of stones in our own village,
> Rain of gold in other people's land,
> However poor we may be,
> We still yearn to go home.[40]

39. In my survey on merantau history, there was only one case during the Dutch time which fits merantu *à la urang siak*. The decline of the traveling *urang siak* was surely due in part to the emergence of modern Islamic schools after 1910s. There was no case in the same survey in which a person migrated as a religious missionary. This may simply mean that religious preaching and proselytizing are not considered occupations.

40. In Minangkabau, *Hujan batu dikampuang awak,/Hujan ameh dirantau urang,/Walau bak mano misikin awak,/Bacinto juo dagang nak pulang.*

Yet it was not until the Dutch period that this ideology was translated into widespread social practice in the form of circulatory merantau.

Merantau patterns after the Dutch period ended continued to be nonagricultural in terms of occupational pursuit. Increasingly it was the nuclear family rather than the individuals who migrated. These tendencies have become especially salient since 1960, as I observed in the survey on merantau history. Partly because of the increase in the numbers of white-collar perantau, merantau by family has become more popular; office workers, owing to their relatively secure jobs and guaranteed incomes, run few risks in taking their families with them to the rantau. The rapid growth of urban centers and the attraction of large markets have induced many merchant perantau to congregate and settle in these cities. *Kaki lima*, roadside vendors, still peddle for a living but they move, not from one market town to another, but from one street corner to the next. The more they tend to settle in one place, the more they feel the need for somebody to look after their daily wants. If they are not yet married, they often go back home to marry and the new bride is immediately taken back to the rantau. If they are already married and if the nuclear family is still in the village, it is frequently sent for once life in the rantau becomes somewhat stabilized. In fact, it is often the case that sending for wives and children is now the first sign, in the villagers' eyes, of a perantau's success in the rantau (he is *sanggup* or financially capable).

Compounded with the above trends is a decreasing tendency to return home. The destination of merantau today is often far away, for example, Java. In many cases, his wife and children accompany the perantau. It is a heavy economic burden to undertake, even occasionally, the long trip to the village with the whole nuclear family. As the convergence of Minangkabau perantau in cities progresses, many perantau associations are being organized in such places as Jakarta, Pekan Baru, Medan, and Palembang. These new associations, sometimes even organized according to the nagari of the perantau's origin, usually function as the setting for adat and religious ceremonies, such as marriages, funerals, and Lebaran, many of which could never have been performed in the rantau in early times and would therefore have provided reasons for visits back home. They also serve as a medium for exchanging gossip and

information between the rantau and the village. Unmarried perantau may still often go home. But once they are married and begin to
form their own nuclear families in the rantau, their physical relationship with their villages becomes remote. In the process the predominant pattern of merantau is changing: from circulatory merantau to Chinese merantau (*merantau Cino*).

5 / Village and Rantau

Historically and culturally, the rantau originated from the darek. Yet, their relation was never unidirectional. The darek did not simply dictate the shaping of the rantau. The rantau also exerted its influence on the darek. As suggested by an adat aphorism referring to "the deer with the golden horns [symbolizing a king] who came from the sea," kingship was presumably introduced to the darek via the rantau (Abdullah 1972a:185). Similarly, an aphorism mentioned earlier maintains that "Islam ascended [from the coast, that is, the rantau, to the darek], while adat descended [from Mount Merapi]." In this mutual interaction, the darek provided Minangkabau identity, while the rantau served as a gateway through which new ideas and practices were introduced to the Alam Minangkabau.

The basis of the rantau's dynamism was its inherent difference from the darek, irrespective of many shared characteristics. The rantau was not simply a geographical extension or replica of the darek. One clear sign of the difference is another adat aphorism which says: "Luhak [darek] has penghulu, rantau has raja" (*Luhak bapanghulu, rantau barajo*). In the cultural heartland of the darek, it was traditionally the penghulu, the lineage heads, who held the highest political and judicial power. But in the more heterogenous rantau bordering on the outside world where kinship proved to have little effect in controlling mixed population, it was the raja, the minor kings, who presided over villages (Datoek Madjolelo and Marzoeki 1951:25). Heterogeneity generated by the contact with the outside world was a major source of rantau's dynamism.

After the middle of the nineteenth century, that is, after the Dutch

154

established their political hegemony over West Sumatra, the locus of rantau began to change. The Alam Minangkabau itself was contained within the administrative boundary of Sumatra's West Coast. As the immediate rantau lost its capacity to expand, the idea of rantau became more and more identified with areas outside West Sumatra to which Minangkabau perantau migrated to earn a livelihood rather than to establish new permanent settlements. In addition, the development of transportation and communication systems allowed the darek and its people to have direct contacts with the outside world without the mediation of the local rantau in West Sumatra. Today, rantau is largely understood as synonymous with areas—particularly cities and towns—outside West Sumatra. Merantau is also increasingly understood in a similar fashion: to leave one's native province, not one's village or the darek.

This shift, however, did not change the nature of interaction between the darek (now primarily West Sumatra as a whole) and the rantau (primarily areas outside West Sumatra).[1] The rantau is still conceived as a zone different from the darek which serves as a source of new ideas and practices. Yet the rantau-darek contrast at the present time has become overlaid to a great extent by the urban-rural or city-village distinction, as the urban orientation of the perantau has grown. Some characteristics of this urban-rural contrast are readily recognizable. By comparison to the West Sumatran villages from which most Minangkabau perantau originate, the urban rantau is crowded, multiethnic, culturally diverse, occupationally differentiated, steeply stratified economically, highly developed in terms of mass communication, abundant in entertainment, and so on.

Inspite of these obvious general differences between village and rantau, we have little understanding of the kind of life a perantau may actually come to lead in the rantau. How different is the perantau's life from that of his compatriots back in the village? How does the perantau organize his family life and household? How does he relate to his matrilineal relatives? Are people who tend to remain in the village systematically different from those who tend to stay in the rantau? Partly in order to answer these questions, a household

1. This is my own metaphorical usage of the terms. Even though rantau may be used to refer to areas outside West Sumatra in daily conversation nowadays, the darek still retains its traditional meaning of the cultural heartland in West Sumatra.

survey was conducted in IV Angkat and in Padang and Pekan Baru. In the survey, IV Angkat represents a microcosm of the village; Padang and Pekan Paru represent microcosms of the rantau.

The respondents in IV Angkat were drawn from four villages, while those in Padang and Pekan Baru were people originally coming from two of the same four villages. The sample size in IV Angkat was 395—a 10 percent random sample of male household heads (husbands) in the four villages. The size of the perantau sample in the two cities was seventy-five. These were male household heads whom I chose from members of the perantau associations of IV Angkat Candung in Padang and Pekan Baru.

Every study of perantau is bound to suffer from sampling problems. The present attempt is no exception. The sample size is very small. Respondents could not be randomly selected. People who become members of perantau associations are more likely to be successful perantau, however modest their success may be, rather than the near-destitute perantau who fail. Even among members of perantau associations, the difficulties encountered in locating and interviewing respondents in large cities necessitated the inclusion of all reachable respondents rather than a sampling of them. With a mean and median length of stay in the rantau of nineteen years, the respondents in the survey had been away from the village for an extremely long time.[2] They also came disproportionately from the highly educated white-collar sector. In no sense, then, are my samples from Padang and Pekan Baru representative of the perantau households found in these two cities, however the universe of perantau households might be defined. This rather dismal situation should not, however, discourage us from drawing some inferences from the survey results at this exploratory stage of our inquiry. There are a number of differences in the way family life is organized between the village (IV Angkat) and the rantau (Padang and Pekan Baru). Some of these differences may be attributed to the weaknesses and the bias of my sampling in the two cities. On the other hand, many of the differences are also intelligible in terms of the general contrast between urban rantau and village.

2. The distribution of lengths of stay in the rantau was as follows: less than 6 years, 4 percent; 6 to 10 years, 14 percent; 11 to 15 years, 27 percent; 16 to 20 years, 17 percent; 21 to 25 years, 17 percent; 26 to 30 years, 7 percent; 31 to 35 years, 7 percent; 36 to 40 years, 3 percent; more than 40 years, 4 percent.

Demographic Characteristics of Household Heads

In order to get acquainted with the characteristics of the people who supplied me with information in the village and the rantau, let us first examine some demographic traits of the two groups of respondents, namely, age, educational level, and main occupation. By comparison with respondents from the village, those in the rantau were on the average younger, better educated, and far less likely to be agricultural or manual in occupation (Table 5.1). These results may be exaggerated due to a sampling bias, but the basic differences, especially as far as educational level and occupation are concerned, are not likely to be factitious.[3] Table 5.2 shows the educational level and occupation of those who were covered in my survey on merantau history and who at the time of the survey were staying in the village or in the rantau. In this instance, both perantau and villagers were drawn from the same 132 sublineages studied in my survey on merantau history. Since information concerning perantau was obtained from their matrilineal kin who still resided in the village, there is little likelihood of a sampling bias caused by the differential accessibility of various perantau.[4] Another difference is that my sample in the household survey consisted of only household heads, while Table 5.2 covers non-household heads as well as household heads. In these respects, the perantau and the villagers involved in the survey on merantau history are more comparable to each other and more representative of those who currently stay in the village or in the rantau than my samples from the household survey.

A comparison of Tables 5.1 and 5.2 shows that my rantau re-

3. Nobody in the rantau was engaged in agriculture as their main occupation; the 3 percent in "agricultural or manual" were manual laborers. The disparity with regard to agricultural occupations widens if we take supplementary occupations into consideration. About 75 percent of respondents in the village were engaged in agriculture either as their main or supplementary occupation. Only one percent of those in the rantau were so engaged. The survey of the Sumatra Regional Planning Study in southern Sumatra also seems to indicate that Minangkabau perantau are younger than those who stay in West Sumatra. The age distribution of their 239 Minangkabau male household heads in cities and towns of southern Sumatra was as follows: 20 to 35 years old, 30 percent; 36 to 45 years old, 36 percent; 46 to 55 years old, 23 percent; more than 55 years old, 11 percent. The mean age was 43 years.

4. Even in this case, people whose close matrilineal kin have all left the village cannot be tapped in the survey. As mentioned before, a male respondent was asked about his children (non-matrilineal kin) instead of his kemanakan.

spondents in the household survey overrepresent the share of college graduates and white-collar workers among the perantau. Nevertheless, a general divergence between perantau and villagers is unmistakable, showing in both tables: in other words, perantau are better educated and far less agricultural or manual in occupation than villagers. (This is also true for female villagers and perantau as seen in Table 5.2.) The seemingly rather simple observation is not without significance for characterizing a specifically Minangkabau migratory pattern. Different from the people who flock in from Bekasi, Cirebon, Indramayu, and other places relatively near to Jakarta, who often become manual laborers (for example, *becak* or tricycle drivers), the Minangkabau perantau in the capital, by comparison with their former fellow villagers, are in general selected people in terms of their educational level and occupational orientation.

Table 5.1.   Age, education, and occupation of household heads in village and rantau

	Village (N = 395)	Rantau (N = 75)
Age		
20 to 35	11%	28%
36 to 45	25%	28%
46 to 55	36%	31%
56 and older	28%	13%
Mean age	49	43
Educational level		
No schooling	3%	0%
Grade school	63%	32%
Junior high	21%	26%
Senior high	11%	14%
College	2%	28%
Main occupation		
Agricultural/Manual	43%	3%
Commercial	21%	29%
Artisanry	16%	11%
White-collar	18%	54%
Other	2%	3%

Source: Household survey in IV Angkat and in Padang and Pekan Baru. Unless otherwise specified, the subsequent tables are all based on the household survey.

Table 5.2. Education and occupation of villagers and perantau

	Males		Females	
	Villagers (N = 157)	Perantau (N = 166)	Villagers (N = 322)	Perantau (N = 90)
Education				
No schooling	15%	4%	27%	10%
Grade school	63%	45%	52%	40%
Junior high	12%	22%	13%	22%
Senior high	8%	17%	5%	15%
College	2%	12%	3%	13%
Main occupation				
Agricultural/Manual	38%	4%	39%	0%
Commercial	18%	46%	4%	12%
Artisanry	22%	16%	24%	10%
White-collar	13%	25%	6%	9%
Housewife	0%	0%	24%	59%
Other	9%	9%	3%	10%

SOURCE: Survey on merantau history.

Household Composition and Management

The question of housing is essential in the Minangkabau society, for the legal status of a house of domicile according to adat determines to a great extent who may live there. In terms of legal status the houses in the villages are more or less evenly divided between ancestral and individually earned properties. By contrast, houses which are ancestral property are very rare in the rantau, as it accounts for only 4 percent; houses in the rantau are overwhelmingly rented (over 50 percent) or individually earned (36 percent).[5] This difference is significant, for the proportion of rented or individually earned houses in the rantau suggests that the occupants have great discretion as to who will stay there with them. In this respect, the term "individually earned house" in the village is a bit misleading.

5. Individually earned properties are the properties acquired entirely by one's own efforts. This tendency was already noted in colonial times. According to the Dutch census (Volkstelling 1930, 4:66), the legal status of houses in the municipality of Padang was as follows: ancestral property, 11 percent; individually earned property, 46 percent; other (mainly rented), 43 percent. This recalculation of the census results does not include houses of unknown legal classification.

It is still relatively rare that ground for building a house has the status of individually earned property even if the house on that ground is classified as such. In such cases, the discretion of any use attributed above to individually earned property does not apply. Suppose that a husband builds a house on the ancestral property of his wife's lineage. Even if the house itself is his individually earned property, there is no way for him to accommodate his parents in the house so long as the house stands on the land of his wife's lineage.

There is little difference in household size between village and rantau: on the average 6.7 and 7.4 persons per house respectively. However, there is considerable divergence in household composition between village and rantau (Table 5.3).[6] The major difference concerns the inclusion or exclusion of either the wife's kin or the husband's. From the table, it is apparent that inclusion of husband's kin seldom happens in the village. Beyond the nuclear family, the household in the village almost exclusively incorporates the wife's relatives. This is not the case in the rantau. There households often include the husband's kin and his wife's. Of twenty-one households in the rantau that included husband's kin, seven actually incorporated both the husband's and his wife's. Thus, among nonnuclear households in the rantau, the inclusion of these two types of kin was relatively balanced: 17 percent had wife's kin, 19 percent husband's, and 10 percent both wife's and husband's. The results show that the matrilineal principle plays an important role in household formation in the village, but household formation in the rantau is more variable.[7]

In terms of generational depth, about 35 percent of the households sampled incorporated parents, both in the village and in the rantau. The only difference between the two spheres is that, as pointed out above, the parents in the village are those of the wife,

6. The meanings of the categories in the table are as follows: stem—a nuclear family with the wife's parent(s) (and her unmarried siblings, usually sisters); joint—household of two married sisters or more (and their parents and unmarried siblings); husband's kin included—all households which include the husband's kin, such as parents and siblings; other—a nuclear family and non-immediate kin of the wife (e.g., wife's sister's child).

7. Although the household survey did not specifically ask this question, another significant difference in household composition between village and rantau is the sleeping arrangement of boys. Boys in the rantau sleep in their parents' house, while those in the village still commonly sleep in the surau or else in coffee shops or empty houses.

Table 5.3.   Household composition in village and rantau

	Nuclear	Stem	Joint	Husband's kin included	Other
Village (N = 393)	53%	27%	13%	1%	6%
Rantau (N = 72)	54%	12%	2%	29%	3%

while in the rantau they are equally divided between the parents of the wife and those of her husband. Only in one household in rantau were the parents of both wife and husband found living together.

Aside from household composition, the management of family affairs also reveals differences between village and rantau. Both in terms of consulting about problems connected with the nuclear family and in making decisions about the children's education, occupation, and so on, wives' participation was more frequently mentioned in the rantau than in the village. This tendency is particularly noticeable in decision-making about the children: 54 percent of the perantau versus 35 percent of the villagers mentioned such participation. Another important observation is that the mamak in the rantau seems to play a less important role in the management of family affairs than he does in the village. The difference is especially pronounced in consultation about nuclear-family problems. Only 14 percent of the respondents in the rantau mentioned the mamak as a primary consultant about such problems, while 38 percent did so in the village.

Perhaps these findings mean that once separated from extensive kin networks in the villages, husbands and wives in the rantau are much more dependent upon each other in the management of family affairs than their counterparts back home. Stronger conjugal ties and mutual dependency in the rantau are also suggested by the lower rates of divorce and polygamy experiences there than in the villages. This is particularly true for the older generations (respondents older than 45 years) among whom both practices are more common than among their juniors.[8]

8. Figures for divorce and polygamy experiences were as follows: in the village (N=390), 24 percent and 38 percent; in the rantau (N=74), 14 percent and 11 percent. Even if the age is controlled (20 to 45 years old versus 46 years or older), the difference essentially persists, although it widens for the older generations.

Matrilineal Kinship Relations

Knowledge of the identities of one's older kin reflects one's genealogical consciousness. Although knowledge of their identities does not necessarily mean intimacy between a person and his or her older kin, we may still assume that it does often reflect a certain psychological proximity. In the survey, respondents were asked to identify the names and adat titles of three male figures two generations above them, namely, mother's father, (any of) the mamak of the mother (if there is more than one mamak), and father's father.[9] The results show that people in the village are slightly better acquainted with the identities of these older kin than those in the rantau; the difference is mainly due to the fact that the former group has a better knowledge of adat titles than the latter. Three observations can be made concerning the respondents' genealogical knowledge. First, many of these male respondents (about 50 percent on the average) could not identify either the name or adat title of people from their grandparents' generation.[10] Second, adat titles were likely to be better known than personal names, especially among people in the village. This conforms to the traditional custom that in the village adult males are addressed by adat titles rather than by personal names. Third, respondents were better acquainted with the identities of older kin from their mother's side than from their father's, signifying better familiarity with matrilineal kin.

As far as financial assistance is concerned, there is hardly any difference between village and rantau concerning the respondents' relationship to their mamak during childhood; in about 20 percent of the cases, mamak provided part of daily expenses, and in about 57 percent of the cases, they offered financial assistance for respondents' education. Differences between village and rantau emerge mainly with regard to marriage. Mamak tended to be less frequently involved in the marriage arrangement of respondents in the

9. Traditionally, every man was given an adat title upon marriage or assumption of an adat position.
10. The women seemed to have better genealogical knowledge than the men. According to interviews conducted in one of the four villages in IV Angkat, only about 25 percent of 85 women interviewed did not know either the name or adat title of their mother's father and mother's mamak. There was no difference, however, concerning father's father: 61 percent did not know either.

rantau (45 percent versus 58 percent) and in providing financial assistance for the wedding ceremony (23 percent versus 48 percent). The first difference, however, is mainly found among those perantau who had already left the village before they were married. Considering the fact that more and more people leave for merantau prior to marriage, future trends seem to be that mamak will be decreasingly involved in the marriage arrangement of perantau.

If there is little difference between village and rantau in terms of the financial assistance received from the mamak, there is a slight difference concerning the financial assistance that respondents in their roles as mamak have rendered to their kemanakan. More respondents in the rantau have given financial assistance to their kemanakan than have those in the village. The difference is slight but consistent over the various fields of education, daily living, merantau, and marriage. On the average, 73 percent of the respondents in the rantau and 62 percent in the village have the experience of giving financial assistance in these fields. In spite of this, however, the mamak in the rantau seem to have more tenuous and remote relationships with their kemanakan than do their village counterparts. The former have, for example, been less frequently involved in the marriage arrangements of their kemanakan (55 percent versus 85 percent, among the respondents whose kemanakan are married). Perantau's idea of their role toward their kemanakan is the rather passive one of "be informed of their well-being" (60 percent), instead of "give advice" (38 percent) or "be their guardian" (2 percent); the same set of figures for the villagers are 39 percent, 42 percent, and 19 percent. Even though mamak in the rantau do give material assistance to their kemanakan more frequently than their village counterparts, their involvement in their kemanakan's lives remains more formal, partly because of their physical remoteness. It seems as if they are possibly paying off their traditional complex moral responsibilities to their kemanakan simply by means of enlarged financial help.

The Two Worlds of the Village and the Rantau

As already noted, an estimated 30 percent of all Minangkabau may currently be found outside West Sumatra. Most Minangkabau who stay in the villages are therefore likely to know some people—matrilineal kin, affinal kin, childhood friends, school friends, former colleagues, and so on who reside in the rantau. According to my survey on merantau history, 86 percent of the 132 houses studied have some members of their sublineages (paruik) now staying in the rantau.

In spite of this closeness of merantau to the everyday lives of most Minangkabau, some people obviously do tend to remain in the village and others to stay in the rantau. The characteristics of these two groups of people are diverse. Some villagers are young, well-educated, and nonagricultural in occupation. Some perantau are old, poorly educated, and manual in occupation. The classification of people as villagers and perantau is not always fixed or permanent. Some villagers will become perantau someday, while some perantau eventually will come back to live in the village. Nevertheless, results from my household survey and my survey on merantau history indicate that perantau and villagers as a group do present somewhat different demographic characteristics: in comparison to those who remain in the village, people who stay in the rantau are on the average better educated, far less agricultural or manual in occupation, and most probably younger.

Just as different types of people leave the village, the consequences of merantau vary among the perantau. Although there are numerous success stories, merantau is essentially a gamble; some succeed, but others fail. Rantau does not always bring good luck, even though there is a popular saying to the contrary (*rantau bertuah,* or rantau abounds with luck). An adat aphorism recognizes these mixed outcomes:

> *Karatau* was expected to be *madang,*
> It turns out that it destroys the rice plants,
> Merantau was expected to make one happy,
> It turns out that it saddens one's heart.[11]

Despite all this, the cities and towns where most of the perantau congregate envelop them with atmosphere, life style, and environment peculiar to the modern rantau. My household survey, albeit

---

11. In Minangkabau, *Karatau disangko madang,/Kironyo maluluah padi,/ Marantau disangko sanang,/Kironyo merusuah hati. Karatau* and *madang* are certain species of trees.

concerned with the quite narrow scope of family life, shows some differences between village and rantau in the way people organize their lives. Household organization in the villages is still governed by the matrilineal principle, while that in the rantau is more variable, allowing easier inclusion of the husband's matrilineal kin. Separated from their respective matrilineal kin networks in the village, the husband and wife in the rantau seem to be more dependent upon each other in the management of family affairs. In terms of matrilineal kinship, their relationships with their mamak in later life, that is, after childhood, seem more remote than for those who stay in the village. Even with regard to their kemanakan, the perantau's involvement is expressed mainly in financial terms; such traditional moral obligations as finding a spouse for the kemanakan are more perfunctorily performed.

These results may well have been influenced by the particular sets of respondents I questioned in IV Angkat and in Padang and Pekan Baru. Yet, many of these findings are also intelligible in the context of difference between urban rantau and village. Whether perantau are successful or unsuccessful, educated or not educated, white-collar workers or manual laborers, young or old, they live in a city or town far away from their village. In the rantau, ties to matrilineal kin and affinal kin diminish in their immediacy in everyday life. Traditional rights and obligations associated with the matrilineal system cease to be as binding in the rantau as in the village. Physically separated from the village, perantau are more susceptible to an urban culture which is in no way Minangkabau. Whether perantau like it or not, the simple fact that they live in the rantau forces some sort of readjustment in the way their lives are organized.

That life style differs between the village and the rantau is clearly perceived by the perantau themselves. There is a popular theory among perantau, especially among males, that it is the adat which prompts Minangkabau men to merantau. In a matrilineal society, there is no room for individual male initiative. Minangkabau go merantau in order to seek self-respect and to be free from adat.[12] Whether this theory is true or not, it reflects an awareness among the perantau that the rantau life is quite different from that in the village.

12. "Karatau Madang Dihulu," *Aneka Minang*, no. 14 (n.d.), pp. 7–10.

A subdistrict head in the darek once told me a story of a Javanese woman who stayed in one of the villages under his jurisdiction near Bukittinggi. She was on a volunteer aid program for rural development and was supposed to stay in the village for a couple of years, helping the village government in its development efforts. Raised in a city and a college graduate, she had worn only Western clothes all her life. She appeared in the village in Western clothes of the type often worn by civil servants—light brown two-piece suits. However, she was strongly advised by the village head to dress like a village woman if she wanted to be accepted by the villagers. In fact, except for schoolgirls, practically no woman, married or unmarried, above the age of about fifteen wears Western clothes in rural areas. Thus, this Javanese woman had to wear indigenous clothes for the first time in her life—not indigenous Javanese female attire, but Minangkabau *baju kurung* or knee-length overall-like garments.

In a nice contrast to that story, there is a recent Minangkabau popular song from the rantau called "Poncho" (*Baju Ponco*):

This present age,
This is the age of all kinds of fashions,
Already known is the fashion of funny clothes,
Which many young people like.
Cut square, with lace around the edges,
It looks like a table cloth,
With flower patterns, it also looks like a Jango blouse,
The famous fashion, the fashion of the poncho blouse.
I want one like that too,
Afraid of being left behind by the age,
I don't care how funny it looks, it's the poncho blouse that I like.
Mother, please buy me one,
I want to wear a poncho blouse,
Let other people say I am crazy rather than being out of fashion.[13]

The Javanese woman who had to wear a *baju kurung* and a Minangkabau girl singer who craves a funny, crazy poncho blouse are symbolic of the distance between the two worlds of the village and the rantau. Whether this difference will be a source of change

13. Jango is the hero of some spaghetti western movies. The song is in *Aneka Minang*, no. 12 (n.d.), p. 35, and is translated here by permission of the composer, Chilung Ramali.

and innovation in contemporary Minangkabau society is contingent on the relations maintained between village and rantau. While the dominant pattern of merantau was circulatory, the rantau was still closely tied to the village. But, as Chinese merantau has gained in importance, village and rantau tend to grow apart.

6 / New Configurations in Minangkabau Society

Changing patterns of migration are closely interrelated with other alterations that have been taking place within Minangkabau society. For example, migration by nuclear family instead of by individual is inconceivable without some realignment of the matrilineal system. Unless the mamak relinquishes his traditional rights and obligations over his female kin, the urang sumando, the husband, cannot take his wife and children to the rantau. Were it not for his attachment to his nuclear family, the perantau might marry women in the rantau as his second, third, or even fourth wives, instead of sending for his wife and children from the village. This, in fact, did sometimes happen, particularly during the Dutch period; being Moslems, Minangkabau men may be polygamous. Conversely, change in the matrilineal system is often instigated by new ideas and economic resources brought back to the village by returning perantau.

In order to understand the process whereby merantau patterns have changed, it is essential to examine many other transformations in Minangkabau society. The discussion in this chapter, therefore, concerns changes in the matrilineal system and social stratification.

The Advent of Individually Earned Property

One of the most significant developments in West Sumatra after the early nineteenth century was the growing economic consequence of *harta pencarian* (individually earned property) and the crystalization of the concept and the practices associated with it.

Previously, the concept of harta pencarian had not been unknown. Harta pencarian referred to those properties which were derived entirely from one's own efforts. A person might produce rice from the rice field by his or her own efforts and labor, but the produce was not regarded as individually earned so long as rice field was an ancestral land.

Aside from its association with nascent commercial and artisanal activities, the concept of harta pencarian traditionally was closely related to the opening of new agricultural land. Newly opened land was of two types: more or less permanent cultivations (sawah or wet-rice fields) and impermanent or shifting cultivations. The former was the basis of the expansion of ancestral land, for usually this type of new land was absorbed into the ancestral property (harta pusaka) of the developer's mother's house after his death (Graves 1971:52; Verkerk Pistorius 1871:45). In this context, one should also remember that the opening of new sawah in particular requires sizable investments of manpower and material: insofar as the developer depended on his lineage or sublineage for help, there would be considerable restraints on his discretion in the disposal of its product.

The second type of new land offered wider latitude in the disposal of its product. The clearing of upland *ladang* (dry fields) was not a major operation like creating new sawah. Its rather impermanent nature made the lineage of its developer less concerned to control it than was the case with sawah. Possibly then the opener of new *ladang* had some freedom in disposing of its product—for example, spending or giving some of it to his wife and children.

But so long as agriculture was mainly of a subsistence nature, harta pencarian of this type probably was not consequential. In the midst of a largely sawah agriculture, the main significance of upland *ladang* was to provide supplemental foodstuffs—rice, bananas, and some root crops. Admittedly, pepper cultivation, gold-panning, gathering of forest products, and rudimentary commercial and artisanal pursuits had existed before as sources of harta pencarian; the practice of these activities had been limited in both scale and areal spread in West Sumatra. It was only after the early nineteenth century, as the money economy spread through the society, that harta pencarian became really significant. As described in Chapter 3, the early nineteenth century saw the proliferation of coffee cultivation, the ravages of the Padri wars, the subsequent imposition of Dutch political control on West Sumatra, and finally the emergence of opportunities for a merantau not of the village segmentation type. For our purposes here the spread of cash crops, mainly coffee at the beginning, and the increasing popularity of nonsegmentary merantau are particularly important. The common denominator underlying the two phenomena was the increasing circulation of money. For cash income, whose acquisition usually depended on the individual's own efforts, was to become the prime modern expression of harta pencarian.

The traditional medium of commodity exchange was barter or gold dust. To be sure, coinage (mainly Spanish dollars) was already known in the seventeenth century. But it was only after the early nineteenth century that American coffee buyers arrived in West Sumatra with large amounts of Spanish dollars and flooded the Minangkabau society with this coinage. Thereafter the spread of a money economy, or at least of its institutional framework, was very rapid. By the Currency Law of 1854, paper currency and coinage in the Dutch East Indies were standardized in accordance with the system in the Netherlands—a complete departure from the confused monetary situation before this time (*Encyclopaedie van Nederlandsch Oost-Indië 2*, 1918:793, 804). A branch of the Java Bank, the bank of circulation of the Netherlands East Indies, was established in Padang in 1864. This was one of the only two branches of the Java Bank founded in the Outer Islands before 1906—the other was in Makasar (*ibid. 1*, 1917:155). Saving banks were also inaugurated in Padang in 1879 (ibid. *4*, 1921:45). The establishment of these institutions reflects the high level of money circulation in Minangkabau society by the latter half of the nineteenth century. The final impetus in the same direction was the introduction of a money tax after 1908 (Schrieke 1955b:98, 112–113).

Coffee cultivation and nonsegmentary merantau made possible a new kind of wealth, that is, money incomes not wholly constrained by adat regulations on matrilineal inheritance. Unlike other forms of wealth, money could, with ease and secrecy, be transferred, accumulated, converted into various goods, and disposed of largely at the individual's discretion. Moreover, this new wealth did not accrue from adat positions such as penghuluship. Coffee was usually grown in wasteland (that is, uncultivated land) and in hedges

NEW CONFIGURATIONS   171

around houses; like upland *ladang*, the usage of such land and the
disposal of its produce were not stringently regulated by adat
(Dobbin 1977:26). Nonsegmentary merantau made possible the
pursuit of wealth beyond the nagari's boundaries, usually through
nonagricultural occupations. In theory, every ambitious and ener-
getic man could seek new wealth by both avenues. As will be described below, the changing role of the man vis-à-vis his wife and
children was contingent upon the growing significance of harta
pencarian and increasing population pressures on limited agricultural land.

It is difficult to document systematically how population pressure
affected the pattern of land utilization. However, it seems to have
proceeded as follows according to my interviews in IV Angkat.
(Also see Kahn 1976:71–75.) As ancestral land became insufficient
to provide for the whole membership of an adat house and the
possibilities for its physical extension narrowed, the sublineage
(paruik) tended to divide into smaller economic units, normally the
samandai (mother and her children). Accordingly, the ganggam
bauntuak, usage rights to ancestral land or sometimes sharing
rights to the product from ancestral land, were allocated to the
various samandai of the house. If the ancestral land was relatively
large, each constituent samandai was given ganggam bauntuak to
particular plots. If the land was too small to be divided this way, it
was used by different samandai in turn, usually on an annual basis
or on the basis of a planting season. The effect of rising population
density in the Dutch period was to make this latter pattern increasingly common, especially in the land-short darek. It meant that the
samandai could no longer survive on. harta pusaka alone. As the
economic centrality of harta pusaka decreased, the samandai began
to turn to the sumando, the husband, as a possible supplementary
provider.

It is not clear why the samandai turned to the sumando instead of
to the mamak for a supplementary livelihood. Possibly the decision
is due to the fact that the sumando-samandai is essentially a one-
to-one relation with the exception of limited polygynous cases. In
contrast, some paruik may have multiple mamak, while some
paruik may not have any direct mamak. Mamak's traditional obligations to kemanakan, direct or classificatory, consisted mainly of
supervision, moral guidance, and cooperation in the enlargement of

harta pusaka—"commodities," if one can make a metaphorical use of the term, not readily measurable, comparable, or evaluable, and thus relatively inexhaustible. Commercial profits, salaries, and incomes from cash crops, all prime examples of harta pencarian, are quantifiable, finite, and scarce. The unequal demographic distribution of direct mamak magnifies these qualities, causing a serious difficulty in the division of mamak's harta pencarian. Even if the paruik have multiple mamak, it is problematic to assemble the harta pencarian of mamak and then equitably redistribute it to their constituent samandai. Under the circumstances, the sumando is a more readily definable, approachable, and possibly even reliable source of supplementary livelihood for the individual samandai. The samandai, above all the mother, must have exerted considerable pressure and charm upon the sumando so that he would expend his harta pencarian on his wife and children rather than on his own sublineage.

The reliance between the samandai and the sumando began to assume real social significance only after the acquisition of harta pencarian on a substantial scale became possible. Harta pencarian not only made such reliance a viable option for the samandai but also opened the way for the sumando to establish an enhanced and more secure position vis-à-vis his wife and children. This in turn raised the man's bargaining position as a mamak for respect and proper treatment from his paruik, as the paruik did not want completely to relinquish its claim over his harta pencarian either.

The sumando still could not belong to the lineage of his wife, nor could he take his wife and children away from their lineage. Nevertheless, he began to wield more domestic authority over the samandai grouping in proportion to his increasing economic contribution to it. The primary economic unit in the society was now more likely to be the conjugal nuclear family than the samandai or paruik. The sumando began to reside in the house of his wife. If we borrow Hazairin's characterization, the sumando batandang (visiting husband) was gradually transformed into the sumando menetap (living-in husband) (quoted by Kemal 1964:222–223). This physical proximity was essential to the psychological proximity required for stabilizing the conjugal nuclear family.[1]

---

1. There is a parallel between change in sumando's residential patterns and change in merantau patterns from circulatory to Chinese merantau. In both cases,

Reflecting the closer ties developing within the nuclear family, men increasingly transferred their harta pencarian to their children by means of *hibah* (gift), lest it fall into the hand of their kemanakan upon their death.[2] This practice became particularly popular in the early twentieth century (Josselin de Jong 1952:115–116); today it is the general custom that harta pencarian is inherited by a man's children. But the Alam Minangkabau witnessed many heated discussions before this present acceptance was really achieved. In 1901, an adat expert was already proposing in *Insulinde*, a magazine published in Padang, that harta pencarian be inherited according to *faraidh* (Islamic inheritance law), which favored wife and children over kemanakan (Abdullah 1972b:9). The same point was reiterated by the Kaum Muda Islamic reformists in the 1910s, and in the 1930s by Perti, a powerful local Islamic educational association (Schrieke 1973:39–40; Abdullah 1972b:9). A resolution to the same effect—that harta pencarian normally be given to the children—was also adopted by a conference of adat functionaries and Islamic experts in Bukittinggi in 1951, and again by a seminar on inheritance law in Padang in 1968. These activities, continued over several decades, show that among both adat and Islamic experts there were strong impulses at work to clarify the concept of harta pencarian and its relation to inheritance practices. Above all, they constitute repeated attempts to draw a hard and fast line between harta pusaka (ancestral property) and harta pencarian (individually earned property): the one a man may not meddle with, but the other he may dispose of as he wishes.

The Decline of the Adat House

While harta pencarian was the basis for the emergence of the nuclear family as the primary economic unit, the increasing popularity of relatively small non-adat houses was the physical basis for

---

men's physical presence was registered in two locations at the beginning: one's mother's house and one's wife's house or village and rantau. In the process of change, men have now largely come to stay in one location, that is, one's wife's house or rantau, yet their psychological ties to the other location, one's mother's house or village, are still strong.

2. *Hibah* is the Arabic term for the gift of one's property to a designated person while one is still alive. The gifts given under *hibah* cannot be contested.

accommodating the nuclear family as a residential unit. Often observed in contemporary paintings and governmental emblems, the Minangkabau adat house, with its characteristic "horned roofs," symbolizes the Minangkabau matrilineal system. In the village, an adat house stands for the prestige, wealth, and continuity of one's matrilineage. It also typically houses an extended family of several related samandai organized according to matrilineal principles. Today, however, despite what postcards and paintings suggest, the adat house is no longer widespread in West Sumatra.

Out of 395 houses visited during my household survey in IV Angkat, only thirteen percent were adat houses. Not only are few adat houses to be observed nowadays, but new adat houses are seldom built. According to my survey on family history among 132 sublineages in IV Angkat, in 77 percent of these sublineages no adat house had been built since the turn of the century; in only five percent of the cases was a new adat house built during the past thirty years.

There is no way to obtain reliable figures concerning the prevalence of adat house in West Sumatra in general. However, in my nagari survey conducted in 232 villages, village heads were asked to estimate the percentage of adat houses among all the dwellings in their villages. Although such estimates can not be accepted at a full value, they should still provide some idea as to the prevalence of adat houses.[3] The results (Table 6.1, which gives percentages of village heads who gave estimates in six different ranges) show considerable regional variation. In general, few adat houses are to be found in the three districts of Padang Pariaman, Pasaman, and Pesisir Selatan, all of which directly face the Indian Ocean. The Minangkabau-style adat house was never common in this coastal rantau (Datoe' Sanggoeno Di Radjo 1955:177–178). Instead, a different type of adat house, heavily influenced by the Acehnese model, seems to have been popular. If these three districts are excluded from the calculation, the average estimated percentage of

3. In two districts of West Sumatra, a comparison can be made between estimates in the present research and other research results. According to my research, the average estimated percentage of adat houses in both Solok and Sawahlunto/ Sijunjung is 12 percent; in other studies (possibly based on actual enumeration of houses), the figures are respectively 8 percent and 12 percent (Sjafei et al. 1971:77; Sjafei et al. 1972:66).

Table 6.1. Prevalence of adat houses in West Sumatran villages, as estimated by village heads

Estimate of prevalence	Tanah Datar	Agam	50 Kota	Solok	Padang Pariaman	Sawahlunto/ Sijunjung	Pasaman	Pesisir Selatan	Total
0%	7%	52%	7%	0%	100%	0%	73%	85%	39%
01–05%	37%	30%	17%	43%	—	21%	23%	15%	25%
06–10%	23%	12%	4%	16%	—	46%	4%	—	13%
11–20%	7%	3%	10%	24%	—	21%	—	—	8%
21–30%	13%	3%	21%	14%	—	12%	—	—	8%
31% +	13%	—	41%	3%	—	—	—	—	7%
Sample size	30	33	29	39	30	25	26	20	232
Mean percentage	13%	3%	27%	12%	0%	12%	1%	1%	9%

SOURCE: Nagari survey.

Minangkabau houses per village goes up from 9 to 13 percent: still a substantially lower figure than one might expect.[4]

It is difficult to ascertain when the decline of the adat house in West Sumatra began. In the 1910s, almost all the houses in Nagari Sumpur in Tanah Datar were of the adat type, according to Radjab (1950:4). According to the 1930 census, 49 percent of the native dwellings in rural West Sumatra were categorized as ancestral property in their legal status (*Volkstelling 1930*, 4:66); most of these are likely to have been adat houses.[5] The general tempo of the decline of the adat house is shown by my research in IV Angkat. In my survey on family history, each respondent was asked to enumerate the total number of houses of his or her sublineage existing in the village today, and the total number of adat houses among them. A related question concerned the situation prevailing at the time when his or her mother and grandmother were married. From a combination of the kin classifications and ages of the respondents, a set of generational categories has been constructed, analogous to those developed in Chapter 4. Classified according to those generational categories, the results of my housing questions can be seen in Table 6.2.[6] The table shows that the adat house was quite prevalent in Generation A, but its popularity rapidly declined thereafter.

The decline was partly due to natural and manmade calamities. An earthquake in 1926 wiped out many houses around Padang Panjang. During the independence war against the Dutch (the late 1940s) and during the PRRI rebellion (1958–1961), many houses were either destroyed or burned down. For example, in the district of Solok, 2,207 houses are estimated to have been destroyed be-

---

4. Yet although adat houses are not numerous in the villages today, new houses are still occasionally built. In 58 percent of the villages surveyed, at least one new adat house had been built during the last thirty years, and in 46 percent of the cases within the last fifteen years. The three districts mentioned above (Padang Pariaman, Pasaman, and Pesisir Selatan) are excluded from the calculation.

5. Excluded from the calculation are Ophir, Gemeente Fort de Kock, Bangkinang, Kota Pajakoemboeh, Kota Padang Pandjang, Fort van der Capellen, Kota Solok, Gemeente Sawahlunto, Afdeeling Padang, and Afdeeling Kerintji Painan; these are either urban areas or outside Minangkabau areas proper. Houses of unknown legal status are not included in the calculation either.

6. The generational categories in the table include the following people: Generation A, grandmothers of respondents older than 35 and mothers of respondents older than 55; Generation B, grandmothers of respondents younger than 36 and mothers of respondents younger than 56; and Generation C, all respondents.

Table 6.2. The decline of adat houses in IV Angkat

	Generations		
	A	B	C
Houses	135	212	349
Adat houses	93	87	44
Proportion of adat houses	69%	41%	13%

Source: Survey on family history (figures from 132 sublineages).

tween 1947 and 1948, and another 5,389 houses during the PRRI (Sjafei et al. 1971:37). Estimates for the same time periods in the district of Sawahlunto/Sijunjung are respectively 1,107 and 1,698 houses (Sjafei et al. 1972:40). Many of the buildings ruined were certainly adat houses. Once destroyed, such adat houses were frequently not replaced. The construction of an adat house is expensive, particularly if one is to adorn the house with the traditional woodcarvings. Materials for the great central pillars are now hard to come by because of deforestation. Proper adat ceremonies, including an expensive feast, have to be carried out before construction. Cooperative activities by lineage members are essential to the actual construction of an adat house; but, it is difficult to obtain such cooperation nowadays because the other lineage members are busy with their own daily pursuits. Besides, *gotong royong* (cooperative activities) may be more expensive than hiring wage laborers; one usually has to provide meals of more than modest quality to those who participate. These are some of the external factors promoting the decline of the adat house.

In addition to the above factors, the adat house also seems to be less popular than the ordinary house as a residence today. If one travels in the interior of West Sumatra, one sometimes encounters a large adat house surrounded by several ordinary houses of smaller size. The adat house is still solid enough for occupancy, but nobody lives there. The members of the adat house have long since moved to their respective houses in the immediate vicinity. As the nuclear family replaced the paruik as the primary economic unit within the adat house, it became more and more a problem to maintain harmony in the house. The tungganai (house elder) was not the sole male authority there any more. In his new role as provider for the samandai the sumando had a great deal to say as to how the life of his wife and children should be managed. Without a single strong authority figure, conflicts and disputes tended to take place between different nuclear families. In the villages, one hears frequent stories of jealousy and feuds between married sisters over whose husband earns more, and the resulting ostentatious attempts to demonstrate their wealth. As a consequence, the majority of houses nowadays are occupied by a single nuclear family or a stem family as will be shown later.

The decline of the adat house has been further influenced by changes in the identity of the financiers of house construction. As is clear from Table 6.3, the financial participation of the sumando in this activity has increased considerably over the last twenty years.[7] In particular, 84 percent of the houses constructed in the last ten years were built with the financial assistance of the sumando. By contrast, 90 percent of the houses built more than sixty years ago were financed either by the women of house or by the mamak— both matrilineal members of the house. This change has a significant bearing on what types of houses are built today, for by adat and by preference, houses built by sumando are almost always non-adat houses (Table 6.4; "*Tungkus nasi*" or rice packet in the table is a house with a similar interior layout to the adat house, but without horned roofs). There is only one case where the sumando built an adat house; in the rest of the cases, the adat houses were all built either by the women of house or the mamak.[8]

A concomitant of the decline of adat house is the small household size observed in the contemporary Minangkabau village (household in the sense of those who live together in one house). According to my household survey in IV Angkat (395 houses), the average size of

7. The categories of financial providers are classificatory: "women of house" refers not only to the present female occupant(s) of the house but also to her (their) mother (and her sisters) or grandmother (and her sisters), and so forth. "Other" are children or cooperation between sumando and mamak. "Sumando (and wife)" means that the husband alone or the husband and wife jointly financed house construction.

8. According to adat, it is the responsibility of the mamak to build an adat house for his kemanakan. However, it is not unknown, though rare, for a sumando to build an adat house. Radjab (1950:4), for example, says that his mother's adat house was built by the husband of his great-grandmother.

Table 6.3. Relation between age of house and identity of financial provider

	Financial provider				
Age of house	Women of house	Sumando (& wife)	Mamak	Other	Sample size
61 years or more	32%	10%	58%	0%	19
41 to 60 years	18%	34%	41%	7%	29
21 to 40 years	23%	39%	23%	15%	26
11 to 20 years	11%	59%	11%	19%	27
10 years or less	4%	84%	4%	8%	25
Average	17%	47%	26%	10%	(126)

SOURCE: Survey on family history.

the household is 6.7 persons.[9] Fifty-four percent of the houses were inhabited by six persons or less, and only 15 percent by ten or more. The largest household in the survey contained twenty-five persons. In terms of household composition, 53 percent of the houses were occupied by nuclear families, that is, husband, wife (and children), and 27 percent by stem families, that is, nuclear families along with the wife's parent(s) (and her unmarried siblings—usually sisters). Only 13 percent of the houses were inhabited by two or more married sisters and their nuclear families (plus their parents and unmarried siblings, where applicable).[10] Joint households maintained by married sisters, the basis of the old extended matrilineal family residence, are clearly not common today. The traditional image of a large matrilineal family living in one adat house no longer corresponds to reality.

9. According to Kahn's study (1976:78), the average household size in Sungai Puar near Bukittinggi was also about six persons in the early 1970s. My figure is probably somewhat inflated. The survey only covered the households with male providers. It is my impression that the usual size of households with female providers is a little smaller. If the household is defined as "a person or a group of persons who stay in part of or in the whole of one house and eat [together] from one kitchen," the average household size in rural West Sumatra was 4.7 in 1971 (Kantor Sensus dan Statistik Propinsi Sumatera Barat). The municipalities (*kotamadya*) are excluded from this calculation.

10. This includes several cases where respondents live with their wives' mothers and maternal aunt(s) in one house. As for generational depth in household composition, 34 percent of the houses surveyed included the wife's parent(s), and one percent the wife's parent(s) and grandparent(s).

Table 6.4.   Relation between type of house built and financial provider

Financial providers	Type of house			Sample size
	Adat	Tungkus nasi	Ordinary	
Women of house	24%	14%	62%	21
Sumando (& wife)	2%	0%	98%	59
Mamak	38%	9%	53%	32
Other	0%	8%	92%	13
Average	14%	6%	80%	(125)

SOURCE: Survey on family history.

The Strengthening of Conjugal and Father-Child Ties

Given the precarious and unimportant position of the husband in the traditional Minangkabau family, the conjugal tie between husband and wife must have been weak in times past. According to the 1930 census, West Sumatra had the highest rates of male and female divorces in the entire Netherlands East Indies: 9.8 and 14.2 per 100 adult persons respectively; the second highest figures for males were 7.2 (Sumatra's East Coast) and for females 10.2 (West Java) (*Volkstelling 1930*, 8:104). Likewise, men in West Sumatra were most frequently polygamous: 8.7 persons per 100 married men ahead of 7.7 (the second highest figure) for "Timor en onderhoorigheden" (*Volkstelling 1930*, 8:106).[11]

Since the early twentieth century, however, divorce and polygamy, which were actually even more frequent than the above figures suggest, came under increasing attack by Islamic reformists and Western-educated intellectuals (Anwar 1967:113). The Kaum Muda, concerned with the education and emancipation of women, admonished men not to divorce their wives lightly and stressed the strict conditions for polygamy (for example, equal treatment of different wives) required by true Islamic teachings (Noer

11. The average divorce rates for the native population of the Indies were 4.3 for men and 7.7 for women (*Volkstelling 1930*, 8:104). Although there are no data available, it seems that high divorce rates were accompanied by high remarriage rates. There was a good reason for men to remarry after divorce; not being married in Minangkabau society meant that men had to sleep in a surau. The average polygamy rate for the Indies was 2.5 (*Volkstelling 1930*, 8:106).

Table 6.5. Generational comparison of divorce experiences in VI Angkat

	Generations			
	I	II	III	IV
Males				
Size of sample	69	113	141	57
Percentage of sample divorced	51%	45%	31%	18%
Females				
Size of sample	119	240	204	58
Percentage of sample divorced	32%	36%	25%	14%

SOURCE: Survey on merantau history.

1973:80–86; Schrieke 1973:99–100, 113–119). The opinions of Western-educated intellectuals on marriage were most eloquently expressed in the popular novels written by Minangkabau authors in 1920s and 1930s. The main themes of these novels were the importance of love, the value of the conjugal tie, the undesirability of the practice of *urang jemputan,* by which a man was "paid" to marry a girl, the father's economic responsibility toward his wife and children, and sympathy for women's plight in contemporary society (for example, see Rusli 1965).

The strengthening of the conjugal tie is reflected in the decrease of divorce and polygamy rates observed from my survey in IV Angkat. Table 6.5 shows the prevalence of divorce experiences among the sublineage members of 132 houses. The results in the table are classified according to the generational categories utilized in Chapter 4. Rates of divorce and especially polygamy experience are likely to be largely influenced by the age factor. For example, usually the older a respondent, the more likely he is to have ecomomic resources to marry the second, third, and fourth wives. Generation IV includes those who are still young and alive, but the age factor in Generations I to III is somewhat less significant. People in these categories are those who are middle-aged, old, or dead. Although the results for females are not conclusive, those for males show a steady decrease in divorce experience from Generation I to Generation IV.[12] Similarly, the percentage of men with polygamy

12. The proportion of multiple divorce experiences for married persons has also declined. Their percentages from Generation I through Generation IV are respectively 23, 22, 9, and 4 for males, and 14, 14, 8, and 2 for females.

Table 6.6.   Polygamy experiences in IV Angkat, males

| | Age of respondents | | | | |
	Below 36 years	36 to 45 years	46 to 55 years	Above 55 years	Total
Respondents					
Size of sample	41	96	141	111	389
Percentage of sample polygamous	7%	15%	38%	69%	38%
Respondents' fathers					
Size of sample	43	95	140	109	387
Percentage of sample polygamous	65%	76%	79%	85%	78%

SOURCE: Household survey in IV Angkat.

experiences has decreased considerably (Table 6.6). As noted above, polygamy rates may reflect the age factor; the older a respondent, the more likely he is to be able to afford polygamy. The information on this question was obtained for both respondents and their fathers, however, and the interpretation of the results is less problematic than for those concerning divorce. On the average, 78 percent of fathers have had the experience of polygamy; the figure has decreased to 38 percent (still very high percentage) among the respondents.[13]

The significance of the decrease in polygamy is that it is highly correlated with the decrease in divorce. If the divorce and polygamy experiences of male respondents are cross-tabulated, the results show that, proportionally speaking, those with polygamy experience are 7.6 times more likely to have divorce experience than those without. Likewise, those with divorce experience are 3.6 times more likely to have polygamy experience than those without. Even if age is controlled, that is, if the results are tabulated only for those respondents 46 years old and older—who are more likely to have both divorce and polygamy experiences owing to their age—the same associations persist. The interconnection shows that not only is the matrimonial tie much stronger now than it used to be, but

13. The wide discrepancy between the 1930 census and my survey results is due to the fact that the former only refers to current civil status while the latter refers to both current status and past experiences.

also that what is strengthened is the bond of monogamous marriage.

One important factor in changing the conception of marriage and matrimonial relationships was the spread of education. For instance, the Kaum Muda tried to propagate new religious ideas and practices, including those concerned with husband-wife relations, through the schools that they established. Ideological impact aside, education also had structural implication for the father-child relationship in Minangkabau society. It is said that "according to adat and religion, the education of the children was 'the duty of the father to his children'" (Abdullah 1967:63). Whether this was always true or not, the education of children had frequently come to be provided by the father rather than by the mamak by early in the twentieth century (Schrieke 1973:56, n. 62; Josselin de Jong:116).[14] Education offered special advantages for a father who cared for his children, for during the period of Dutch rule, it became the most important avenue for bureaucratic advancement. Investment in one's children's education produced fruits of harta pencarian that by their very nature could not be contested by one's matrilineal relatives after one's death. Thus, the increasing provision of education for his children by the father was both a stimulus and a response to the strengthening of the father-child relationship.

As mentioned before, one sign of a stronger father-child relationship has been the increasing acceptance of the practice that individually earned property is given to children, rather than to kemanakan. In a study on inheritance cases conducted by Sa'danoer (1971) in Padang and in twenty-one villages in 1970, this trend is clear (Table 6.7). Before 1920, individually earned property was given to the children in about half of the cases. By 1970, the figure had reached 74 percent. In contrast, the instances of kemanakan receiving individually earned property decreased from 51 percent to 18 percent in the same period.[15]

14. However, it would not be correct to assume that the mamak do not help in the education of their kemanakan. According to my household survey in IV Angkat, 45 percent of the respondents answered that they had received some financial assistance from their mamak for their education.
15. The figures in parentheses in Table 6.7 refer to the number of cases, not respondents. The researcher asked a respondent (i.e., village head, hamlet head, and penghulu) to enumerate those cases of inheritance of individually earned property he remembered. Although the table indicates increasing inheritance by children rather

Table 6.7. Inheritance of individually earned property over time

Years of inheritance transaction	Inherited by			Total
	Children	Kemanakan	Other	
1878–1919	48%	51%	1%	100% (73)
1920–1944	60%	33%	7%	100% (373)
1945–1959	65%	29%	6%	100% (393)
1960–1970	74%	18%	8%	100% (428)
Total	66% (832)	28% (351)	6% (84)	100% (1267)

SOURCE: Recalculated from Sa'danoer (1971:12).

There are also indications that the father is now more involved in ensuring the well-being of his children. According to my household survey in IV Angkat, a sizable majority (70 percent) of the male respondents answered that during childhood they were mainly supported by their fathers; moreover, there is a slight increase over generations in the proportion of respondents who gave this answer (Table 6.8). Conversely there is a steady decrease in the proportion of respondents who received financial assistance from the mamak on a regular basis.[16] As mentioned in Chapter 5, today it is predominantly the father and mother, not the mamak, who make decisions concerning the children's future.

Summarizing the above observations, we may conclude as follows concerning change in the Minangkabau matrilineal system. The conjugal nuclear family increasingly constitutes the basic economic and residential unit rather than the extended matrilineal family. The emergence of harta pencarian is closely related to the ascendancy of the nuclear family as the prime economic unit. So long as ancestral land was sufficient for the members of an adat house, there was little chance for a sumando to have any significant economic role in the lives of his wife and children. However, the

than by kemanakan, this does not necessarily mean a decline in matrilineal inheritance of individually earned property (although this is a strong possibility), for the researcher does not distinguish the sex of the property donor and the property recipient. If the donor and the recipient are both females, the inheritance pattern still follows the matrilineal principle even if the recipient is the donor's child.

16. Excluded from the calculation in Table 6.8 are those respondents who did not have any direct mamak. "Other" means sibling, aunt, or grandmother. "Assisted by mamak" means financial assistance from the mamak on a regular basis.

increasing inadequacy of ancestral land, due to population pressures, created room for the sumando to make a real economic contribution to his wife and children. But it was only after the appearance of opportunities to amass harta pencarian on some scale (notably through commercial agriculture and nonsegmentary merantau) that the nuclear famliy became a truly viable economic unit. For as long as a man's economic livelihood was tied to ancestral property, specifically to his mother's ancestral land, there were no resources at his disposal which he could expend on his wife and children.

In conjunction with the ascendancy of the nuclear family as an economic unit, the residential pattern began to change. The visiting husband (*sumando batandang*) transformed himself into the living-in husband (*sumando menetap*). Residential arrangements today are more properly identified as uxorilocal than duolocal. Household composition is generally small (on the average about six persons per house) and it often consists of only the nuclear family. The adat house, bastion of the large extended family residence pattern, is in decline; instead, village houses nowadays are ordinary small structures which usually accommodate either a nuclear or a stem family (nuclear family with wife's parents and her unmarried siblings).

The above tendencies are not comprehensible without taking into account the growing solidarity of the conjugal nuclear family. The strengthened conjugal tie is attested to by decreasing divorce and polygamy rates. It is important to note here that this strengthening of the conjugal tie was not necessarily based on the Western notion of marriage for love. According to my household survey in IV Angkat, marriages in the villages are still mostly arranged; only a handful of villagers (7 percent) actually chose their own spouse.

Table 6.8. Provider for respondent during childhood in IV Angkat

Age of respondents	Father	Assisted by mamak	Other	Sample size
Above 55 years	60%	29%	11%	96
46 to 55 years	73%	17%	10%	106
36 to 45 years	74%	15%	11%	74
Below 36 years	77%	14%	9%	35

SOURCE: Household survey in IV Angkat.

The decrease in divorce and polygamy was in a great measure influenced by economic factors. Women, now more economically dependent on their spouses than they used to be, certainly have every reason to cultivate amicable relations with their husbands. Previously, descendants of original settlers (*urang asa*) and Islamic teachers were "invited" to marry (*dijemput*) into different houses. Their economic responsibilities toward their wives and children were minimal since the latter were mainly supported by their ancestral land. Nowadays, this type of subsidized polygamy is extremely rare; polygamous men have to support their wives and children by themselves. There are only a few men who can afford polygamy today.

In addition to the conjugal tie, the father-child relationship is much more important now than before. The individually earned property of a father is generally inherited by his children instead of by his kemanakan. The father wields great influence over future plans of his children. It is mainly the father, not the mamak, who looks after their material well-being. A famous adat aphorism says "The child is to be embraced [in one's bosom], the kemanakan to be guided [by the hand]" (*anak dipangku, kemanakan dibimbing*). Even though it is not certain how old this aphorism is, it captures the nature of contemporary family relationships in the Minangkabau society. The mamak is the moral custodian of the kemanakan according to adat; he leads his kemanakan by giving him advice and by teaching the wisdom of the adat. In contrast, the affective tie is between father and child. It is the father who warms the child in his bosom and feeds it.

New Trends in Social Stratification

Despite the fact that the Dutch government was essentially interested in maintaining the status quo in West Sumatra, traditional social stratification in fact was eroded in step with the increasing direct control of the colonial government. The incorporation of West Sumatra into the Dutch East Indies brought about the centralization of the political and administrative structure in the Minangkabau society. This process of centralization, however, could not be stopped there. The higher authorities began to intervene increasingly in internal village affairs; administrative personnel were professionalized and their qualifications standardized; administrative hierarchies were rigidly demarcated both within and outside the village. The introduction of the *laras* system (a pseudo-adat administrative structure) and later the *demang* system (a more bureaucratized administrative structure) robbed many penghulu of political power. Under these systems, a penghulu usually became a village head. However, by appointing a single penghulu to the key position of recognized local authority, the system relegated the other penghulu to secondary status. The prestige of these penghulu diminished from opposite directions. On the one hand, they now needed the mediation of the village head to reach the higher authorities. On the other, their lineage members could, if necessary, bypass them and appeal directly to the village head or to a Dutch authority in dealing with their problems, even though the Dutch administrator usually sent adat problems back to the village or lineage concerned. Even the newly created powerful position of village head was far from free of limitations. For one thing, the village head was not the final authority to the villagers. Above him, the chain of authority extended through the subdistrict head and the district head to the governor. The village head, as well as penghulu, often had to act as the lowest cogs of this administrative machine rather than as protectors of the villagers or of their kemanakan. Western criminal law was introduced in 1875, thus divesting the penghulu of any punitive power (Abdullah 1972a:43). The Agrarian Law of 1915 denied penghulu territorial rights over unoccupied lands by declaring that henceforth they belonged to the government (Abdullah 1971:23). The penghulu themselves became divisive when an attempt was made in 1912 to distinguish government-recognized penghulu from those not so recognized (Schrieke 1955b:136–138).[17]

The onslaught of higher political powers on the village did not stop after the Dutch period. Since the period of the Japanese occupation, many non-penghulu have come to be elected or appointed to the position of village head. The village has been subdivided into the smaller territorial unit of the hamlet (*jorong* or *korong*). Ham-

17. For a more detailed discussion of Dutch influence on the decline of penghulu power, see Schrieke (1955b:135–143). The Agrarian Law, which was preceded by the Domain Declaration of 1874, was not and could not be strictly applied in West Sumatra (Oki 1977:108–117).

let chiefs have become important mediators in settling intrahamlet disputes and sometimes even problems related to adat. The intensification of political party activities in the 1950s brought into the village a new source of power—careers and positions in political party hierarchies. A penghulu and his kemanakan were sometimes pitted against one another by differing political allegiances. As a result of the alleged communist coup attempt of 1965, penghulu accused of involvement were either replaced or expelled from their adat positions in response to directives from the higher authorities. Clearly, the penghulu no longer wield anything like the political and judicial power they used to have.

The increasing intervention of higher political powers in nagari affairs is symbolically expressed in the decline of the *balai adat* (adat council hall). Twenty-seven (12 percent) of the nagari in my nagari survey do not even have a council hall, traditionally considered one of the essential conditions for establishing a nagari.[18] In these villages, the adat council is now held at the office of the village head. It is becoming more popular to build a two-story office for the village government, modeled after the architectural style of balai adat. The first floor is for the village office, and the second the adat council; the arrangement symbolizes the latter's respected but shoved-upstairs position.[19]

The erosion of the penghulu's status is not limited to the political sphere. Previously, penghulu were the wealthiest people in the nagari, with their claims to adat fees (for example, for opening new agricultural land) and with their traditional rights to the produce of *sawah kagadangan* (sawah for greatness). In general, adat fees for penghulu had disappeared by the early twentieth century (Oki:19–22). In response to mounting population pressure, the special rice land for penghulu began to be subdivided for lineage members in order to overcome land shortages. Today a majority of the penghulu in 73 percent of the villages in my nagari survey do not have any *sawah kagadangan* left; in half of the villages, not a single penghulu has *sawah kagadangan* anymore. As the economic privileges of the penghulu were being eroded, merantau created

18. This does not include ten nagari which do not have to have any council hall according to their adat. Instead, they use an open field for an adat meeting.
19. The adoption of balai adat architecture is not limited to the offices of village heads. Today the offices of subdistrict and district heads and even the governor's office itself are built on the model of the Minangkabau balai adat.

new sources of wealth from outside the nagari. Even if one were not
a penghulu, one could go away for merantau; depending on one's
efforts and luck, one could become as rich as or richer than a
penghulu. Nouveaux riches began to emerge.

The power of these nouveaux riches can be seen in the novels of
Minangkabau authors from the early part of this century. One of
the most famous stories from this period is *Sitti Nurbaja*. The novel
was written in 1922—in probably the most prosperous period of
the entire Dutch era—and was set in Padang, the commercial as
well as the administrative center of Sumatra's West Coast. Datuk
Meringgih, the villain of the story, is a merchant of low social
origins yet one of the richest persons in Padang. Despite his bad
character and conduct, everybody obeys him because of his wealth.
The author of the novel, Marah Rusli, muses: "Isn't the power of
money great? Certainly what could be more powerful than money?
This world revolves around money. At the root of everything is
money" (Rusli:11).

Another Minangkabau author, Muhammad Radjab, recalls in his
autobiography occasions when successful perantau merchants tried
to show off their newly acquired wealth upon their return to the
village. One person with many gold-capped teeth smiles all the time
just so that his gold teeth will be visible to others. Another marches
around the village wearing an expensive fashionable raincoat from
the rantau, even though it is not raining and very hot. A successful
perantau smokes "Westminsters" or cigars, and takes his gold
watch out of his pocket every five minutes, pretending to check the
time (Radjab 1950:206).

These characterizations are far from being respectful. Datuk
Meringgih, his datuk title being only a form of address, not denot-
ing a penghulu position, is lowly in social origin and bad in character. Radjab's perantau are all laughable in their vain efforts. These
characterizations are due partly to the lack of prestige accorded to
the powerful nouveaux riches and partly to the social background
of the two authors. Both Rusli and Radjab were Western-educated
intellectuals, originally from well-established families in their villages.[20] Their disdainful descriptions of the nouveaux riches are

20. Marah Rusli, a son of *demang* (subdistrict head), belonged to the coastal
nobility in Padang. He studied in the Sekolah Raja in Bukittinggi and later at a
veterinary school in Bogor (Usman 1961:39). Muhammad Radjab was a son of a

themselves testimony to how much their power was felt by the society of the time. In fact, Radjab recounts that when he was a child, successful perantau merchants were often discussed between mothers and their marriageable daughters. In times past, it was adat nobility, the penghulu, who were most often coveted as husbands. After the Padri wars, Islamic teachers were often preferred. As the economic conditions in the villages declined, it was successful merchants who became the most sought after as prospective urang sumando (Radjab 1950:202–205).

Another important change in social stratification after the middle of the nineteenth century was caused by the introduction of formal education. Formal education had been an essential condition for bureaucratic success since the late nineteenth century. Although access to education was not completely free of ascriptive privilege, education and school diplomas proved to be decisive for entering and advancing in the expanding bureaucracy. Education was a symbol of progress, and a kind of passport for the newly emerging intelligentsia and bureaucrats:

> Education was becoming a respectable alternative path on a par with being a rich merchant in terms of its economic prospects, and with being a learned *ulama* [Islamic teacher] in terms of its prestige. By the late nineteenth century, according to Minangkabau villagers, three occupations had overwhelming status: *angku doktor, angku laras, angku guru* (lord doctor, lord larashoofd [subdistrict head], lord teacher) (Graves:339).

By joining the bureaucracy, the educated could be socially mobile within an administrative hierarchy which stretched far above the village head and penghulu in the village. By so doing, they were gaining an enhanced status in the eyes of villagers at the same time. Nowadays, even the conferral of a special penghulu title on an educated man sometimes occurs in the village.[21]

The spread of education also brought about conflict between the

---

famous Islamic teacher in his village. After studying at an Islamic school (Sumatera Thawalib), he went to a Particuliere Middlebare School in Bandung, and finally to Universitas Indonesia after the Second World War (Radjab 1969:66).

21. I was told in one village in Tanah Datar that their first *sarjana hukum* (a holder of a master's degree in law) was accorded such a title for his knowledge and achievement. A special penghulu title is honorary and lasts only for one generation.

better educated younger generation (kemanakan) and the less-educated older generation (mamak). Previously, the penghulu were the only intellectuals in the village aside from the Islamic experts; their knowledge and learning of adat were very much respected.[22] As the younger generation became educated at Western-style schools, they grew less respectful of the penghulu and their knowledge of adat. In their eyes, the penghulu were, after all, simple village folk without any modern sophistication. Kemanakan were thus less likely than before to heed with respect the advice and opinions of the penghulu (for example, see Moeis 1967, on this type of conflict).

These trends mentioned above have created new bases of social stratification and undermined the traditional social hierarchy. Reflecting the decreased power and status of the penghulu, a number of the once coveted and prestigious penghuluships are today unoccupied. In IV Angkat, only 8 percent of 132 lineages interviewed have a living penghulu, while in 58 percent of the cases the lineage's penghuluship has been unoccupied for at least the last fifty years (survey on family history). Among the same lineages, only one penghulu has been inaugurated according to adat in the last ten years, and only four penghulu since the Dutch colonial era.[23]

This situation in IV Angkat obviously is an extreme one within West Sumatra. However, the empty penghuluships are not infrequent elsewhere, especially in the three central districts of Tanah Datar, Agam, and 50 Kota (Table 6.9).[24] In these areas, more than 20 percent of the penghuluships are vacant. If one counts those

22. This does not mean that the penghulu were mostly literate. According to observation of one Dutch official in 1829, perhaps two out of a hundred penghulu would be able to read and write (cited in Dobbin 1974:327, n. 68). Most probably the alim ulama fared much better in this score because of their Islamic education.

23. Major reasons for the vacancies are disputes among lineage members over who should be a new penghulu; candidates being still too young; and extinction of penghulu lineages. The most frequently mentioned reason in IV Angkat, however, is economic. According to the adat of the area, each penghulu inauguration requires the slaughter of a water buffalo and 100 *sukat* (some 1,200 liters) of rice.

24. The figures in Table 6.9 are for the average per nagari. Some of the information is based on estimates, particularly if there are many penghulu positions in a village. The percentage figures of vacancy and merantau are calculated from original non-rounded results, and thus there may be discrepancies between the percentage figures listed and the figures one might obtain by calculating the rounded figures in the table, for example, "no. of vacancies" divided by "average no. of penghulu."

Table 6.9. Vacancy rates of penghuluships per nagari in West Sumatra

	Tanah Datar	Agam	50 Kota	Solok	Padang Pariaman	Sawahlunto/ Sijunjung	Pasaman	Pesisir Selatan	West Sumatra
Average no. of penghulu	64	73	92	34	22	19	25	26	46
No. of vacancies	13	19	23	2	3	1	2	2	8
Vacancy rate	21%	26%	25%	5%	13%	5%	6%	6%	18%
Penghulu in rantau	7	14	5	2	1	1	1	2	4
Merantau rate	11%	20%	5%	7%	4%	3%	2%	6%	9%
Nagari in sample	30	33	29	39	30	25	26	20	232

SOURCE: Nagari survey.

penghulu currently in the rantau, in 27 percent of the cases in West Sumatra, either the penghuluship is unoccupied or its holder does not live in the village. Although in these latter cases there are usually acting penghulu in the village, one can not help but feel the deterioration of the once prestigious penghuluship. As if in step with the lowered status of the office, the pomp and circumstance once associated with the inauguration of a new penghulu is increasingly rare. Traditionally, a water buffalo had to be slaughtered for a communal feast in order to make the inauguration of a penghulu official. Now in many villages, the inauguration of several penghulu is possible with the slaughter of only one water buffalo—in 48 percent of the nagari surveyed, such a simplified ceremony is acceptable, according to the nagari survey. In some cases, even the head of a buffalo now suffices to fulfill the condition.

In sum, social stratification in contemporary Minangkabau society is more variable and fluid than before. Because of political centralization, because of the prevalence of circulatory merantau, and because of educational progress, penghulu (and Islamic teachers) no longer have monopolistic control over political and judicial power, wealth, knowledge, and prestige. As if to mirror the decline of the penghulu's status, once coveted penghulu positions are often left unoccupied. The pomp and circumstance previously associated with the inauguration of penghulu are rarities nowadays. Achievement has become more and more important for attaining high status even in the village. The power and prestige of penghulu (and Islamic teachers) have been increasingly contested by intellectuals, politicians, bureaucrats, and nouveaux riches.

Merantau and Social Change

Lacking a centralized political structure and courtly aristocracy, the social stratification system in traditional Minangkabau society was contained within the village. Power and prestige recognized in one village could not be transferred to another, nor could achievement outside the village be translated into enhanced status within the village unless the attempt was made to attain high status according to adat, that is, as penghulu. Even in this case, one has to be aware of limitations. Unless a person is genealogically related to a penghulu lineage, however minor the relation might be, the attainment of penghuluship was very difficult.

Exceptions to this pattern were the Islamic teachers and the Minangkabau royalty whose high status extended beyond their locality. Islamic teachers, who usually traveled as students from one religious school to another, in fact often went back to their native villages to enjoy added respect. However, even in the case of religious teachers and royalty, their supravillage status mainly conferred prestige, not power. Their lack of power is exemplified by the failure of the Regent system (Graves:148–157), which was introduced by the Dutch in the early nineteenth century. Not wishing to be involved in costly direct control, the Dutch initially hoped that the end of the Padri wars would restore the position of the "paramount chiefs" through whom they would be able to continue their profitable trade with West Sumatra. It need hardly be said that these hopes were based on a serious misunderstanding of the position of paramount chiefs. In order to carry out this policy, Regents were appointed, out of the traditional local nobles, as native administrative heads of pacified areas. Supported by the Dutch government, they were accorded titles, honors, and entourages appropriate to their new positions. Among these Dutch-appointed Regents were both royal and Islamic figures: "the King of Minangkabau" as Regent of Tanah Datar, Tuanku Mudo (the chief lieutenant of Tuanku Imam Bonjol in the Padri wars) as Regent of Bonjol, and Tuanku Halaban (an Islamic leader in the Padri wars) as Regent of Payakumbuh (Abdullah 1967:207, n. 87). Despite the appointment of these impressive figures, the Regent system, so successful in Java, completely failed in West Sumatra for lack of a tradition of government by a supravillage ruling class (ibid.:35). The system was eventually replaced by the afore-mentioned *laras* system in the middle of the nineteenth century, and then by the *demang* system in 1914.

Social mobility before the nineteenth century was above all centrifugal. People dissatisfied with the situation in a village sometimes went away to create a new settlement so that they could be original settlers, and thus become the most powerful and respected figures in the new village (Abdullah 1971:18; Junus 1971:246; Datoe' Sanggoeno Di Radjo 1955:87–89). By the same token, merchants and adventurers, who were active along the Straits of Malacca and elsewhere between the seventeenth and nineteenth centuries, often seem to have become *nakhoda* (ship's captain), *orang kaya* (nobles), and other great men by dissociating themselves from their villages and attaching themselves to a sultanate outside West Sumatra (perhaps Johor and Siak)—or creating their own *negri* (state). Examples of these patterns are the cases of Nakhoda Muda (see Chapter 3) and the creation of Negri Sembilan in the Malay Peninsula. In either case, geographical mobility could lead to vertical social mobility. However, this vertical mobility was attained outside one's home village and within a new framework, for instance, a new nagari, a non-Minangkabau sultanate, or a circle of merchants and ship's captains.[25] While the penghulu in the home village still maintained a solid basis for their claims to power and prestige in the traditional stratification system, outside achievement could seldom be transplanted back home. Social mobility was realized and attained by going away and staying away.

Just as social mobility and geographical mobility were centrifugal, Minangkabau ideology was also centrifugal and outward-looking. Lacking political, economic, and religious centers of much significance, the Alam Minangkabau did not have any centripetal focus to draw its population or ideology.[26] The Alam was still amorphous and not circumscribed by clear-cut boundaries. As its frontier was expanding through village segmentation and population movement, the mental horizons of the Minangkabau were also expanding. There were little incentive and inclination to go back home after once leaving the village.

The establishment of Dutch hegemony in the middle of the nineteenth century was crucial in two ways for promoting a different pattern of geographical mobility and ideology, namely, circulatory merantau. First of all, the Dutch government founded a locus of centralized supravillage power for the first time in the Minangkabau history. Village social stratification, as well as such

25. Non-Minangkabau here is used in the sense of a sultanate outside West Sumatra. Although I can find no specific reference to the existence of a "community" of merchants and *nakhoda* trading along the Straits of Malacca, it is most likely that those working in the same trade routes eventually came to form some sort of community of their own. Concerning such a community in the western coast of Sumatra in the nineteenth century, see Kato (1980).

26. For a comparison, see Anderson (1972b) concerning the importance of the center (*pusat*) in the idea of the traditional Javanese polity.

other aspects of village life as politics, economy, and communications, were incorporated into a larger framework beyond the nagari. For the first time, social mobility achieved outside the village could be now infused back into the village. The bureaucracy provided a model in this respect. By joining it and by advancing in its hierarchy, one could be socially mobile both in the organization and in the village. After all, a *demang* (subdistrict head) was higher in status than a village head or penghulu.

The advancement of communication and transportation systems made possible relatively easy exchanges of information, goods, and people between the village and the rantau. Villagers could now keep informed of a perantau's success in Medan, Jambi, or some other place. A perantau could make sure that villagers knew of his achievements. Villagers could witness a perantau's success in the sudden prosperity of his lineage in the village or in his person when he came back to visit. The shortened distance between village and rantau made a perantau's success in rantau more accessible to village both psychologically and physically.

So long as villagers were still sufficiently provided for by ancestral land, the perantau's endeavors, even if successful, did not register much special meaning for their lives. But as economic scarcity affected the nagari, villagers became more appreciative of the fruits of the perantau's labors. The erosion of the penghulu's power bases made the competition for power and prestige in village more dynamic than it could otherwise have been. Merantau experiences themselves became an important criterion of one's status. Radjab tells the story of a certain Lebai Saman in his native village (1950:26, 202). Lebai Saman had never been married in his life, but not because he disliked women. He had once been on the rantau to Lampung, but stayed for only six months. He could not stand living in a "foreign country." Since then, he had never gone merantau again. He was not married because no mother asked him to marry her daughter. He was little respected because of his lack of true merantau experience.

Another important consequence of Dutch control was the geographical enclosure of the Alam Minangkabau. After the Padri wars, the "Minangkabau land" was confined within the administrative boundaries of Sumatra's West Coast. Previously, there had been already signs of constraints on the outward expansion of the frontier, for example, clashes with the Batak to the north, and with Acehnese, British, and Dutch on the west coast. The drawing of a tight administrative boundary put a final end to the idea of the ever-expanding Alam Minangkabau. In the days of the frontier spirit the overriding concerns were "what will one become?" and "where will one go?" Increasing contact with non-Minangkabau and the cessation of frontier expansion brought about new and more introspective concerns to the fore, namely, questions of identity ("what am I?") and of origin ("where do I come from?"). It was against this social background that circulatory merantau came to be significant in the society.

Circulatory merantau had a far-reaching influence on Minangkabau society. The idea that one not only left the village behind but also later came back to it gave the perantau a different perspective on their relation to the village. They became more involved in improving conditions in the village to which they expected or were expected to return eventually. The perantau thus launched movements to reexamine and to reflect more deeply on Minangkabau adat, and they also introduced new ideas and practices from the rantau.

Through merantau, Minangkabau came into contact with different ethnic groups in Indonesia with various languages and traditions—in faraway markets, plantations, schools, and offices. The contact heightened the perantau's awareness and his scrutiny of Minangkabau adat. This heightened consciousness of Minangkabau as a society is clearly reflected in the novels written by Minangkabau authors during the 1920s and the 1930s, which share certain striking features. The authors almost invariably had merantau experiences. Likewise, the major figures in the novels are perantau. Their inner and outer lives are not confined to West Sumatra, let alone to the village. They move freely out from West Sumatra to Batavia, Makasar, Aceh, and Medan. Yet they are irrevocably tied to their homes because of their pasts—relatives, memories, and childhood incidents. Often they meet their destinies back in their villages after having been away for a long time (see, for example, *Sitti Nurbaja* and *Salah Asuhan*). By their own intent or by fate, they come face to face with members of other ethnic Indonesian groups during their stay in the rantau. In passing, these novels often discuss Minangkabau customs such as cross-cousin marriage, forced marriage, polygamy, and the matrilineal system in general in a way that points up the contrast to other societies in Indonesia. In Hamka's *Merantau Ke Deli* (Merantau to Deli), a young Minangkabau perantau marries a Javanese coolie on a Dutch plantation. After describing the initial difficulties in their marriage, the author attributes them to the difference between the Minangkabau idea of married life and that of the Javanese. The author's sentiments are clearly on the side of the latter where close husband-wife relationships and mutual cooperation are more stressed than in Minangkabau society.

Stories of interethnic marriages are not limited to *Merantau Ke Deli*. In *Apa Dajaku Karena Aku Perempuan* (What Can I Do, Being a Woman) by Nur Sutan Iskandar, the heroine marries an Acehnese merchant, albeit against her will. In Kedjora's *Karam dalam Gelombang Pertjintaan* (Foundering in the Waves of Love), a Minangkabau man marries a Jakarta girl. In Adinegoro's *Asmara Djaja* (Love Victorious), one finds a marriage between a Minangkabau perantau and a Sundanese girl (concerning these stories, see Teeuw 1967:58–61). Whether interethnic marriage was actually frequent among perantau does not concern us here. But it served as a useful literary device to present a comparative framework for reexamining Minangkabau adat and for describing the encounter between the Minangkabau and non-Minangkabau worlds. The crux of the matter was that the goodness and validity of Minangkabau adat were not taken for granted any more; adat had to be examined and compared.

As some of the titles suggest, another characteristic of these Minangkabau novels is that many revolve around love and marriage, where modern and traditional ideas, young people and old, individual desires and societal codes clash most fiercely. "Modern and young" people usually try to regard marriage as a personal affair which should be decided on according to love. "Traditional and old" people, by contrast, view marriage as the fulfillment of social obligations and responsibilities, which should therefore be arranged according to propriety; for example, cross-cousin marriage, forced marriage or *kawin paksa* in the understanding of the modern and young, is from the traditional perspective most desirable since it cements the relationship between a man's matrilineage and his mamak's wife's. Again it does not really concern us whether love marriage was in fact more frequent among the modern and young than arranged marriage—pretty clearly it was not. "Love" and "love marriage" were codes which stood for the conflict between Minangkabau society and the individuality which the perantau heroes of these stories came to discover in the rantau.

As a typical example of the Minangkabau novels of this time, let us review briefly what was probably the most popular story written during the Dutch period, namely, *Salah Asuhan* (Wrong Upbringing) (Moeis 1967, originally 1928). The main figure of the story is Hanafi, an office clerk in Solok. Because of his Dutch education in Batavia, he is, or at least he thinks he is, thoroughly Westernized in his behavior and attitudes. He only associates with Dutch friends, because his compatriots are not up to his standards. He falls in love with Corrie, a friend since childhood. However, following her French father's advice that "East is East, West is West, and the two will never become one [sic]," Corrie leaves for Batavia instead of responding to Hanafi's love. His love not being accepted, Hanafi marries Rapiah, a daughter of his mamak. Even after they have a son, Sjafei, Hanafi never feels any love for Rapiah; she is an unsophisticated village woman to him. He goes to Batavia for treatment when he is bitten by a mad dog. There he meets Corrie again. His love for her flares up. Hanafi secures a job in Batavia, divorces Rapiah, legally "becomes an European," changes his name to Christiaan Han, and marries Corrie whose father has died in the meantime. Their marriage, however, is not happy. Neither their Indonesian nor their Dutch friends want to associate with them any more. In this misery, rifts develop in their marriage because of the insinuations of other people and misunderstandings between Hanafi and Corrie themselves. Finally, Corrie leaves Hanafi and finds a job in Semarang. By the time Hanafi realizes his mistake and goes to Semarang to see Corrie, it is too late; she is dying of cholera. Hanafi eventually goes back from Java to West Sumatra. In spite of his wrongdoing, his mother and Rapiah are willing to take him back. But Hanafi knows only too well that his love belongs to the decreased Corrie even though he now sees how fine a woman Rapiah is. He also realizes that as long as he stays with his mother, she, Rapiah, and Sjafei (his son), who love each other dearly, cannot live together. (For Rapiah's parents will not continue to permit this rather unusual arrangement in a matrilineal society unless Hanafi remarries Rapiah.) Hanafi's life was burned up when Corrie died; he is already spent. He finally commits suicide, asking his mother never to let Sjafei follow his path.

Salah Asuhan clearly embodies many characteristics of the Minangkabau novels written during the 1920s and 1930s. Hanafi was educated at a Dutch school in Batavia, and his predicament arises from the fact that he is caught between the East (Minangkabau) and the West (Dutch or non-Minangkabau). His self and his individuality, awakened through Dutch education and love for a Eurasian girl, estrange him from both native and Dutch societies. When he tries to cross the racial and cultural boundary by changing his name from Sutan Pamenan (his adat title upon marriage to Rapiah) to Christiaan Han, he in fact loses his identity; he is neither Minangkabau nor Dutch because regardless of his personal desires, neither society responds to him any more. Despite his will to the contrary, Hanafi can never get free from Minangkabau society. When Corrie dies, he finds himself back in West Sumatra even though his immediate wish was only to leave Batavia. After returning from the rantau to West Sumatra, he realizes that he has at long last finished his education—after so many sufferings. He now understands that there is nothing wrong with Dutch education. Let his son Sjafei pursue Dutch education as much as he desires. Let him discard bad Eastern customs and adopt good Western customs. However, since he is an Easterner, his upbringing (*asuhan*) should be according to proper Eastern ways. He should never forget his Eastern origin and character which are part of his flesh and blood as if he had drunk them with his mother's milk. Hanafi's mistake was that he thought he could become a European by means of personal effort—Dutch education, "naturalization," and marriage to Corrie. Yet even after realizing all this, Hanafi knows that he can not fit back into his native society; the only solution is suicide. Irrespective of whether one agrees with this ending or not, *Salah Asuhan* projects, in the guise of the traumatic personal history of Hanafi, the painful encounter between the Minangkabau and the non-Minangkabau worlds, and an all-too-lopsided clash between society and the individual.

As revealed in *Salah Asuhan*, Minangkabau novels from the 1920s and the 1930s exemplify the relationship between perantau and the Minangkabau society when circulatory merantau was predominant. Perantau left their villages to make their living in Batavia, Medan, Deli or elsewhere. Some of them (like most of the Minangkabau novelists) stayed in the rantau year after year. Yet Minangkabau society remained the frame of reference of their thinking and behavior. As an adat aphorism says, "However high one jumps, one falls down to earth in the end" (se-tinggi-tinggi melambung, jatuhnya ketanah juga); the psychological orientation of the perantau remained focused on the Minangkabau society. This orientation was not that of sentimental reminiscence but was committed and active in terms of exerting changes on Minangkabau society. Circulatory merantau opened up new paths to power, wealth, knowledge, and prestige. Through education and encounters with other ethnic groups, perantau became acquainted with family relationships different from those of matriliny. Armed with new experiences in the rantau, returning perantau often acted as the vehicle for social change in the Alam Minangkabau. It is within the context of this organic relation between rantau and village that the changes in the family system and social stratification should be understood.

The interaction between merantau and social change continued after the Dutch period. At the initial stage of circulatory merantau, out-migration was mainly by individual men, partly because the conjugal tie was not yet strong and partly because the mamak still maintained relatively tight control over their female relatives. But as the conjugal tie grew stronger and as husband's individually earned property assumed more and more importance in supporting his wife and children, the mamak slowly relinquished his traditional obligations toward his female kin. So merantau by the nuclear family became increasingly popular, particularly after independence. While their nuclear family and matrilineal relatives were left behind in the village, there was every reason for perantau to go back home to their native village once in a while. The present popularity of nuclear family merantau, the prevalence of long-distance migration, and the mushrooming of perantau associations, however, militate against maintaining this circulatory arc between the rantau and the village. Chinese merantau (merantau Cino)—a more permanent kind of migration than circulatory merantau—is now ascendant.

Despite improved communication and transportation systems, the village seems very far away from the rantau nowadays.

The shift of emphasis from circulatory to Chinese merantau has profound significance for the relationship between village and rantau, and by implication for the course of social change in contemporary Minangkabau society and the society of the future.

7 / Matriliny and Migration

Noticing change in Minangkabau adat during the Padri wars and the subsequent direct contact with the colonial power, Francis (1839:111), a Dutch official in Sumatra's West Coast in the late 1830s, commented on its "bastardization," particularly with regard to inheritance practices along the coast. A famous Dutch scholar on adat law, Snouck Hurgronje, observed in the 1910s: "the belief that the [matrilineal] Minangkabau family system should be changed in accordance with the religious law, is becoming more influential on their [the people's] attitude" (quoted by Abdullah 1967:209, n. 111). In his analysis of the communist uprising of 1927 in West Sumatra, Schrieke summarized as follows the symptoms of decline in the "matriarchical" system: "The establishment of the [nuclear] family, the one-family dwelling, inheritance laws, the relaxation of the rules governing land tenure, the lessening of sacred family property—all these are factors combining to slacken the matriarchical family ties" (Schrieke 1955b:119).

Despite these comments, and despite all the changes described in the last chapter, there are many aspects of Minangkabau adat which have actually remained relatively unchanged. Different people set foot in West Sumatra with different expectations and ideas about Minangkabau society. Those with the idea that the Minangkabau still practice communal living in adat houses will find that this is not generally true any more. On the other hand, if a person were to arrive in West Sumatra with the expectation of finding the "Disappearance of Matriclan Survivals in Minangkabau Family and Marriage" (Maretin 1961), he would be surprised to find many "vestiges" of the old customs. It is noticeable that the three Dutch commentators mentioned above made their observations during two periods in recent Minangkabau history when powerful Islamic reform movements (the Padri and the Kaum Muda) swept across West Sumatra. It is understandable, then, that these Dutch men expected a continuing decline of a matrilineal system which (they thought) was strongly challenged by a revived Islam in one way or another.[1] Since the colonial era, however, Minangkabau society has demonstrated a remarkable resilience in accommodating to changing times and circumstances. Until now, the nature and extent of this accommodation have not been clearly spelled out. It is my intention in this concluding chapter to provide a description of this accommodation and at the same time to try to explain why it has been possible.

The Matrilineal System in Contemporary Minangkabau Society

Change and continuity in the family system can best be understood if we refer back to the four main characteristics of the Minangkabau matrilineal system mentioned in Chapter 2, namely, descent and descent group formation are organized according to the female line; a matrilineage is a corporate descent group; the residential pattern is duolocal; and authority is in the hands of the mamak.

Among these characteristics, the first is basically unchanged. Descent is still traced through the female line and descent groups such as suku (clan), payung (lineage), and paruik (sublineage) are formed around it. A person's suku name is still an important part of his or

1. In addition, Schrieke's influential report (1955b) is misleading on two accounts. First, most of his observations on the changing economic situation in West Sumatra come from areas such as Kerinci, Indrapura, Tapan, Muara Labuh, Alahan Panjang, Pariaman, Talu (Ophir area), Bangkinang, and Mapat Tunggal (in the north of Lubuk Sikaping). Because of the cultivation of cash crops (coffee, coconut, sugar cane, tobacco, and rubber), "the revolution in outlook" supposedly was taking place in those areas. However, these are the sparsely populated areas outside of the Minangkabau heartland or the areas where sawah, the most important communally-held property, was relatively insignificant. Second, his statement "In some negeris (such as Air Dingin and Solok) all the family land has been done away with and has been transformed into self-earned land as a consequence of pledging" (p. 110) is based, at least partially, on incorrect information. When a Dutch official made an investigation in Air Dingin (Alahan Panjang area) in 1934, he found harta pusaka there to be intact. Apparently about half of the ancestral rice land was pawned to build new adat houses after a big fire in 1910; most of the sawah had been redeemed by the time the investigation was made (Oki 1977:61–64, 126).

her identity whether in the village or in wider circles. Adult males are still often addressed in the village by their matrilineally-derived titles: "Hi, Tumanggung, where are you going?" Women are likewise identified by their suku affiliation. If one wants to locate the house of a certain Mother Rabiah, it is best to specify her suku as well as the hamlet of her residence, for example Mother Rabiah of Suku Tanjung in the hamlet of Kapalo Koto. Beyond the village, various government documents in West Sumatra make use of identification by suku name together with personal name. Some form of suku exogamy is still strictly upheld. Depending on the adat of the village, suku endogamy may be completely prohibited, prohibited only between members of the same suku in one village, or merely between members of one payung within the same suku. The strength of suku exogamy is exemplified by an incident I observed in Nagari Sulit Air, a village famous for its merantau activities. The village traditionally prohibited any kind of suku endogamy. In 1972, however, the adat council of the village passed a resolution that suku endogamy was permissible so long as it took place in the rantau. Yet when such a marriage was actually performed between two young leaders of the perantau association in Jakarta in 1973, it caused a great commotion: many persons both in the village and in the rantau were extremely critical.[2]

As for the other three characteristics of Minangkabau matriliny, there have been considerable alterations, as described in the last chapter. However, a closer scrutiny of these changes reveals, as I will try to show below, that they do not necessarily jeopardize the matrilineal system itself.

With regard to the matrilineage as a corporate group, the alterations can be characterized as follows. Ancestral property remains the most important foundation of the Minangkabau matrilineage. Although ancestral property, above all land (or more properly speaking, its usage rights), is now likely to be divided among samandai (or their corresponding nuclear families), it is inherited in a pattern that is essentially the same: it is transmitted according to the female line and is in principle inalienable from the matrilineage or sublineage.

2. *Singgalang,* no. 367 (March 1973), no. 370 (April 1973), and no. 390 (June 1973).

At the same time, the rise of individually earned property has added complexity to inheritance practices. It has been already pointed out that in contrast to ancestral property, individually earned property can be and is inherited by one's children instead of by one's kemanakan. In fact, according to my nagari survey, 96 percent of 232 village heads replied that it was far more common in their villages that individually earned property be given to the children rather than to the kemanakan. Nevertheless, it should be noted that even today, the disposition of individually earned property is sometimes influenced by matrilineal inheritance patterns. If we recall the survey of Sa'danoer (1971:12), mentioned in Chapter 6, in 18 percent of 428 inheritance cases studied for the 1960–1970 period, individually earned property was actually given to kemanakan.

In addition, the apparent discretion permitted in the disposition of individually earned property is generation bound, for the status of such property is not permanent according to Minangkabau custom (Benda-Beckmann 1979:194–196). Minangkabau adat basically distinguishes between two types of property, ancestral and individually earned.[3] Ancestral property belongs to a lineage and is inherited according to matrilineal principles over generations (*turun temurun*). Individually earned property is acquired by one's own effort and may be given to a person or persons of one's own choice. This classification and conceptualization does not recognize "perpetual harta pencarian" which may be inherited from generation to generation with discretionary disposal rights (that is, the inheritor of the property at each generation may dispose of it as he or she wishes). In Minangkabau adat, inherited individually earned property is "liminal" at best: it is no longer individually earned property, but it is not yet ancestral property either. It poises in this ambiguous and "uncomfortable" limbo, in between stages, until it becomes ancestral property. Accordingly, individually earned property, especially immobile property such as houses and land, becomes low (that is, new) ancestral property (*harta pusaka rendah*) in two or three generations even though it may initially be given to children. Again, according to my nagari survey, 63 percent of 232

---

3. In addition, *harta suarang* (jointly earned property between husband and wife) has been legally distinguishable since 1930, according to Jahja (1968:85).

village heads said that in their villages individually earned property
generally became ancestral property after one generation, that is, in
the generation of the children of a property-purchaser. The figure
would be even higher if a longer generational span, two or three
generations from the original purchaser, were taken into account.
Not only is the status of individually earned property
generation-bound but immobile individually earned property tends
to be given to daughters in preference to sons (Kahn 1976:73), and
from them to their daughters and so on according to the matrilineal
principle; as will be discussed shortly, the fact that Minangkabau
houses usually have identification plates bearing female names is
one manifestation of this tendency. Individually earned property
inherited by sons rather than by daughters is also likely to be given
to daughters alone in the grandchildren's generation (counted from
the original owner of the property) and from then on to their
daughters following the female line (see Figure 7).[4] Evidently, then,
sizable amounts and proportions of individually earned property
cannot be accumulated over the generations so long as these principles are retained. Even in Padang, the provincial capital and the
largest urban center in the province, the proportion of registered
individual land—the approximately 40 percent of the total land in
the city which was formerly under Dutch ownership and is now
controlled by Chinese—has remained virtually stable for the last
fifty years. The remaining 60 percent is unregistered; these lands
seem to repeat the cycle of individually earned to ancestral land
(Evers 1975).[5]

Coupled with the increasing importance of individually earned
property, the prevalent practice of giving it to children has misled

4. The three circled groups in Figure 7 represent different matrilineal groups,
while dotted lines indicate possible lines of inheritance in case individually earned
property is given to children.
5. Because Evers cites only two cases of diachronical data, further study is
necessary to substantiate this contention. Probably the best and most involved work
on Minangkabau property relationships is that of Benda-Beckmann (1979). He
detects a symptom of the emergence of "perpetual harta pencarian" (my terminology) which could eventually chip away the existing harta pusaka (pp. 344–350). The
legal case he cites, as he is well aware, is not representative of currently popular
practices. Furthermore, even if individually earned property maintains its status, for
example, for two generations from its original purchaser, the property is likely to be
eventually converted into harta pusaka as long as immobile individually earned
property tends to be given to daughters in preference to sons.

Figure 7. Inheritance of individually earned property by children

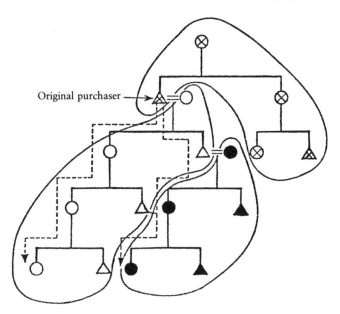

some scholars into either pointing out or predicting the dissolution of ancestral property, and thus the dissolution of matrilineage, and even of the Minangkabau matrilineal system itself. None of this, in fact, is actually happening.

Admittedly, in everyday village life in West Sumatra, it may not be easy to discern the cooperate nature of descent group in the sense that the descent group, be it paruik, payung, or suku, acts as a body and controls its constituent members and their share of ancestral property. Nevertheless, the Minangkabau do still understand that the ownership of ancestral property essentially belongs to the descent group rather than to its individual users and that its use and disposition are ultimately not free from cooperate constraints and matrilineal principles. Should pledgings or sellings of ancestral land—still relatively rare in West Sumatra—occur, every effort is made to confine the transactions within the sublineage, lineage, or suku concerned, lest the land fall into the hands of another suku's members, let alone into those of another nagari's members. If a paruik dies out (*punah*), its ancestral property is generally taken over by its most closely related paruik. Although an increasing number of disputes concerning harta pusaka seem nowadays to be brought to the court, most of them are still settled within the circle of paruik, payung, or suku under the guidance of house elders or lineage elders. Even such a seemingly more personal decision as marriage is also still subjected to descent-group scrutiny. All in all, I maintain, the cooperate nature of the descent group, albeit in more flexible form, is still very binding in West Sumatra.

As suggested earlier, residential arrangements are now more properly identified as uxorilocal than duolocal. A husband may still visit his mother's house rather regularly (once a week), particularly if his wife's house is nearby, in order to keep informed of the situation at his natal house. Nevertheless, with his time mostly spent at his wife's house, his life (though not kin affiliation) belongs there rather than to his mother's house. The pervasiveness of uxorilocal residency is clear from my survey in IV Angkat. Among 395 houses, there were only five cases where a wife had moved to the house of her husband. These rare cases were generally explained in terms of expediency. For example, in one case, all of the members of the husband's residence had migrated from the village and he had been asked to take care of the house in the meantime.[6]

Although the shift from duolocal to uxorilocal residence has altered the nature of a man's relation to the matrilineal kin of his wife, this shift does not in itself mean that Minangkabau society has become less matrilineal.[7] In uxorilocal as in duolocal residence patterns, women still remain with their matrilineal relatives after their marriage.

Not only are households still basically formed around women and the network of their matrilineal kin, but the ideology (and the practice) that the house essentially belongs to its female members remains strong. In one of the villages in IV Angkat, the village government recently proposed that all the houses display a plate

6. Even if a house is built by a husband, it is usually built on the ancestral property of his wife. Because the wife does not move out of her own kin network, such cases should still be considered as uxorilocal rather than neolocal.

7. According to the study of Aberle (1961:667), uxorilocal or matrilocal residence is modal (49 percent) for his sample of 84 matrilineal societies from different parts of the world; only four percent are duolocal.

with the name of the owner on it. Although more than half of the houses in the village are individually earned property, and thus most probably belong to husbands or jointly to husbands and wives, the names are without exception female. Hamka (1963:35) also tells the story of a Javanese visitor to Padang who was surprised to find that in the advanced provincial capital of West Sumatra most of the names on house-plates were feminine.

Since the house continues to belong to its female members, the custom of boys' sleeping in the surau (prayer-house) is still commonly practiced. If there are not enough surau in the village, boys also sometimes sleep in coffee shops or empty houses. Sixty-seven percent of the 232 village heads interviewed in my nagari survey replied that almost all of the unmarried boys in the village slept outside their mothers' houses. In response to a similar question asked in a study by Naim (1973a:21), 77 percent of 157 penghulu interviewed said that their unmarried sons and male kemanakan did not sleep at their mothers' houses.[8]

One concomitant of uxorilocal residency is the increasing involvement of the husband with the kin of his wife. Previously, a man's obligations to his children, let alone to his wife's relatives, were generally limited to intermittent gift giving on ceremonial occasions. Uxorilocal residency was both a cause and a consequence of closer ties between a man and his wife and children. It also entailed more frequent contact between a man and his wife's kinsmen and the former's growing involvement, more likely by persuasion than by choice, in the welfare of the latter. Nowadays, it is very common for a sumando to be expected to make some kind of economic contribution to his wife's matrilineal kin (for example, helping to send his wife's nephew to school), especially if he has his own source of income. Tanner (1971:34) is even of the opinion that nowadays the focus of a man's involvement increasingly shifts from the matrilineal family of orientation to the matrilineal family of procreation. This contention may be a little exaggerated, but there is no doubt that a man's socioeconomic obligations are no longer directed solely to his own matrilineage; that of his wife can also become very demanding of his help indeed.

8. Naim addressed a questionnaire to penghulu from 129 different villages in West Sumatra who attended an adat conference in Padang in 1970.

Next to the confusion over ancestral and individually earned property mentioned already, much of the misunderstanding about the present Minangkabau matrilineal system is concerned with the sphere of authority. Some people seem to argue that because the solidarity of the nuclear family is strong and because the father, and not the mamak, takes care of the children, the matrilineal system must have been replaced by a patrilineal or bilateral type of system. This interpretation is clearly inaccurate. For here the distinction between authority within the domestic group and authority within the descent group is crucial (see, for more details, Schneider 1962). The descent group we are concerned with is a group defined by the matrilineal principle, corporate property and an appointed leadership; the domestic group, on the other hand, is a household which handles the care of children.

Previously both the domestic group and the descent group were formally under the authority of one person, the tungganai (house elder); probably it is more accurate to say that the domestic group was to a great extent under the authority of the oldest woman in the adat house. Today the father and the mother are primarily responsible, although it is not unusual for them to be assisted by the mamak, in looking after the material welfare of the children. The mamak is by no means completely left out of the domestic group sphere. He is kept informed of what is happening to his kemanakan: their educational plans, their occupational plans, and their plans for migration, not to mention marriage.[9]

In the sphere of the descent group, all adat matters which deal with the lineage as a corporate group are the concern of the mamak. Decisions related to ancestral properties and the conduct of lineage members are taken by the matrilineage or sublineage as a whole under the guidance of the mamak. Examples of such decisions concern disputes over ancestral property and titles, infringements of adat customs and misbehavior by lineage members. In these matters, the sumando may be consulted but final authority is unquestionably in the hands of the mamak.

9. For example, according to Naim's research (1973a:16), about 50 percent of the penghulu surveyed answered that they were currently taking care of some of their kemanakan. In my household survey in IV Angkat, 79 percent of the respondents who had ever been on merantau replied that they had asked for the permission of their mamak before leaving the village.

The mamak still plays an important role in the marriage arrangements of his kemanakan. Even if he is not directly involved in seeking a prospective spouse, it is customary to ask the permission of the mamak before marriage. Courtesy aside, this custom has its practical side. All adat ceremonies are arranged by the mamak—for example, the protocol, the exchanges of speeches and so forth. Marriage is usually celebrated by two rituals: the adat wedding ceremony and the *nikah* wedding ceremony. The former symbolizes Minangkabau matriliny and the role of the mamak, while the latter symbolizes Islamic law and the role of the father—for in Islamic law, the father of the bride is the principal witness to the marriage. The adat wedding ceremony is preceded by the *nikah,* but without it the marriage is not legitimate in the eyes of the villagers. The adat ceremony is by far the more expensive of the two. Thus it sometimes happens that the adat ceremony is postponed for some time after the *nikah* ceremony until it is economically feasible. Even in these instances, it is rare, particularly in the village, that consummation of the marriage takes place before the adat ceremony is carried out. The mamak's consent to the marriage is thus crucial, for without it no speaker will appear for the adat ceremony and, as a consequence, it will not take place.

Naturally these two spheres of authority are not always distinct. (When I was conducting interviews in the villages, I used to ask for the "head of the family" [*kepala keluarga*] at the houses I visited. Oftentimes, I, in turn, was asked by the sumando, who now stays at his wife's house most of the time, which head of the family I meant, the sumando or the mamak.) Sometimes an attempt is made by one side to venture into the other's sphere. Nevertheless, people are aware of the distinction and some semblance of order prevails. Perhaps it is helpful to conceive of domestic group authority and descent group authority as parts of a continuum rather than as discrete categories. At opposite ends of the continuum the preeminence of the mamak or the father is relatively clear. But as one approaches the middle of the continuum, the distinction becomes blurred and potential conflicts between mamak and father, or between matrilineage and nuclear family may emerge. I remember an incident I observed in Padang which shows under what circumstance authority relations between descent group and domestic group can get rather obscure. A noted government official died leaving a will to the effect that his body be buried in Padang itself rather than in his native village nearby. The will was a manifestation of the deceased's attachment to his wife and children; he wanted them to look after his grave. However, his kemanakan wished to take his body back to the village according to the adat, while the surviving wife and children intended to fulfill his wishes. The kemanakan were concerned that they might be gossiped about if they failed to perform their adat obligations to their mamak. The wife and children, as good Moslems and as loving survivors, wanted to respect the deceased's wishes (*wasiat*) as Islam admonishes. These conflicting positions created acute tension between the two sides, especially since a proper Moslem has to be buried as soon as possible after his death. In the end, a compromise was reached to the effect that his body would be buried in Padang, but without the grave being cemented; and it would be transferred to his native village after one year. (This move actually never took place.) The incident shows that when adat and Islam prescribe different behavioral expectations and when there is no widely accepted procedure of reconciling this discrepancy, conflicts between descent group authority (mamak-kemanakan) and domestic group authority (father-mother-children) are likely to emerge.

Another story I heard exemplifies the case where authority relations are clearly distinguished, even though an attempt is made by one side to intervene into the other's sphere. A former minister of the central government from a famous perantau village near Bukittinggi once tried to influence the selection of a new penghulu for his wife's lineage. Despite his political power and stature in the rantau, he, as a sumando, could not win favor for his candidate. In the end, he had to yield to the opinion of a penghulu from a lineage related to his wife's, who was a mere goldsmith in the village.

In sum, there have certainly been significant changes in the Minangkabau matrilineal system. The increasing importance of the nuclear family as an economic and residential unit is undeniable. Concurrently, the bonds between husband and wife, and between father and children have obviously been growing. Yet it is premature to suggest the disappearance of the matrilineal system itself.

It is true that nowadays some educated Minangkabau men in the cities pass on part of their names to their children as the "family name." However, the principle of matrilineal descent-reckoning is still practiced in West Sumatra, and suku affiliation is still important in terms of establishing a person's identity and determining the range of possible marriage partners. Property is now given to children instead of kemanakan, but it is only individually earned property. The usage rights of ancestral land are now more likely to be divided between paruik members, but people still uphold the principle that the ownership of ancestral land ultimately belongs to descent groups, not to individual users. Residential arrangements are now more uxorilocal than duolocal; but this change does not jeopardize the matrilineal system. The father wields strong influence over the lives of his children, but only in the sphere of the domestic group; the mamak still dominates the sphere of the descent group. If we observe the balance struck between change and continuity in the Minangkabau matrilineal system, then we are likely to be impressed by how successfully the system has managed to survive by accommodating to changing times and circumstances. This accommodation is all the more remarkable when we consider the extent of the transformations the Minangkabau village has experienced since the beginning of the nineteenth century.

Continuity in Social Stratification

The ascent of nouveaux riches in the "marriage market" noted by Radjab, if taken too literally, may make one overlook an important consistency in Minangkabau social stratification. For the nouveaux riches were sought after as husbands not so much for their enhanced social prestige as for the practical benefits they could bring to the matrilineal kin of a bride—financial assistance, souvenirs from the rantau, material as well as moral support for those wanting to go merantau, aid for education, and so on. At the same time, traditional elites, such as the penghulu, the Islamic teachers, and the coastal nobility, were far from being supplanted by these nouveaux riches as desirable husbands. They are still coveted for the social prestige they can bestow upon the lineage they marry into, even if they do not bring any special financial benefits. According to Naim's study of 170 penghulu from different areas in West Sumatra, about 20 percent were currently polygamously married (as of 1970) (Naim 1973a:12–13). In contrast, 8.7 persons per 100 married men in West Sumatra were polygamously married in 1930

(*Volkstelling 1930*, 8:106). Under changed economic conditions, polygamy rates can be expected to be much lower today than in 1930. Naim's figure suggests that the penghulu still possess strong bargaining power in marriage arrangements in West Sumatra. It still often happens that traditional elites are "paid" (*dijemput*) to marry a prospective bride, their price being negotiated according to their status: for example, if a person is a Bagindo (traditional coastal nobility), so many gold dollars, and if he is a Bagindo and a Doctor, a car.

As the last example indicates, a great amount of prestige is now accorded to academic titles. As one person put it, those with an "appendage r" (Dr., Ir., Drs., Mr.) at the beginning of their names "sell well" (*berlaku*) in the contemporary marriage market.[10] Nevertheless, even here, one has to be aware of the limitations the adat imposes. However successful a person may be in the rantau and however high an academic title he may acquire, he is not likely to be asked to marry the daughter of an urang asa (descendants of original settlers) so long as he is not an urang asa himself. To be sure people in the village are reluctant to admit that any distinction still exists between the descendants of original settlers and those of latecomers. In ordinary daily life no discrimination is apparent between the two groups. Sometimes the distinction can be observed in residential arrangement whereby descendants of the so-called kemanakan beneath the knees (*kemanakan dibawah lutut*) live in a separate place from others. The distinction is most clear, however, in marriage arrangements. Kemanakan beneath the knees, particularly males, seldom have any prospect of marrying daughters of urang asa, irrespective of their success and fame in the rantau. They often have to marry among their own kind in the village or with those of similar status from another village.[11]

10. "Benarkah Jodoh Harus Dibeli di Minangkabau?," *Aneka Minang*, no. 16 (n.d.), p. 8. Ir. is an engineering degree. Drs. (generally in social sciences and humanities) and Mr. (Dutch law degree) are equivalent to a master's degree.

11. The study of Thomas (1977:14–17) in one of the hamlets (*jorong*) in a village near Batu Sangkar shows that "newcomers" (*urang datang*) there lived in their separate settlements. "A larger proportion of the people in the outlying settlements" came to the hamlet a couple of generations ago. As Thomas's study was concentrated on the main settlement of the hamlet, his observations about the outlying settlements are cursory. They indicate, however, that their population differed from that of the main settlement in several important respects, for example, residen-

In addition, traditional status positions (penghuluship) are still relatively difficult to achieve by means of success in the rantau unless a person belongs to the urang asa. It is true that a person outside the proper line of inheritance sometimes captures the position of penghulu because of his money, fame, academic title, or other distinction. In such cases, the irregularity means someone from a minor lineage superseding a candidate from a major lineage where both belong to the urang asa. Such occurences are not frequent; the common practice is that penghuluship is inherited by brothers or direct kemanakan. In 70 percent of the villages studied in my·nagari survey, penghuluship is typically transmitted in this way. According to Naim's research (1973a:20), 92 percent of 166 penghulu, representing some 120 villages, inherited their positions from their direct mamak. The persistence of this rigid inheritance pattern for penghuluship does not permit any easy translation of outside success into traditional high status in the village.[12]

I mentioned in Chapter 6 that there are now many vacant penghulu positions: ninety-seven (42 percent) of the 232 villages studied in my nagari survey had one or more of their penghulu positions unoccupied. This does not necessarily mean that penghuluship is no longer eagerly sought after because of the decline in its power and prestige. In fact, the prevalence of direct mamak to direct kemanakan inheritance notwithstanding, the succession to a penghuluship often causes serious disputes among contending aspirants. Thus, in 34 percent of ninety-seven villages where I found vacant penghuluships, the major problem was lack of lineage or sublineage consensus and disputes among candidates (see also Benda-Beckmann:365–366). It even sometimes happens that a desperate candidate may forge the signature of an opponent in order to win the coveted position.[13]

tial pattern (neolocality is not uncommon), land ownership (very few owned land), number of penghuluships (few penghulu in proportion to the population size), sex and age composition (sex ratio is more balanced and there were fewer old people), and rates of merantau (fewer people seem to merantau).

12. Benda-Beckmann (p. 414, n. 25) is doubtful of the prevalence of "direct inheritance" of penghuluship. Unfortunately this question cannot be settled without the scrutiny of actual inheritance cases.

13. "Karena Ingin Hendak Djadi Penghulu, Dipergunakan Tanda Tangan Palsu," Haluan, 9 October, 1957. The most pressing problem in filling vacant penghuluships is the lack of economic capability: 37 percent of the 97 villages

I remember a young doctor I met in West Sumatra, from a very prosperous and proper family in a village in the darek area. He had been trained to be a doctor in Jakarta and subsequently returned to West Sumatra to work for an Islamic hospital in the establishment of which his family was deeply involved. A few years after his return to West Sumatra, he went on the pilgrimage to Mecca, thus becoming a haji. Today, his relatives are thinking of eventually placing him in a long-vacant penghulu position belonging to their lineage when he is more mature and knowledgeable about adat. Acquisition of a penghulu title will be the final feat to cap the accomplishments of this young doctor, for he will then have accumulated titles of prestige in the three most important areas of Minangkabau life, education, religion, and adat. The fact that penghuluship will come to him last may be sheer accident. Yet the order in which his titles will have been acquired is symbolic of the degree of difficulty involved. The right combination of brains, wealth, and effort will produce a doctor. With the proper religious orientation and money, one may become a haji. However, no one can become a penghulu, no matter how hard he tries, unless he comes from the right family line and a penghuluship is vacant or vacated. For Minangkabau intellectuals who stay permanently in the rantau, aspiring to penghuluship may seem anachronistic and unattractive. But for this young doctor and his relatives, whose lives are set in West Sumatra, it still matters a great deal that he become a penghulu in the near future along with being a doctor and a haji.

The continuing attraction of penghuluship—though it is admittedly less prominent than it used to be—derives partly from the

mentioned this as the prime reason for existence of vacant penghuluships. Because the proper inauguration ceremony involves slaughtering of at least one water buffalo and entails a series of banquets for members of related lineages and influential people in the village, it can indeed be very expensive. According to Oki's estimate (p. 192), the inauguration ceremony in the Batu Sangkar area, which lasted for three days to one week, could sometimes have cost more than 1,000 Dutch guilders before the Great Depression. (No comparable figures are available for the present situation.) It seems that individually earned property, not ancestral property, is sometimes used for financing the inauguration ceremony but it is not considered to be very proper. Kahn (1974:91) tells a story about an event in the village he studied: a "penghulu-elect" persuaded his classificatory sisters to pledge ancestral land in order to finance the inauguration ceremony, and the land was pledged to no other than the future penghulu himself! If there is a definite candidate for penghuluship yet the position is not filled for economic reasons, it is likely that he will nevertheless act as a provisional penghulu.

prestige and influence still enjoyed by penghulu in the villages. Penghulu still maintain some measure of punitive power over those who violate adat regulations, such as suku exogamy and nagari endogamy. Punishment for violation of adat may range from the payment of retribution money to the offering of a communal feast asking for a pardon; in former times it could also mean expulsion from the nagari.[14] Penghulu (together with Islamic teachers) are considered the most respected people by many in IV Angkat. They are also regarded as very influential (Table 7.1).[15] It is significant that in both categories, the penghulu are rated above the subdistrict head (*camat*), the most visible representative of the national administrative hierarchy for the villagers.

One of the most significant changes after the Dutch period was the opening of political positions in the village to non-penghulu. During Dutch times, the village head was generally appointed from among the penghulu. From the onset of the Japanese occupation, this policy was no longer strictly followed. The assumption of village headmanship by non-penghulu continued to spread after independence, for the position has remained largely elective in West Sumatra. In 1969, elections were held for two village political positions, village council members (*dewan perwakilan rakyat nagari*) and village head (*wali nagari*).[16] Although election results are not

14. For an example of expulsion from the nagari before World War II, see the case of a woman from Kota Gedang who married a Javanese man against the nagari adat regulations and without her mamak's permission (Anwar 1967:130–132). Although the marriage took place in Tebing Tinggi after elopement from Medan (where she and her husband-to-be worked), she was expelled from the nagari, deprived of all the adat rights pertaining to her and prohibited from coming back to the village. The same punishment was further declared to be applicable to those who would receive and shelter her in the village.

15. The results in Table 7.1 are based on the following question: "Here are mentioned eight occupations or positions. Please think of their general characteristics, for example, wealth, age, etc. This is not concerned with individuals but occupations or positions in general. Generally speaking, which occupations/positions are more respected (influential) than the others? Please choose four occupations/positions which are most respected according to your opinion." The figures show the proportion of the 395 respondents who chose particular occupations/positions as "being respected" and as "being influential." The totals of these percentages are 400, since four choices were made by each respondent.

16. The village council is a legislative body consisting of a minimum of ten and a maximum of twenty elected members; the number depends on the size of the village population. In 1969, the village head had to be elected by and from among the village council members.

Table 7.1. Villagers' perceptions of respected and influential occupations and positions

Occupations and positions	Respected	Influential
Penghulu	71%	77%
Civil servant (*pegawai negeri*)	31%	20%
Merchant (*pedagang*)	38%	27%
Islamic teacher (*alim ulama*)	83%	89%
Subdistrict head (*camat*)	60%	51%
School teacher (*guru sekolah*)	43%	34%
Village head (*wali nagari*)	62%	84%
Rich farmer (*petani yang berharta*)	12%	18%

SOURCE: Household survey in IV Angkat.

available from all the villages in West Sumatra, I was able to collect a substantial portion of them from the governor's office and the offices of district heads. The roster of elected village officials generally lists names, adat titles, ages, occupations, and final education, though the information is sometimes incomplete.

The election results show a surprising number of penghulu and other traditional elites (Table 7.2). Among the village heads, 38 percent use the title of Datuk (generally the title of penghulu), 5 percent hold such coastal noble titles as Bagindo, Sutan, Sidi, and Marah (which are often more highly regarded than penghulu titles along the coast), and 9 percent possess Islamic titles according to adat. A similar finding, albeit less conspicuous, is observable in the case of the village council members: datuk, 27 percent; coastal noble title, 3 percent; and Islamic title according to adat, 11 percent.[17]

17. Among the titles in Table 7.2, Sutan (different from a coastal noble title) sometimes indicates a deputy-penghulu in areas such as central Agam (Agam Tuo). "None" means that no adat title was mentioned in the government document; it is quite possible that in some of these cases adat titles were advertently or inadvertently omitted by village heads themselves or by the government officials who filled the roster. "Not applicable" indicates that the council members were either Javanese, Batak, or females who do not have Minangkabau adat titles. Not all penghulu use Datuk titles (particularly in outer areas beyond the darek), nor do all Datuk titles indicate penghuluship. However, the overlap between Datuk title and penghuluship is generally so close that occasional irregularities can be ignored for our present purposes. Islamic titles according to adat (e.g., *pakih*, *malim*, and *labai*) are inherited according to matrilineal principles. Depending on the particular location in West Sumatra, the titles may or may not connote specific functional roles associated with Islamic rites (such as marriage).

Table 7.2. Adat titles of village heads and village council members, 1969

	Datuk	Coastal noble title	Sutan	Islamic title	Other	None	Not applicable	Total sample
Village heads	38%	5%	8%	9%	11%	29%	0%	397
Village council members	27%	3%	8%	11%	12%	36%	3%	4480

SOURCE: The governor's office and offices of district heads.

The representation of penghulu among village political leaders can be better appreciated if the proportion of penghulu to the total adult male population of West Sumatra is taken into consideration. According to my nagari survey, there are on the average 45.8 penghulu positions in each nagari, out of which 8.4 positions are unoccupied and 4.2 are deputized because the real penghulu are in the rantau. One thus arrives at an average figure of 33.2 men per village who currently occupy penghuluships. From the 1971 census, one finds that there are on the average 858.1 adult males (25 years of age or above) per nagari in West Sumatra. Thus, the proportion of active penghulu among adult males is 1 to 26. Table 7.2 shows that the proportional representation of penghulu among elected village officials is 1 to 2.6 for village heads and 1 to 3.7 for village council members. Penghulu are thus represented among elected village officials on a scale extremely disproportionate to their share of the adult male population of West Sumatra. This result is all the more remarkable since village officials of penghulu status do not seem to have any other advantage over their non-penghulu counterparts. For example, in terms of age and occupation, village council members of penghulu status are slightly older and more likely to be farmers than the others. The mean age of those in the Datuk category among the village council members is 43 years, while that of the others is 40; the representations of farmers are 57 percent Datuk and 49 percent other. The age of village heads does not differ significantly between the two groups; the mean age is forty-two. Village heads of penghulu status are slightly more likely to be farmers than the others: Datuks, 53 percent and the others, 49 percent.

Moreover, village council members of penghulu status are less educated than the others: 57 percent of those in the Datuk category
versus 42 percent of the others graduated only from grade schools.
The same tendency is observable among village heads: the proportions of grade school graduates are Datuk, 50 percent and others,
35 percent.[18]

There is no denying that the Minangkabau social stratification
has undergone considerable change, especially since the end of the
Dutch period. Today the penghulu no longer enjoy the kind of
power and high status that they did in previous times. Bases of
stratification have diversified. White-collar workers, merchants,
and intellectuals contend for high status. Achievement in the rantau
is an important factor in enhancing one's position in the village.
Nevertheless, the penghulu still command a great deal of prestige
and influence. They still seem to possess strong bargaining power in
marriage arrangements. Their access to village political office is far
greater than that of any other group in the village (with the possible
exception of Islamic teachers).[19] The attainment of penghuluship
thus remains very attractive to many people who stay on in West
Sumatra.

Part of the reason for this continuity in social stratification is the
pivotal importance of the mamak-kemanakan tie in matrilineal
Minangkabau social relations. The father-child relation, whether
increasingly strong or not, is essentially an affective tie of a largely
personal nature. Within the framework of a social structure defined
by adat, it does not carry much significant social connotation. It
may be that "[one's] behavior is judged on the basis of the father-
son network" (Abdullah 1972a:196). Children may gain access to

18. Another significant fact about education is the general importance of Islamic
education among these elected village officials. Twenty-nine percent of both village
heads and village council members attended Islamic schools. There is no way to
estimate how much of the adult male population of West Sumatra has received
Islamic education. In my survey in IV Angkat, only 15 percent of 395 male household heads had attended Islamic schools. This figure is probably higher than in other
villages, for there are three Islamic secondary schools in the area, not to mention easy
access to Islamic schools in Bukittinggi. Among the three title groups, "Islamic" have
the highest proportion of attendance at Islamic schools—33 percent for village heads
and 43 percent for village council members.

19. However, the 1969 election results may have been strongly influenced by the
policy of the New Order (*Orde Baru*) under President Suharto. The policy in this
election generally favored traditional elites in West Sumatra.

education, wealth, and high position—outside the adat structure—
through their father. But a father can not bestow adat-based social
status on his children in the village. It is only the mamak who is
capable of this. Adat-based social status, adat titles, and ancestral
property are all mediated through the mamak-kemanakan network.
This network is ordered hierarchically on the basis of adat. Because
it is also based on generational difference, it does not allow room
for change in the inner organization of the hierarchy. However rich,
educated, and highly positioned a kemanakan may be, he remains a
kemanakan to his mamak until his mamak dies. "A kemanakan in
Minangkabau, although he may have cleverness as high as the sky
and have whatever position, yet for his function as kemanakan to
his mamak the adat aphorism 'the kemanakan follows the order
of the mamak, the mamak follows the order of truth' always
holds."[20]

The durability of the mamak-kemanakan tie is actually facilitated
by change from circulatory to Chinese merantau. While the
mamak-kemanakan relation is based on ascription, merantau in-
culcates achievement. When circulatory merantau was predominant, returning migrants could and did challenge the power and
status of mamak on the basis of their achievement in the rantau. As
Chinese merantau has become more popular, ascription and
achievement have largely ceased to be in competition with one
another. The growing importance of achievement does not necessarily lead to a decrease in the significance of ascription. Rather,
ascription and achievement are increasingly identified with two relatively self-contained localities, namely, ascription for the village
and achievement for the rantau. Admittedly, achievement in the
rantau still commands high respect in the village. However, achiev-
ers in the rantau no longer contend for power in the village. On the
contrary, there is an increasing tendency for achievement in the
rantau and ascription in the village to become mutually supportive.

Two Worlds, One Adat

On the basis of his research results in a village near Bukittinggi in
the early 1970s, Kahn proposes an assessment of Minangkabau
matriliny diametrically opposed to mine. He argues: "While

20. "Minangkabau Adatnja Kokoh," *Haluan*, 19 November 1957, p. 3.

ideologically matriliny and Minangkabau *adat* remain important for most Minangkabau, in fact there is little substance to matrilineal organization. In a very real sense Minangkabau social and economic organization is no different from that of other Sumatran groups. . . . The great difference, I would suggest, is ideological." His conclusion is: "This elaborate ideology concerning Minangkabau *adat* is retained only because there is no pressure against it. If, for example, agriculture in West Sumatra underwent a revolutionary transformation—i.e., if it were capitalized, then *adat* would all but disappear. The principles of matrilineal kinship might be compared to the remnants of feudalism which still persist in Western Europe" (1974:102, 104).

It seems that both of us are observing the same phenomena, the strength of adat in West Sumatra. However, I see Minangkabau matriliny as substantial, and I stress Minangkabau social and cultural dynamism, for example, merantau and flexibility of adat. Kahn, a Marxist-oriented economic anthropologist, views Minangkabau matriliny as an "empty shell" (my terminology); he emphasizes the importance of external forces, originating from beyond the nagari, West Sumatra, and Indonesia, which have in general thwarted Minangkabau society's internal economic processes (in particular, capitalization of agriculture and commodity production) and its thorough transformation.

In many ways, the revolutionary transformation or capitalization of agriculture is synonymous with the disappearance of adat in West Sumatra. Their relationship is more like two sides of a coin than like a cause-effect relation. One of the best indicators of agricultural capitalization is, precisely, decreasing control of adat over land tenure. The two elements are interdependent. While lack of agricultural capitalization helps the perseverance of adat, adat in turn reinforces lack of agricultural capitalization. Minangkabau adat is more than simply an elaborate ideology. Adat influences various facets of Minangkabau life, including land tenure, and societal process in West Sumatra. It is a decisive social factor to be reckoned with whenever we try to contemplate the future development of Minangkabau society.

The resilience of Minangkabau adat derives, at least in part, from its continuing relevance to the Minangkabau—both in the village and in the rantau. It is my task to explain how this is so.

From my research, IV Angkat proved to be an area that did not

depend very heavily on agriculture for its livelihood: only 43 percent of 395 males and 29 percent of their wives gave farming as
their main occupation. These figures are extremely low for nonurban areas in West Sumatra. According to a survey on occupations
conducted in all of West Sumatra in conjunction with the 1971
census, 75 percent of males and 68 percent of females 25 years old
or above in rural West Sumatra are engaged in agriculture (Thamrin 1973:IV, VII). The low figures I found are partly due to land
shortage and partly due to the unusual availability of nonagricultural occupations for villagers in IV Angkat. People in the area are
relatively well educated, they have a well-developed tradition of
handicrafts, and they live near Bukittinggi, the most important
urban center in the interior.

     These results might be interpreted as evidence that agriculture
plays an insignificant role in the lives of a majority of the villagers in
IV Angkat. If this were the case, the finding would be important in
its social implications. It would mean that more than half the villagers lead their lives without any essential relationship to ancestral
land for sustenance. But nothing could be less accurate than such an
interpretation. In rural West Sumatra, as in many other places in
Indonesia, people frequently have more than one means of livelihood to supplement their income. One may, for example, tend a
village coffee shop, occasionally bring artifacts from the village to
Bukittinggi, and, in season or if time allows, work on a rice field. In
my survey in IV Angkat, about 50 percent of both male respondents
and their wives turned out to have supplementary occupations. If
these supplementary occupations are taken into consideration, the
proportion of agriculturalists in the population increases considerably: to 76 percent for males and 70 percent for their wives. Moreover, only a few households are completely detached from agriculture. Eighty-four percent of 356 households (where heads are
currently married) in my sample draw at least part of their income
from agricultural activities; in only 16 percent of the cases are
neither husband nor wife so engaged. Considering that IV Angkat is
clearly less dependent on agriculture than many other areas in West
Sumatra, the results indicate how important farming still is to contemporary Minangkabau society.[21]

     21. It is difficult to ascertain from my research the extent of agriculture's con-
tribution to the household economy. Sixty percent of the 395 households in IV

In addition to the continuing economic importance of agriculture for the Minangkabau rural household, the characteristics of landholding patterns in West Sumatra have remained relatively unchanged. Landholdings are small and fragmented. Yet there are only a few landless households. Ancestral property continues to occupy a predominant portion of agricultural land in the village. Transfers of land are still relatively difficult and infrequent.

According to the 1963 agricultural census, farms in West Sumatra are very small indeed. Fifty-three percent of the farms surveyed had less than 0.5 hectares of agricultural land, 80 percent less than one hectare and 95 percent less than two hectares.[22] This distribution of farms by size of landholdings resembles that of land-hungry Java (Table 7.3). The average size is 0.85 hectares per farm in West Sumatra, a figure lower than anywhere else in Indonesia except the provinces in Java, where the average ranges from 0.58 hectares in Yogyakarta to 0.76 hectares in East Java (Biro Pusat Statistik 1964:10).

In contrast to Java where landlessness and tenancy are prevalent, both phenomena are still rare in West Sumatra. In my survey in IV Angkat, information was collected only on the landholdings of each respondent's wife, on the assumption that a man's wife's land is generally more important than that of his mother to the livelihood of his household.[23] According to the results of this survey, 12 per-

---

Angkat produce enough rice to feed themselves for four months or more in the year, but only 17 percent produce an annual surplus. Ten percent of the households do not have any rice produced by themselves, whether on their own land or that of others.

22. The size of West Sumatran landholdings is even smaller in the densely populated interior. In the district of Agam, where the land is most fragmented, 81 percent of the farms have less than 0.5 hectares of agricultural land, and 96 percent of them less than one hectare. The average size is a mere 0.35 hectares per farm (Biro Pusat Statistik 1964:6, 15). According to the survey of the West Sumatra Regional Planning Study, conducted among 1,353 sample farms in West Sumatra in 1971–1972, the landholding is less fragmented than in the agricultural census; 31 percent of the farms are less than 0.5 hectares in area, 65 percent less than 1.0 hectare and 89 percent less than 2.0 hectares. The average size is 0.95 hectares per farm (recalculated from Junghans and Budianto c. 1974:333).

23. If a respondent was not currently married, information was obtained concerning his mother's land. Also included in my consideration was land purchased by the respondent himself. According to a study among 45 farmers in Nagari Sumpur of Tanah Datar, 65 percent cultivate the wife's land, 26 percent the husband's mother's land, and 9 percent both. Unfortunately, this is the only case where this type of information was available to me from the study of the West Sumatra Regional Planning Study.

Table 7.3. Distribution of farms by size (in hectares)

	0.10–0.49	0.50–0.99	1.00–1.49	1.50–1.99	2.00–2.99	3.00–3.99	4.00–4.99	5.00+	Total farms
West Sumatra	53.3%	26.5%	10.9%	4.1%	2.7%	0.8%	0.4%	1.3%	323,381
Central Java	52.6%	27.9%	10.5%	4.3%	3.0%	1.0%	0.4%	0.3%	2,623,343

SOURCE: Biro Pusat Statistik (1964:1).

cent of the households had no access to agricultural land, and 17 percent no access to sawah (wet-rice land). This proportion of landless farmers is much larger than that given in the survey of the West Sumatra Regional Planning Study (W.S.R.P.S.) mentioned in Chapter 4, which suggested that only 2 percent of the 1,353 agricultural households studied owned no agricultural land (Junghans and Budianto:336).[24] Other than the fact that IV Angkat suffers from one of the most acute land shortages in West Sumatra, the discrepancy between the two survey results arises partly from differing research procedures. In my survey, a husband's mother's land was not considered, while in the W.S.R.P.S. study, households cultivating only a husband's mother's land were not included in the category of the landless. In any case, the two surveys do show that landless farmers are still a relatively rare phenomenon in the Minangkabau village.[25]

One implication of these findings is that despite the increasing importance of nonagricultural occupations and the money economy, there has been little differentiation in landholding in the village. Minangkabau rural society has not seen a handful of landholders controlling large agricultural areas, nor a vast number of land-

24. Note the possible difference in nuance in the meaning of "landlessness" in Java and in West Sumatra. The West Sumatran cases may include those people whose sublineages own ancestral land but who cannot partake in it because the land is already too small in comparison to the number of sublineage members.

25. Kahn's study (1974:443) suggests that the proportion of landless farmers may be very large in some, I presume few, extremely land-short villages in West Sumatra. Among his sample in Sungai Puar near Bukittinggi (the subsection of the village he studied is known for its blacksmith "industries"), 43 percent of the villagers surveyed (both males and females) did not have any access to land through their home of origin.

less peasants subsisting as tenants or laborers, nor a numerous nonagricultural population driven from the land. Whether farmers, merchants, or white-collar workers, almost everyone in rural West Sumatra also still works on agricultural land, whose size may be small or medium but is rarely extensive.

This observation assumes special significance when we recognize that most agricultural land in West Sumatra still seems to be ancestral property. In my survey in IV Angkat, respondents were asked to estimate how much of the wet-rice land they worked was individually earned property and how much ancestral. The results (Table 7.4) show that ancestral property clearly predominates (see also Benda-Beckmann:283–285). This predominance, certainly in relation to sawah and possibly to other agricultural land, is related to the relative infrequency of land transactions. According to the W.S.R.P.S. survey, only 4 percent of 1,353 agricultural households studied had ever purchased sawah, only 3 percent upland, 3 percent ground for building a house, while another 3 percent held pledged land (Junghans and Budianto:336) Although the frequency of land transactions might be expected to be higher in the overpopulated interior, these figures indicate that land sales are still uncommon in West Sumatra as a whole.[26]

The importance of the concept of communal ancestral property is underscored by the failures of various decrees aimed at land control in West Sumatra, both during the Dutch period and after independence. According to the Domain Declaration, issued in 1874, all land in West Sumatra, except for privately owned land in and around Padang, was theoretically categorized as a domain. However, this "judicial fiction," as Governor Ballot called it, was kept secret from the Minangkahau population, because the Dutch gov-

26. In the W.S.R.P.S. survey, only pledging was slightly higher in the interior than in the outer areas: 3.8 percent versus 1.9 percent respectively. Reportedly, the survey conducted by the Fakultas Hukum dan Pengetahuan Masyarakat of Universitas Andalas, Padang, in 1964–1965 also indicates similar results. Two of the conclusions of the province-wide survey are: holding of pledged land, especially for long periods, is inconsequential in West Sumatra; and it is social (helping other people) in nature rather than commercial (Sihombing 1968:77–78). These results do not necessarily negate the possibility that land transactions could be (or could have been) "considerably" high in some land-short villages. Benda-Beckmann's study in a village near Bukittinggi does indicate that although land sales are rare, pledgings of land and transfers of pledged land could be more common than suggested here (pp. 218–273, 285–288).

Table 7.4. Status of sawah among land-owning households in IV Angkat

All individually earned	1 to 49% Ancestral	50 to 99% Ancestral	All sawah ancestral	Sample size
9%	2%	15%	74%	328

SOURCE: Household survey in IV Angkat.

ernment was afraid of confrontation if the declaration were made known to the public. After the introduction of the Agrarian Law of 1915, which deemed unoccupied lands henceforth to be government property, the colonial government ordered the registration of all land transactions in West Sumatra, but the directive was little heeded at the village level. In 1922 the Dutch government considered the introduction of a land tax but had to abandon the plan the following year. Experience with two previous armed confrontations in West Sumatra, the Padri wars of the early nineteenth century and the anti-tax rebellion of 1908, and awareness of strong local opposition against any government control of land most probably made the Dutch wary of enforcing these decrees (Oki:92, 108–111, 117, 266–267).

After independence, the Indonesian government introduced the Agrarian Law of 1960. In spite of a directive from the central government that land be registered under the names of individual owners, only a tiny fraction of land outside Padang and Bukittinggi has ever been registered in West Sumatra to this day (Benda-Beckmann:281, 320–321). Even in the provincial capital, Padang, Evers (1975) found that the proportion of registered land had not increased since colonial times. Adat still controls landholding and land utilization in Minangkabau society.[27]

To a great extent, this pattern of adat-controlled landholding has, rather paradoxically, been assisted by the spread of a money economy and of nonagricultural occupations. Today, many Minangkabau villagers do not depend solely on land for their livelihood; this new flexibility has alleviated competition for control of land, which tends to lead to commercialization of land and to dif-

27. Land registration would obviously have a serious effect on Minangkabau matriliny; it would mean the specification of individual land ownership on record and eventually would probably undermine the concept of communally-held harta pusaka. Land registration and measurement of land will be inevitable if the central government hopes to introduce a land-based taxation system to rural Indonesia.

ferentiation in land ownership. On the other hand, only few of the villagers who do not have to depend solely on agriculture for a living, forgo land completely. For "ownership" of land, specifically ancestral land, is the primary sign of being an urang asa. To lose it is to invite doubts about one's traditional status in the future. Land ownership reflects primarily status and prestige and secondarily wealth, precisely because land has been little commercialized and can rarely be bought. Concern with this social significance of land is still strong in the contemporary Minangkabau society. Tanner (1971:359–360) cites the case of a man whose main motive for going to court was to show his fellow villagers that his sublineage used to have ancestral land. According to the plaintiff the ancestral land in question was pawned in 1921; the land was then pawned by its new holder to another person (the current holder) in 1944. The plaintiff now claimed the right to redeem this land (sawah). Apparently, he did not need to use the land itself. He was more concerned with showing other villagers that he came from an urang asa family.

If Minangkabau adat and the matrilineal system have a close bearing on the social and economic life of villagers, this is not the case with the perantau. Some land-rich families may send rice from the village to their kin in the rantau. Perantau who are not yet established in the rantau may count on the economic security of the village, at least temporarily, if they fail in their independent efforts.[28] However, the perantau do not depend on agricultural land or ancestral property. The adat possesses less influence and immediacy in regulating their lives than those of their compatriots in the village. For example, perantau not only live far away from the village and its extensive kin network, but even have a tendency to marry outside it (Table 7.5).[29] While villagers usually marry within the small geographical circle where similar adat is shared and the

28. This provision of security is sometimes applicable even after a long absence from one's native village. A man from Alahan Panjang returned home in 1930 after spending 30 years in the rantau. He could still claim his rights over ancestral land in this case (Oki:127).

29. The information in Table 7.5 is about the latest wife if a respondent has married more than once. "Agam" means both husband and wife come from villages in this district (where IV Angkat is located) but from different subdistricts; "West Sumatra" means husband and wife are from different districts in West Sumatra; "Other" means husband and wife come from different provinces in Indonesia, and so forth.

230   MATRILINY AND MIGRATION

Table 7.5. Relation between birthplaces of husband and wife

	Same hamlet	Same village	IV Angkat	Agam	West Sumatra	Other	Total
Villagers	50%	23%	20%	2%	4%	1%	100% (391)
Perantau	25%	14%	29%	12%	19%	1%	100% (73)

SOURCE: Household survey in IV Angkat, Padang, and Pekan Baru.

kinship network is concentrated, perantau find their spouses much
further away. They usually live in an urban environment where the
Minangkabau adat has little relevance. Jakarta, Medan, Pekan
Baru, and even Padang are inhabited by a conglomeration of different ethnic groups—Javanese, Batak, Sundanese, and Buginese,
just to mention a few. The Minangkabau thus are only one of the
many ethnic groups which form the heterogenous population in
these cities. Urban influences leave profound marks on the way the
lives of the perantau is organized. Whether they are high government officials, affluent shopowners, petty roadside vendors, or
pickpockets, perantau have different life styles, indeed live in a
different world, from the villagers.

   Yet even though their world is so different, perantau are no less
attached to the Minangkabau adat. As far as I am aware, there have
been two notable instances in recent Minangkabau history where
the abolition of matriliny was publicly proposed; in both cases, the
proposal was made by a perantau Islamic leader. In the late
nineteenth century, Ahmad Chatib launched a propaganda campaign
from Mecca against Minangkabau matrilineal adat, particularly
its inheritance practices (Schrieke 1973:34-37). Because matrilineal inheritance violated Islamic law, he maintained, those following local tradition were infidels and were destined to go to hell.
He vowed that he would never go back to West Sumatra until the
adat was abolished. He married locally and died in Mecca, never
returning to his native land. Although some of his students were
later to initiate the Kaum Muda movement in West Sumatra and to
influence inheritance practices in relation to individually earned
property, his radical proposals were little heeded in Minangkabau
society.

   In 1946, Hamka (Haji Abdul Malik Karim Amrullah), the famous son of a respected *ulama* known as Haji Rasul, published a book called *Adat Minangkabau Menghadapi Revolusi* (The Minangkabau Adat Faces a Revolution). In it, he proposed replacing the matrilineal adat with a patrilineally-oriented system more appropriate, in his opinion, to contemporary conditions. There is a well-known aphorism which describes the unchanging nature of the Minangkabau adat:

> The old adat, ancient heritage,
> Neither rots in the rain,
> Nor cracks in the sun.[30]

Of this aphorism, Hamka said: "The Minangkabau adat neither rots in the rain nor cracks in the sun—this saying is very appropriate, for what does not rot in the rain nor crack in the sun is stone. And this stone is now already covered with moss. Let us put this stone into a museum so that it is stored and is always valuable. There in the museum, there are many friends of this stone in various forms (Hamka 1963:62)." Apparently, the book aroused great hostility toward the author in West Sumatra, especially among adat functionaries (Hamka 1963:12; Hamka 1968:41). Thus in the cases of both Ahmad Chatib and Hamka, proposals made by prominent Minangkabau Islamic leaders for abandoning the matrilineal adat were firmly rejected or ignored, in the village and in the rantau alike.

As mentioned before, when a young perantau couple from Nagari Sulit Air carried out an intrasuku marriage, which had been approved by the adat council of their village only a year before, strong protests were filed by both villagers and other perantau. I was often told that cross-cousin marriage is still idealized among perantau—sometimes, in fact, two sides arrange a "casual" meeting between cross-cousins in the hope that a marriage may eventually come of it. These examples indicate the importance of adat to perantau as part of their ideology, sentiment, and identity.

In addition to their ideological attachment to Minangkabau adat, perantau's concern for the welfare of their villages is generally very high. If a development project is announced in a village, for exam-

---

30. In Minangkabau, *Adat lamo, pusako usang,/Indak lapuak dek ujan,/Indak lekang dek paneh./*

ple, the building of a school, a clinic, or a mosque, many perantau are more than willing to pitch in by sending money and construction materials. They are also mindful of their relatives' well-being back home. They frequently send money back to their families of origin through friends visiting home or the post office ("*kirim wesel pulang*" or literally "send money orders go home" as one perantau put it). The money flow from the rantau to West Sumatra usually reaches its peak shortly before or during Ramadan, the fasting month. Although sending money orders via the post office is thought to be the less popular means of remitting cash (Naim 1973b:306), data collected at the main post office of Bukittinggi in 1972 give us some intimations of the magnitude of the money flow from the rantau. In case of the post office at Maninjau in Tanjung Raya, which is further away from Bukittinggi and is very famous for its merantau activities, the total amount of money sent from the rantau over the five years between 1967 and 1971 reached about 62 million rupiah (about $150,000 at the contemporary conversion rate of Rp. 145 to the dollar). Considering that postal money orders capture only a part of the money flow between the rantau and the village, the entire transfusion must be very substantial indeed.

If their kemanakan are to marry, perantau are usually willing to extend financial assistance for the wedding even though they themselves may not go home to attend it. If their ancestral land is pledged, they will try to reclaim it with whatever financial resources they might acquire in the rantau. If the house of their origin is run down, they will try to rebuild it for their kemanakan. It is not uncommon to see many expensive-looking, new cement houses when traveling through the West Sumatran countryside, especially the darek. These houses, often a token of perantau's success in the rantau, are mainly built by perantau for their matrilineal kin or those of their wives. It sometimes even happens that nobody of immediate kin or nobody at all lives there. Kahn recounts the case of a certain Zulfa in Sungai Puar. She and her three brothers built a small house in their village. When the house was built, two of her brothers, retired civil servants, lived in their wives' houses, while the third brother lived in Bukittinggi. Kahn (1974:238) observes:

> Zulfa, however, lives in Java, where she went only a few years after the house was built, and to which she always intended to go. When

the house was built she was past the child bearing age, and had had no daughters. Thus, as expected, the house was locked up and left empty when she went to Java. When I asked the second brother why they had built the house, if it was to remain unoccupied ... he replied it was not right that their family should have no home of origin. Their parents had been dead for a long time, and all the children had lived most of their lives in the *rantau*. The house in which they had been brought up was disintegrating. For this family, building a house on family land, even if it was not to be used, was the only way of establishing an identity in Sungai Puar.

Just as agricultural land is more than a source of livelihood, a house is more than a domicile in Minangkabau society—both for villagers and for perantau.

Naim (1972:20) tells the story of a petty merchant (kaki lima) whom he met in Singapore. He sold *kopiah* (a black hat worn by Moslems), which he and his wife made, by the roadside. When Naim asked him about his relations with his village, he proudly said he had visited home several times and had bought and held pledged sawah for his sisters and kemanakan—though he himself spent years and years in Singapore as a mere kaki lima. Naim also tells of a Minangkabau barber in Malacca. The barber once went back home as the representative of his perantau friends from the same village, taking with him some money to complete a construction project in their village. In appreciation of his and his friends' contribution, the villagers held a party in his honor. For the occasion, they invited musicians who played classic Minangkabau music, and he had made a cassette tape recording of the event. He told Naim that he always wept when he listened to the tape.

To be sure, not all perantau maintain similarly strong attachment to Minangkabau adat. Some perantau—for example, western-educated intellectuals and not-too-successful *becak* (tricycle) drivers—may not and even may not want to remain Minangkabau. Once a reporter from the *Tempo* magazine asked a Minangkabau perantau merchant in Bali what he thought about the past performance of then outgoing Governor of West Sumatra, Harun Zain. He replied: "There is an old saying of our ancestors, isn't there?: 'Whichever land we stand on, the sky above that land we respect deeply' (*Dimana bumi dipijak, disitu langit dijunjung*). Look, I am more interested in seeing who will be a replacement of Pak Karmen [then Governor of Bali] later."[31] Nevertheless, to most perantau, Minangkabau identity seems to continue to be important. Perantau may long for their village. They may be proud of their Minangkabau traditions. They may help their compatriots uphold their adat—the adat of both villagers and perantau—in whatever way they can, morally and materially. They may subsidize their relatives in the village so that the latter can maintain their ancestral house and property. Previously many perantau retired to the village in their old age—"*Minang maimbau*" or "Minang is calling" as perantau say. Today they seldom wish to go home to stay, except for an occasional visit. After interviewing various perantau in Jakarta, a reporter for *Aneka Minang,* a magazine devoted to communication between the rantau and West Sumatra, asked them if they intended to go home to live eventually. Generally, the answer was "no" or an evasive "don't know, maybe later." "They leave their villages in throngs and those who go back can be counted by one's fingers. Even those who go back are not from the circle of the successful ones. The largest percentage of those who 'retreat' are people who have had their hopes already crushed."[32]

As they stay in the rantau, perantau become accustomed to a new urban life style which has little to do with Minangkabau adat in practice. While perantau previously came back home for long visits of one, two, and sometimes three months (often around Lebaran or the ending of the fasting month), the perantau of today, if ever they go back, pay only a short visit and after one or two weeks, return to the rantau, where their life now belongs.[33] Why do they not stay any longer? Maybe because they can not afford the time and have more important needs in the rantau. And maybe they do no longer feel comfortable with village life and its practice of the adat. For perantau, "to go home [to stay]" (*pulang*) is "to disappear" (*hilang*) or to lose oneself (Hamka 1968:39). While I was staying in West Sumatra, Governor Harun Zain made a public appeal to Minangkabau perantau to come back and help in the development of West Sumatra—apparently to no avail whatever.

Yet, even though they tend to be separated from their village by

31. "Harun Zain: Fondasi, Menjelang Isi," *Tempo,* 8 October 1977, p. 24.
32. "Karatau Madang Dihulu," *Aneka Minang,* no. 14 (n.d.), p. 11.
33. For a description of the return home of a prewar perantau, see Hamka (1962:106–110).

longer distances and periods of time in this era of Chinese merantau, there is no equivalent separation in the perantau's psychological orientation. One of the most remarkable developments after
independence has been the sprawling of Minangkabau culture in
the rantau. As migration patterns have tended to become more
"Chinese" than circulatory, there has developed a large market of
clientele who crave contact with *urang awak* (our people) and with
Minangkabau culture. This is particularly true in the major cities of
Jakarta, Bandung, Medan, Pekan Baru, and Palembang, where
many perantau are concentrated and are in frequent contact and
competition—economic, political, cultural, and intellectual—with
other Indonesian ethnic groups. Perantau do not live in an ancestral
house nor do they draw part of their living from ancestral land.
Nevertheless, their sense of Minangkabau identity in the midst of
multiethnic cities is as strong as or possibly stronger than that of
their counterparts back home.[34]

Manifestation of strong ethnic identity in urban settings is not the
monopoly of the Minangkabau. The Toba Batak, for instance, are
also known to be very "ethnic" in Jakarta, Medan, and elsewhere.
However, there are two important reasons why the assertion of
ethnic identity is increasingly visible among the Minangkabau
perantau, particularly since the 1960s. First, there has been the
change in migration patterns from circulatory to Chinese merantau,
increasing the magnitude of migration and concentrating it in several major cities in Indonesia. As migrants increased in number,
ceased to be constantly on the move, and began to converge in
several major cities, it has become feasible to foster and express the
sense of ethnic identity and solidarity among the Minangkabau
perantau in an organized fashion.

Secondly, the PRRI regional rebellion (1958–1961), which
started in West Sumatra, resulted from and in the hightened awareness of Minangkabau ethnic identity against other groups, primarily the Javanese. This rebellion against the central government is
thought to have been anticommunist (the communists were
strongest in Java), to have been opposed to "guided democracy" of
Sukarno, and to have been against Javacentrism in the allocation of

---

34. Bruner (1963:10) makes a similar observation that "the sense of ethnic identity is stronger among Toba Batak in the city [Medan] than in the village."

financial resources. Although the PRRI affair was termed as "the
politest, most ambiguous civil war in modern history" (Mossman
1961:forenote) and "half a rebellion" (Harvey 1977:152–154),
West Sumatra did not escape physical destruction inflicted by the
rebels and the central government army. The aftermath of the rebellion was more than physical destruction. "It was not just there were
people who rebelled and then were slapped on the side of the head
for a minute" as Harun Zain observes. When he, himself a
Minangkabau, assumed the position of governor of West Sumatra
in early 1966, the utmost priority he assigned to himself was to
restore self-esteem of the Minangkabau.[35] It is not clear what kind
of effects the PRRI rebellion had over Minangkabau perantau. Possibly it strengthened their ethnic solidarity as they suffered the same
humiliation and hardship, and helped out their family members,
fellow villagers, and the like who fled West Sumatra to the rantau.
Also the post-rebellion period was a time when the Minangkabau
perantau could reassure themselves only through their ethnic identity, their cultural uniqueness, and their past glory, since in general
they had lost social, political, and economic influences on the national scene. Most probably it was several years after the demise of
the alleged communist coup of 1965 and the subsequent downfall
of Sukarno (both of which in a way vindicated the West Sumatran
rebellion in the Minangkabau mind) that the Minangkabau perantau began to truly restore self-esteem and to express openly their
ethnic identity and solidarity in the rantau.

It is not difficult to find examples of perantau's efforts to assert as
well as reascertain their Minangkabau identity in the rantau. In the
major perantau cities (for example, Jakarta), one encounters a radio
station which broadcasts Minangkabau music and news during certain days of the week.[36] Magazines such as *Aneka Minang* and
Varia Minang, which claim to be communication media between
the rantau and the village, are published there.[37] Some leading
Minangkabau intellectuals in Jakarta established Yayasan

35. "Harun Zain: Fondasi, Menjelang Isi," *Tempo*, 8 October 1977, pp. 19–20.
36. "Djakarta Rantau Bertuah," *Tempo*, 15 January 1972, p. 44; "Caro Awak
dilangik Batawi," *Aneka Minang*, no. 8 (n.d.), pp. 30–31.
37. In a pattern typical of many Minangkabau endeavors, conflicts on the staff of
Aneka Minang led to one group splitting off to produce *Varia Minang*. Both
magazines closed down a few years after their inception in the early 1970s.

Kebudayaan Minangkabau (Institute of Minangkabau Culture) in 1972.[38] As part of its activities, the organization began in 1974 to publish the *Majalah Kebudayaan Minangkabau* (the Journal of Minangkabau Culture). The journal's motto is to "cultivate the regional culture in order to develop national culture."

In urban centers where many Minangkabau perantau are concentrated, numerous perantau associations have been established, usually organized territorially, that is, according to place of origin in West Sumatra. Even the existence of a Minangkabau association abroad is reported. In 1957, a Kesepakatan Mahasiswa Minangkabau (Minangkabau Students' Association) was founded in Cairo. Since then the association seems to have incorporated a growing number of Minangkabau perantau, Islamic students or otherwise, in Egypt. The association even organized a wedding ceremony of two *urang awak* (our people) according to Minangkabau adat in the early 1970s.[39]

If there are not many perantau in a particular rantau area, the association may be simply a single body encompassing all the local Minangkabau perantau irrespective of their place of origin. As the rantau area becomes more crowded, the association tends to break up into smaller segments, organized by home district, subdistrict, and even village if there are enough people available.[40] In addition to looking after the social welfare of the members living in impersonal and cold cities where social infrastructure is not yet adequately developed, these associations keep some of the Minangkabau adat alive in the rantau. For example, a wedding ceremony according to adat most probably can not take place in the rantau without the assistance of an association. The increase in nuclear family merantau has expanded the importance of perantau associations in performing adat rituals; adat rituals for children of

---

38. The establishment of this institute was stimulated by the Seminar on Minangkabau History and Culture (Seminar Sejarah dan Kebudayaan Minangkabau). The seminar took place 1–8 August 1970, in Batu Sangkar, West Sumatra; it was attended by local adat experts and Minangkabau intellectuals both from within and from outside of West Sumatra. Numerous papers presented at the seminar were later published in multiple volumes in mimeographed form.

39. "Urang Awak di Kairo," *Aneka Minang*, No. 7 (n.d.), p. 32.

40. A limited number of observations made by Kahn (1974:230) seems to indicate that even regular associational patterns of Minangkabau in Jakarta may be largely structured by village allegiance.

"Chinese perantau" are most likely to take place in the rantau. Perantau associations almost exclusively deal with social functions and they are seldom, if ever, used for commercial pusposes, such as for organizing a cooperative business enterprise. *Halal-bil-halal* (the celebration after the end of the fasting month) is the most important occasion for members of these associations to gather together, as is the case in the village. In addition, this celebration is the most important "solidarity day" for the whole Minangkabau community in Jakarta, usually marked by a huge meeting of West Sumatrans in a stadium in Jakarta. In 1972, such a meeting at the Istora Senayan stadium attracted more than 20,000 people.[41]

In recent years, traditional Minangkabau art forms, such as dancing, plays (*randai*), music, and *silat* (a mixture of dancing and karatelike martial art) have flourished more in the rantau than in the village of West Sumatra, where such activities were still essential parts of ritual life forty or fifty years ago.[42] Some Minangkabau art groups have already been formed in the rantau. They put on performances in theaters and hotels, at charity-shows, and on television both for Minangkabau and non-Minangkabau audiences.[43] The flourishing of Minangkabau cultural activities in the rantau is partly a response to commercial demands for the exhibition of ethnic cultures in cosmopolitan and multiethnic cities. It is also a gesture by Minangkabau perantau to assert their unique culture and identity to themselves and to non-Minangkabau. Without any tangible symbols or practices such as the adat house or the matrilocal residential arrangements which stand for Minangkabau adat, the display of and empathy with traditional art forms play a significant role in preserving the perantau's sense of Minangkabau identity. Once when I was visiting a village near Bukittinggi, I was

41. "Halal Bil Halal Sumbar 2 Januari 1972," *Aneka Minang*, no. 1 (1972), p. 16.

42. For example, see Radjab (1950:69, 77), for a description of a performance after the harvesting. *Randai* is a mixture of play, dance. music, and *silat*.

43. Some of the Minangkaban art groups are Kesenian Minang Rantak Kudo and Kesenian Minang Nan Tongga in Jakarta; and Dance and Music Group Sabai nan Aluih and Group Kesenian Lenggo Geni in Bandung. Concerning their activities, see "Sabai Maimbau di Bandung," *Aneka Minang*, no. 5 (n.d.), pp. 15, 31, 33; "Malam Minang di Bali Room," *Aneka Minang*, no. 6 (n.d.), pp. 22–23; "Kesenian Minang di TV. RI," *Aneka Minang*, no. 7 (n.d.), pp. 28–29; "Tjindua Mato," *Aneka Minang*, no. 8 (n.d.), pp. 25–27.

struck by an incident which seemed to symbolize the contemporary stance taken by villagers and perantau toward their tradition and traditional culture. A group of amateur *randai* players was visiting the village the night I was there. This itself is not curious, for only a few villages have their own *randai* groups nowadays and performing troupes are often invited from outside. What was curious on this particular occasion was that this troupe, which included young and middle-aged men, was from Pekan Baru, and, moreover, they were perantau coming back to perform *randai* in their native village. It almost seemed as if the perantau were now preserving the tradition for the villagers.

Taufik Abdullah, a noted historian in Jakarta and himself a Minangkabau, once stressed to me the romantic conservatism of Minangkabau perantau. Though these perantau may change a great deal in their ways of living and thinking, yet they maintain romantic ideas and ideals about how Minangkabau society and village should be. Perantau live in a different world from that of villagers. They change. Their lives have little to do with Minangkabau adat. But most perantau, though not all, struggle to hold on to adat as an important part of their identity. How long this situation will continue is a serious question. When the second and third generations of Minangkabau born in the rantau grow up, they may be more Indonesian or Jakartan than Minangkabau. At least as for everyday language, the proportion of those conversant with Minangkabau drops substantially between the parents' generation and their children's generation in the rantau: from 78 percent to 26 percent according to one study (Naim 1972:36). Though the numbers are still small, perantau, especially the educated, seem to have been increasingly marrying into other Indonesian ethnic groups. Emerging *Minangkiauw* or overseas Minangkabau, the term taken after *Hoakiauw* or overseas Chinese, and children of mixed marriages will certainly add a new facet to the future interaction between the village and the rantau. For the time being, however, perantau and villagers are united by one adat.

Conclusion

At the outset I mentioned the scholarly confusion that exists on the question of whether or not the matrilineal system has disappeared. One of my aims was therefore to clear this question up by specifying change and continuity in Minangkabau matriliny. From the preceding descriptions, it should be apparent that the matrilineal system in West Sumatra has undergone significant change. This change, however, can not be understood in terms of the replacement of one family system by another. Since the beginning of this century, the importance of the conjugal tie and the strengthening of father-child relations have been increasingly salient. Yet, these trends do not indicate the "nuclearization" of the Minangkabau matrilineal family or the transition from matrilineal extended to bilateral nuclear family systems.

Previously, the large adat house embodied many aspects of Minangkabau matriliny. This adat house accommodated people of one descent group. It represented a corporate body in control of ancestral property. It also indicated the locus of the mamak's socioeconomic obligations and his authority vis-à-vis his lineage members. In this sense, the widely popular ordinary houses built in recent years do not represent matriliny any more. Nevertheless, the decline of the adat house does not at all signify the disappearance of the matrilineal system.

The prevalence of non-adat houses is a concomitant of the emergence of the nuclear family in Minangkabau society. The nuclear family in this case, however, is primarily important as an economic and residential unit; nuclearization does not apply to other aspects of the family system. Although the father-child relation is now decisive in the disposition of individually earned property, the matrilineal principle in the inheritance of ancestral property is still intact. Today the father and mother are the principal custodians of children in the sphere of domestic group, yet the mamak continues to wield authority in the sphere of the descent group. A man's obligations have not shrunk to the small circle of the nuclear family; they have expanded to encompass the matrilineage of his wife as well as his own. Nuclearization has in no way undermined the matrilineal basis of descent reckoning and descent-group formation. In short, the solidary nuclear family has so far not superseded the matrilineal tradition in Minangkabau society. On the contrary, the conjugal nuclear family seems to be intricately related to the persistence of that tradition. For the economic basis of matriliny is to a significant degree underwritten by the nuclear family, which today supports itself both by ancestral and individually earned properties. The continuation of the present Minangkabau matrilineal system is in fact contingent on the strength of nuclear families not solely dependent on ancestral property for survival.

The remarkable resilience of Minangkabau matriliny has been greatly facilitated by the society's custom of migration. Looking back on its history, one can not help but be impressed by the close interplay between merantau and the preservation of the adat. Village segmentation as the initial mode of migration was an essential ingredient of Minangkabau tradition and society. During this early stage, migration was largely stimulated by population pressures. Through village segmentation, the balance between population and ancestral land—the cornerstone of the matrilineal system—was maintained. Furthermore, village segmentation enabled population pressure to act as the vehicle for the spread of Minangkabau adat from the darek to the rantau.

The advent of circulatory merantau in the late nineteenth century presented a new mode of migration at a time when village segmentation became increasingly difficult owing to the disappearance of the traditional frontier. The frontier had been pushed further and further away from the darek, and the rantau itself had become relatively crowded. Contact and conflict with other expansionary groups had been already experienced to the north (the Batak) and on the west coast (the Acehnese and Dutch) by the eighteenth century. Expansion to the south was precluded by the inhospitable mountains. And the migratory route to the east coast was closed by the Dutch in the middle of the nineteenth century.

The opening up of new economic opportunities, largely in Sumatra, since the late nineteenth century has enabled "superfluous" Minangkabau men in land-short villages to find alternative sources of livelihood outside their nagari or even West Sumatra. The matrilineal system itself probably encouraged Minangkabau men's tendency to migrate. For example, because land belonged to women, men were not strongly attached to land as small land holders. Yet communally-held land provided merantau aspirants with security in case of failure in migration. Also the matrilineal kinship relationship could be utilized for the recruitment and placement of new migrants.

Different from village segmentation, migration of this era was mainly by individual males, circulatory, and involved relatively short distances. Minangkabau men left the village in search of wealth, while their wives and children stayed behind. Perantau came back to the village once every year or two in order to see their nuclear and matrilineal families and to bring back wealth to supplement the livelihoods of those who remained behind. Circulatory merantau transfused wealth from the rantau into those villages where land alone could no longer provide adequately for the growing population. At the same time, circulatory merantau planted seeds of change in the society of the Minangkabau heartland.

Probably the years between 1900 and 1930 marked one of the most critical eras in Minangkabau history. Circulatory merantau brought in not only new wealth but also new ideas and ambitions acquired in the rantau. As their wives and children were usually left behind in the village, the male perantau were strongly oriented to the village back home, even though they might spend most of their time outside West Sumatra. Achieving new successes and nurturing new ambitions in the rantau, these perantau often aspired to a higher and more respected status in the village. After assimilating new ideas and practices in the rantau, they hoped to introduce change in Minangkabau society, for example, by stressing closer conjugal ties and father-child relations. The Islamic Kaum Muda movement in the early twentieth century and communist uprising of 1927 in Nagari Silungkang, both of which were mainly instigated by returning perantau, were in part manifestations of this interaction between perantau and village when merantau was still largely circulatory in nature.[44]

Since independence, another mode of merantau—Chinese merantau—has gained widespread popularity. Merantau Cino means the movement of whole nuclear families rather than of individuals. Perantau Cino tend to travel even further away from the village, stay away from the village for even longer periods, and come back home ever more rarely. The increasing popularity of Chinese merantau has made less likely a serious confrontation between the perantau and their native society. Perantau now tend to

44. Concerning the Kaum Muda and the communist uprising, see respectively Abdullah (1971) and Schrieke (1955b).

take their wives and children with them to the rantau or at least desire to do so if their means permit. Unmarried perantau tend eventually to take their brides to the rantau even if they get married in the village. Together with their nuclear families, perantau are thoroughly committed to their life in the rantau. Changes in adat in the village are not their immediate concern anymore. For the recent perantau the village has ceased to be a field for contestation. Instead, it is a place which the perantau cherish from a distance as the source of their identity in increasingly multiethnic and cosmopolitan urban centers.

This shift in the perantau's relation to the village is exemplified by Hamka, one of the most prolific perantau writers in Indonesia today. The son of a famous Islamic leader, at one time an organizer of the nation-wide Islamic organization Muhammadiyah, and now a highly respected Islamic leader, Hamka has also been a successful novelist. Through *Tenggelamnja Kapal van der Wijck* (The Foundering of the Ship van der Wijck, 1938), *Merantau Ke Deli* (Merantau to Deli, 1939), and *Adat Minangkabau Menghadapi Revolusi* (The Minangkabau Adat Faces a Revolution, 1946), Hamka was for a long time perhaps the most vocal critic of Minangkabau adat and its matrilineal system. It was he who maintained that the adat should be stored in a museum as valuable stones usually are kept. When he visited Batu Sangkar for a seminar on Minangkabau history and culture in 1970, it was, so I was told, a different Hamka from preindependence times. When he was given an opportunity to address the audience, he burst into tears saying how glad he was to live long enough to see that the Minangkabau adat was still strong and sound. I was also told that nowadays Hamka usually can not talk about Minangkabau society for more than five minutes without his voice being choked with emotion. Yet he seldom visits West Sumatra, let alone his native village. Nor is there any indication that he plans to spend the rest of his life in the Minangkabau society of West Sumatra. For Hamka, tradition and adat seem to be something to cherish and long for but not something to live by.

In this age of Chinese merantau, forces both from the village and from the rantau contribute to the preservation of Minangkabau tradition. The matrilineal adat is still very much a part of people's lives in West Sumatra, particularly in the villages. Many of those who are not happy with matriliny as a way of life leave for merantau. Once in the rantau, the Minangkabau adat tends to assume a different meaning, irrespective of whether the perantau were attached to it or not while in the village. Instead of a way of life, the tradition becomes a means of assuring identity. Even though the perantau themselves do not live by matriliny, it is important for them that their compatriots in West Sumatra do. To this end, the perantau are always ready to render material as well as moral support.

Throughout its history, Minangkabau society has evinced a strong interdependency between the darek and the rantau. The rantau was essential to the darek as an outlet for excess energy—whether overpopulation, discontent, curiosity, or ambition—generated within the darek. The darek also benefited from the wealth and innovations which were brought back from the rantau. On the other hand, the darek itself proved to be important to the rantau. The excess energy supplied by the darek was the basis of the rantau's expansion. The darek also furnished the rantau with a solid identity as part of the Alam Minangakbau, the Minangkabau World. Without it, rantau settlements would have ended as amorphous human clusterings like those, vaguely termed Malay, which have commonly been observed along the east coast of Sumatra. This interdependency continues to the present day, when the darek is more properly identified with West Sumatra and the rantau with areas outside. They are two separate geographical entities, yet in combination they constitute the whole of the Alam Minangkabau.

Merantau and the persistence of adat are integral parts of Minangkabau societal process. Adat remains strong and survives, albeit with accommodations, because of merantau. It is as if by dispersing populations in different fashions, merantau at each historical stage provided the means for successfully maintaining the matrilineal system. Matriliny and migration thus form the core of Minangkabau traditions which, rather than stagnating or involuting, have evolved through their history.

Whether or not the matrilineal system will be viable in a future Minangkabau society remains to be seen. After appraising changes observed in Minangkabau property relationships over the last one hundred and fifty years, Benda-Beckmann notes the resilience of matriliny in West Sumatra (pp. 376–380). On the other hand, he points out "the growing individualization of social and property relationships" (pp. 376–383). That is to say, the prevalence of solidary nuclear families signifies that people increasingly devote their energy and attention to the welfare of their nuclear families rather than their matrilineages. At the same time, the development of a money economy has encouraged the autonomy of individuals over harta pusaka, as pledgings of land, transfers of pledged land, and redeemings of pledged land with individually earned property have become more common than before. Moreover, he sees a symptom of the emergence of "perpetual harta pencarian" (my terminology) which could eventually undermine harta pusaka and the matrilineal system itself. Although his analysis is more elaborate and cautious than I may have implied, one cannot help but feel rather pessimistic about the future of Minangkabau matriliny after reading his diagnosis.

Personally I am more optimistic about the future prospect of matriliny in West Sumatra—so long as the internal dynamics of the society is allowed to operate without extensive outside political intervention in such matters as land tenure. One reason for my optimism is the ideological importance of matriliny to the Minangkabau. To borrow Kahn's expression, matrilineal adat is "a conscious model that villagers hold of their own social organization" and a model that helps "to perpetuate a myth of the Minangkabau as a distinct and unusually ethnic group" in their minds. Since Kahn does not find any structural substance, either social or economic, in this model in contemporary Minangkabau society, he suggests that "this elaborate ideology concerning Minangkabau *adat* is retained only because there is no pressure against it," that is, no capitalization of agriculture and commodity production (1974:102–104). As is apparent from my previous descriptions, I still recognize social and economic substance in contemporary Minangkabau matriliny: descent reckoning, land tenure, marriage, postmarital residential arrangement, and inheritance are all yet regulated by matrilineal adat.

The interaction between ideology and social structure is not one-sided. Social structure influences the shape and relevance of a particular ideology. On the other hand, an ideology, once endorsed, often sustains a particular social structure and influences the course of society's structural change, as the ideology embodies the idealized image of a social structure compatible with it. It is in this vein that the Minangkabau's ideological adherence to matriliny should be appreciated. For example, Benda-Beckmann observes (p. 321):

> It is obvious that a conversion of *adat* rights to *hak milik* [private ownership] rights would be the doom for the *adat pusako* [institution of ancestral property], and this is fully realized by the villagers and lineage elders. In spite of frequent exhortations by the Government, nobody has had his or her *kaum*'s [matrilineal descent group's] land registered, for one "is afraid that the land will be *hak milik* and then be inherited by the children," as several informants in CKL [Candung Kota Lawas, a village near Bukittinggi] put it.

The fact that Islam and matriliny in combination largely define the essence of Minangkabau identity makes it all the more likely that the matrilineal ideology will prove important in determining the future of Minangkabau adat. For Islam feeds the Minangkabau's fervor to uphold and practice the ideology. In Minangkabau history, Islam was often the catalyst in modifying adat. However, the belief widely held by outsiders that adat contradicts Islam is not seriously entertained by the Minangkabau themselves. In my household survey in IV Angkat and in Padang and Pekan Baru, the following question was asked the respondents: "Some people say that Minangkabau adat and Islam contradict each other, for Minangkabau adat is based on matriliny (*sistem keturunan ibu*) while Islam is based on patriliny (*sistem keturunan bapak*). What is your opinion on this matter? Do you agree with it?" About eighty-five percent of both villagers and perantau disagreed. The late Mohammad Nasroen, a noted perantau law professor, once went so far as to maintain that the Minangkabau do not and can not violate Islamic inheritance law (*hukum faraidh*) by following adat inheritance practice, for adat does not recognize the father-mother-children unit on which Islamic inheritance law is based (1968:51).

Significantly, the history of the Minangkabau since the Padri wars has been a process of reascertaining the inseparability between Islam and matriliny in their minds. The Padri wars witnessed the birth of a new aphorism: "Adat is based on Islam, Islam is based on the Holy Text" (*adat bersendi syarak, syarak bersendi Kitabullah*). The Kaum Muda movement of the early twentieth century succeeded in offering a solution to the question of the inheritance of individually earned property—potentially a divisive issue between Islam and adat. As mentioned before, the PRRI rebellion of 1958 in West Sumatra resulted from and in the hightened awareness of Minangkabau ethnic identity. After the humiliating defeat of the rebellion and its consequences (the occupation by the central government forces and the loss of social, political and economic influences on the national scene), the Minangkabau efforts to restore their ethnic pride and self-esteem have been directed to the cultural arena, which is politically relatively not so sensitive. Strong adherence to Islam and matrilineal adat has thus come to be emphasized as distinctively Minangkabau, setting them apart from other ethnic groups such as the Javanese. To most Minangkabau, Islam and adat are mutually supportive of the conception of their ethnic identity, and both elements will remain important to them unless some revolutionary transformation takes place in their thinking about themselves.[45]

Matriliny will surely continue to accommodate changing times and circumstances but it is not likely to disappear in the foreseeable future (unless there is massive intervention by higher political authorities, for instance). The growing individualization of social and property relationships is indeed observable. However, land transactions are still limited in West Sumatra. "Perpetual harta pencarian" is not perceptible either; harta pencarian are still eventually converted into harta pusaka. The growing individualization of social relationships is also matched by men's increasing involvement in the welfare of their wives' matrilineages; social relationships are not simply contracting to nuclear families. In any event, the adherence to the matrilineal ideology, the existence of harta pusaka and the close ties between West Sumatra and the rantau will certainly all be significant factors in predicting the future of Minangkabau matriliny.

The nature of change in this centrifugal society offers various lessons to those of us who are interested in the problem of social change. Social change is not a linear progression, for instance, from

45. Yet we have to be aware that the relation between Islam and adat is double-edged. Islam could be a powerful ideological weapon against adat under different circumstances, for example, in the hands of higher political authorities determined to do away with harta pusaka.

extended to nuclear family systems, or from matrilineal to bilateral descent reckonings. Change in Minangkabau society is not intelligible if we look simply into the internal societal process. Had the Alam Minangkabau been an independent or insulated country and had there been no interlinkage and interaction with the rantau—whether the rantau within or outside West Sumatra—social change in Minangkabau society would have taken a quite different course; probably the much anticipated disappearance of matriliny would have become a reality, as social forces would have been contained within the society. As Chinese merantau exemplifies, neither village nor city can be properly studied by itself in this age of easy communication and transportation. A strong sense of ethnicity does not necessarily evaporate in the process of urbanization. On the contrary, urbanization might actually promote it as people meet and compete against other ethnic groups in social, political, and economic spheres in a multiethnic urban center. The outward characteristics and inner values of a person may not overlap neatly. A Minangkabau perantau in Jakarta may be a "modernist" in terms of, for example, his education, occupation, mass-media contact, and political sophistication. Yet, he may be a diehard "traditionalist" in so far as the Minangkabau adat is concerned. Social phenomena of similar natures may be brought about by very different causes. Increasingly strong conjugal ties in the Minangkabau family have developed mainly from economic considerations, rather than from a new stress on romantic love in mate selection. A society can be both "dynamic," geographically mobile and enterprising, and at the same time "conservative," strong in tradition.

The resilience of Minangkabau adat is especially remarkable since the practice of circulatory and Chinese migration has infused into the villages such modernizing experiences as formal education, a money economy, occupational differentiation, and increasing contact with the outside world. Yet Minangkabau tradition has not simply succumbed to these disturbing forces. On the contrary, the continuation of matriliny hinges upon the custom of migration.

Watson (1958) and Watson (1975) indicate that the Minangkabau are hardly an isolated case in this respect. The Mambwe of Northern Rhodesia and the people of San Tin in Hong Kong are geographically highly mobile. Because of high migration rates, rather than in spite of them, these people have managed to maintain their traditions. Watson (1975:213) concludes: "It is apparent from this study that emigration is a very complex, if not paradoxical, agent of social change. Instead of contributing to the demise of the Man lineage, emigration has had the reverse effect of preserving the traditional organization in a modified form. As I hope to demonstrate, emigration has helped maintain many other aspects of San Tin's traditional culture besides the lineage.

There are certain similarities among the Mambwe, the people of San Tin, and the Minangkabau. All have relatively well-defined kinship groups: matrilineal descent groups of various levels for the Minangkabau, patrilineages for San Tin, and agnatic groups for the Mambwe. These kinship groups function as a recruitment agency for migrants and at the same time offer them a basis of solidarity in the destinations of their migration. On the other hand, these groups bind the social, psychological, and economic orientations of the migrants to their villages of origin. In every case, migrants generally desire to see traditions prevail in their native villages. Traditional kinship obligations offer security to the family members of the migrants who remain in the villages as well as security to the migrants upon their failure abroad or upon retirement. The destinations of their migration are cosmopolitan and multiethnic, so that migrants are unable or unwilling to be totally assimilated there. As if partly to compensate for the lack of assimilation, migrants aspire for good names and reputations within the migrant communities and their native villages. This often means that the migrants try to behave like a proper Minangkabau, a proper son of San Tin or a proper Mambwe, channeling part of the fruits of migration into redeeming lineage land, contributing to the construction of an ancestral hall, or strengthening their agnatic groups' rights to the use of tribal land. Most of all, migration in these three cases provided expanding economic opportunities which did not involve the danger of intensified competition for the existing economic resources within the village. Wealth was transfused from the outside world without necessarily disturbing seriously the village status quo.

Despite these similarities, the Minangkabau are unique in the historical depth of interplay between tradition and migration. The history of migration is relatively short among the Mambwe and the

San Tin inhabitants: since the early twentieth century for the former and the early 1960s for the latter. Whether or not their practice of migration will continue to be an agent of accommodation under changing circumstances is moot. Meanwhile, the Minangkabau serve as a primary example of how tradition can be resilient and how the changing patterns of migration bolster such resilience.

Undoubtedly, change and continuity are always present in any society at any time. Yet it is the continuity and strength of tradition which have been neglected in studies of societal processes, which, ideologically influenced by modernization theory, have tended to conceive of tradition as morally bad or wrong. No society exists without its traditions and no study of societal process is complete unless it takes into account continuity as well as change in those traditions. The present study, it is hoped, constitutes a contribution toward an equitable consideration of both.

Glossary

Adat	Custom and tradition.
Alam Minangkabau	The Minangkabau World.
Alim ulama	Religious teacher or expert.
Balai	Council hall.
Bilik	Sleeping compartment in an adat house.
Bodi-Caniago	One of the two Minangkabau political traditions which is supposedly "democratic," for example, stressing the equal status among penghulu.
Darek	The cultural heartland of the Alam Minangkabau, specifically, Luhak Tanah Datar, Luhak Agam, and Luhak 50 [Limapuluh] Kota.
Demang	A subdistrict head in the Dutch administrative hierarchy in West Sumatra after 1914.
Dijemput	A traditional custom in some parts of West Sumatra in which a man is invited or sometimes paid to marry.
Ganggam bauntuak	Usage right to ancestral agricultural land or sometimes sharing right to the product from ancestral land.
Haji	A title given to a person who has completed the pilgrimage to Mecca.
Harta pencarian	Individually earned property, which is entirely derived from one's own efforts.
Harta pusaka	Ancestral property.
Kaki lima	Roadside vendor or peddler.
Kaum Muda	Young Group, which instigated an Islamic reformist movement in West Sumatra in the early twentieth century.
Kemanakan	A man's sister's children.
Koto-Piliang	One of the two Minangkabau political traditions which is supposed to be "autocratic," for instance, recognizing the hierarchical ranking among penghulu.

Luhak nan Tigo	Three central areas in the Minangkabau heartland, namely, Tanah Datar, Agam, and 50 [Limapuluh] Kota.
Mamak	One's mother's brother(s) or the classificatory kin of the same order.
Merantau	To leave one's village (in search of wealth, knowledge, and fame).
Merantau Cino	Chinese merantau, a pattern of merantau popular after 1950s in which men migrate with wives and children to faraway cities and stay there more or less permanently.
Nagari	Village in West Sumatra.
Paruik	A group of matrilineally related people generally living in one adat house.
Payung	A group of matrilineally related people under the supervision of a lineage head (penghulu).
Penghulu	Matrilineage head.
Perantau	Out-migrant.
Raja	King or minor king.
Rantau	Originally areas outside the darek in the Alam Minangkabau, and sometimes the non-Minangkabau world in general.
Rantau Hilir	Downstream rantau or areas to the east of Luhak 50 Kota and beyond.
Rantau Pasisir	Coastal rantau or areas along the west coast of West Sumatra.
Rumah adat or rumah gadang	Traditional Minangkabau house with its characteristic horned roofs.
Samandai	People of one mother or a group consisting of a mother and her children.
Sawah	Wet-rice field.
Sawah kagadangan	Wet-rice field for greatness or ancestral field which is set aside specifically for the position of penghulu.
Suku	Matrilineal clan or a group of people who share the same unknown ancestress in a nagari.
Sumando	See Urang sumando.
Surau	Prayer house-cum-religious school.
Syarak	Islamic law.
Tambo	Traditional Minangkabau historiography.
Tuanku	Part of title often used by famous Islamic teachers.
Tuanku laras	Adat and administrative head of a nagari federation under the Dutch administration in the nineteenth century.
Tungganai or tungganai rumah	House elder.
Urang asa	Descendants of original settlers in a village.
Urang datang	Descendants of latecomers in a village.
Urang sumando	In-marrying husband.

Selected Bibliography

Abdullah, Taufik. 1966. "Adat and Islam: An Examination of Conflict in Minangkabau." *Indonesia,* no. 2 (October), 1–24.

———. 1967. "Minangkabau 1900–1927: Preliminary Studies in Social Development." M.A. thesis, Cornell University.

———. 1971. *Schools and Politics: The Kaum Muda Movement in West Sumatra.* Monograph Series. Ithaca, N.Y.: Modern Indonesia Project, Cornell University.

———. 1972a. "Modernization in the Minangkabau World: West Sumatra in the Early Decades of the Twentieth Century." In *Culture and Politics in Indonesia.* Edited by Claire Holt, with the assistance of Benedict R. O'G. Anderson and James Siegel. Ithaca, N.Y.: Cornell University Press.

———. 1972b. "Beberapa Masalah Struktur Masjarakat Islam dan Pembangunan." *Loka-Karya Pola Kebudajaan Islam Indonesia.* Padang: Projek Pembinaan Perguruan Tinggi Agama I.A.I.N. Imam Bondjol Padang.

Aberle, David F. 1961. "Matrilineal Descent in Cross-Cultural Perspective." In *Matrilineal Kinship.* Edited by David M. Schneider and Kathleen Gough. Berkeley and Los Angeles: University of California Press.

Ahmad, Fachri, et al. 1970. *Potensi Sosial Agronomis Kabupaten Pesisir Selatan.* Padang: Fakultas Pertanian, Universitas Andalas.

Ahrens, J. c. 1972. *Rural Market Systems of West Sumatra.* Report of West Sumatra Regional Planning Study. Bonn and Jakarta: West Sumatra Regional Planning Study.

Alamsjah, Sutan Rais. 1952. *Sepuluh Orang Indonesia Terbesar Sekarang.* Djakarta: Bintang Mas.

Allen, G. C., and Audrey G. Donnithorne. 1957. *Western Enterprise in Indonesia and Malaya: A Study in Economic Development.* New York: Macmillan.

Andaya, Leonard Yuzon. 1975. *The Kingdom of Johor, 1641–1728.* Kuala Lumpur: Oxford University Press.

Anderson, Benedict R. O'G. 1972a. *Java in a Time of Revolution: Occupation and Resistance 1944–1946.* Ithaca, N.Y.: Cornell University Press.

253

———. 1972b. "The Idea of Power in Javanese Culture." In *Culture and Politics in Indonesia*. Edited by Claire Holt, with the assistance of Benedict R. O'G. Anderson and James Siegel. Ithaca, N.Y.: Cornell University Press.

Anwar, Chairul. 1967. *Hukum-Hukum Adat di Indonesia: Menindjau Alam Minangkabau*. Djakarta: Segara.

Bachtiar, Harsja. 1967. "Negeri Taram: A Minangkabau Village Community." In *Villages in Indonesia*. Edited by Koentjaraningrat. Ithaca, N.Y.: Cornell University Press.

Barlett, Anderson G. III, et al. 1972. *Pertamina: Indonesian National Oil*. Djakarta: Amerasian.

Benda-Beckmann, Franz von. 1979. *Property in Social Continuity: Continuity and Change in the Maintenance of Property Relationships through Time in Minangkabau, West Sumatra*. The Hague: Martinus Nijhoff.

Bickmore, Albert. 1868. *Travels in the East Indian Archipelago*. London: John Murray.

Biro Pusat Statistik. 1964. *Sensus Pertanian 1963*. Djakarta: Biro Pusat Statistik.

———. 1972. *Sensus Penduduk 1971: Penduduk Menurut Ketjamatan Diluar Djawa-Madura*. Seri B. No. 3. Djakarta: Biro Pusat Statistik.

Boerhan, Boerma, and Mahjuddin Salim, eds. 1972. *Tanah Ulajat dalam Pembangunan*. Padang: Fakultas Hukum dan Pengetahuan Masjarakat, Universitas Andalas.

Bruner, Edward. 1963. "Medan: The Role of Kinship in an Indonesian City." In *Pacific Port Towns and Cities*. Edited by Alexander Spoehr. Honolulu: Bishop Museum Press.

Castles, Lance. 1967. "The Ethnic Profile of Djakarta." *Indonesia*, no. 3 (April), 153–204.

———. 1972. "The Political Life of a Sumatran Residency: Tapanuli 1915–1940." Ph.D. dissertation, Yale University.

———. 1975. "Statelessness and Stateforming Tendencies among the Batak before Colonial Rule." In *Pre-Colonial State Systems in Southeast Asia*. Monographs of the Malaysian Branch of the Royal Asiatic Society, no. 6. Edited by Anthony Reid and Lance Castles. Kuala Lumpur: The Malaysian Branch of the Royal Asiatic Society.

Cortesão, Armando, ed. and trans. 1944. *The Suma Oriental of Tomé Pires: An Account of the East, from Red Sea to Japan, written in Malacca and India in 1512–1515*. London: The Haklyut Society.

Cunningham, Clark E. 1958. *The Postwar Migration of the Toba-Bataks to East Sumatra*. Cultural Report Series, no. 5. New Haven: Southeast Asia Studies, Yale University.

Dasgupta, Arun Kumar. 1962. "Acheh in Indonesian Trade and Politics: 1600–1641." Ph.D. dissertation, Cornell University.

Datoek Batoeah Sango. c. 1966. *Tambo Alam Minangkabau: Jaitu Asal Usul Minangkabau Segala Peraturan Adat dan Undang-Undang Hukum*

Disegala Negeri Jang Masuk Daerah Minangkabau. 5th ed. Pajakumbuh: Limbago.

Datoek Madjolelo, Dawis, and Ahmad Marzoeki. 1951. *Tuanku Imam Bondjol: Perintis Djalan ke Kemerdekaan.* Djakarta and Amsterdam: Djambatan.

Datoe' Sanggoeno Di Radjo (Datue' Sangguno Diradjo). 1919. *Kitab Tjoerai Paparan 'Adat Lembaga 'Alam Minangkabau.* Fort de Kock: Snelpersdrukkerij "Agam."

——. 1955. *Mustiko 'Adat 'Alam Minangkabau.* Djakarta: Kementrian P. P. dan K. (Originally published in 1921.)

Datuk Batuah, Ahmad, with the assistance of A. Datuk Madjoindo. 1956. *Tambo Minangkabau dan Adatnya.* Djakarta: Balai Pustaka.

Datuk Maruhun Batuah, A. M., and D. H. Bagindo Tanameh. c. 1954. *Hukum Adat dan Adat Minangkabau.* Djakarta and Amsterdam: Poesaka Aseli.

Datuk Nagari Basa, Bahar. 1966a. *Falsafah Pakaian Penghulu di Minangkabau.* Pajakumbuh: Eleonora.

——. 1966b. *Tambo dan Silsilah Adat Alam Minangkabau.* Pajakumbuh: Eleonora.

Datuk Nagari Basa, H. Mansur. 1968. "Hukum Waris dan Tanah dan Peradilan Agama." In *Menggali Hukum Tanah dan Hukum Waris Minangkabau.* Edited by Mochtar Naim. Padang: Center for Minangkabau Studies.

Datuk Pamuntjak, A. n. S. 1961. *Pertemuan.* Djakarta: Balai Pustaka. (Originally published in 1927.)

Datuk Radjo Penghulu, Idrus Hakimi. c. 1970. *Pokok-Pokok Pengetahuan Adat Alam Minangkabau.* Padang: Sekretariat L.K.K.A.M. Sumatera Barat.

——. 1972. "Bandingan." In *Tanah Ulajat dalam Pembangunan.* Edited by Boerma Boerhan and Mahjuddin Salim. Padang: Fakultas Hukum dan Pengetahuan Masjaraket, Universitas Andalas.

Daulay, Zahara. 1960. "Minangkabau: A Preliminary Study of the Culture and People." M.A. thesis, Cornell University.

de Moubray, G. A. 1931. *Matriarchy in the Malay Peninsula and Neighbouring Countries.* London: G. Routledge.

Dobbin, Christine. 1972. "Tuanku Imam Bondjol (1772–1864)." *Indonesia,* no. 13 (April), 5–35.

——. 1974. "Islamic Revivalism in Minangkabau at the Turn of the Nineteenth Century." *Modern Asian Studies,* 8:319–356.

——. 1977. "Economic Change in Minangkabau as a Factor in the Rise of the Padri Movement, 1784–1830." *Indonesia,* no. 23 (April), 1–37.

Echols, John M., and Hassan Shadily. 1963. *An Indonesian-English Dictionary.* 2d ed. Ithaca, N.Y.: Cornell University Press.

Effendy, Tenas, and Nahar Effendy. c. 1972. *Lintasan Sejarah Kerajaan Siak Sri Indrapura.* Pekan Baru: Badan Pembina Kesenian Daerah Propinsi Riau.

Encyclopaedia van Nederlandsch-Indië. Volumes I–IV. 1917–21. 's-Gravenhage: Martinus Nijhoff.

Encyclopaedisch Bureau. 1920. *Sumatra's West-Kust in beeld.* No. 1. Uitgave: Weltevreden.

Evers, Hans-Dieter. 1975. "Changing Patterns of Minangkabau Urban Landownership." *Bijdragen tot de Taal-, Land- en Volkenkunde,* 131:86–110.

Evers, Hans-Dieter, and Sjofjan Thalib. 1970. *Penduduk Kotamadya Padang.* Padang: Center for Minangkabau Studies.

Fisher, Charles A. 1964. *South-East Asia: A Social Economic and Political Geography.* London: Methuen.

Francis, E. 1839. "Korte Beschrijving van het Nederlandsch Grondgebied ter Westkust Sumatra 1837." *Tijdschrift voor Neerland's Indië,* 2e Jg. I, 90–111.

――――. 1860. *Herinneringen uit den Levensloop van een Indisch' Ambtenaar van 1815 tot 1851, Derde Deel,* Batavia: H. M. van Dorp.

Fritz, Joachim. c. 1972. *Infrastructure of West Sumatra.* Report of West Sumatra Regional Planning Study. Bonn and Jakarta: West Sumatra Regional Planning Study.

Funke, W. W. 1972. "Abung." In *Ethnic Groups of Insular Southeast Asia Volume 1: Indonesia, Andaman Islands, and Madagascar.* Edited and compiled by Frank M. Lebar. New Haven: Human Relations Area Files.

Furnivall, J. S. 1967. *Netherlands India: A Study of Plural Economy.* London: Cambridge University Press. (Originally published in 1939.)

Geertz, Clifford, 1965. *The Social History of an Indonesian Town.* Cambridge, Mass.: Massachusetts Institute of Technology Press.

――――. 1968. *Agricultural Involution: The Process of Ecological Change in Indonesia.* 3d printing. Berkeley and Los Angeles: University of California Press.

Geertz, Hildred. 1967. "Indonesian Cultures and Communities." In *Indonesia.* Rev. ed. Edited by Ruth T. McVey. New Haven: Human Relations Area Files.

Geertz, Hildred, and Clifford Geertz. 1975. *Kinship in Bali.* Chicago and London: University of Chicago Press.

Goode, William J. 1963. *World Revolution and Family Patterns.* New York: The Free Press.

Gould, James W. 1961. *Americans in Sumatra.* The Hague: Martinus Nijoff.

Graves, Elizabeth E. 1971. "The Ever-Victorious Buffalo: How the Minangkabau of Indonesia Solved their 'Colonial Question.'" Ph.D. dissertation, University of Wisconsin.

Hale, A. 1909. *The Adventures of John Smith in Malay: 1600–1605.* Leiden: E. J. Brill.

Hall, D. G. E. 1970. *A History of South-East Asia.* 3d ed. New York: St. Martin's Press.

Hamka (Haji Abdul Malik Karim Amrullah). 1962. *Merantau Ke Deli.* Djakarta: Djajamurni. (Originally published in 1939.)
———. 1963. *Adat Minangkabau Menghadapi Revolusi.* Djakarta: Firma Teka. (Originally published in 1946.)
———. 1966. *Kenang-Kenangan Hidup.* 2d ed. Kuala Lumpur: Pustaka Antara. (Originally published in 1951.)
———. 1967. *Ajahku: Riwajat Hidup Dr. H. Abd. Karim Amrullah dan Perdjuangan Kaum Agama di Sumatera.* 3d printing. Djakarta: Djajamurni.
———. 1968. "Adat Minangkabau dan Harta Pusakanja." In *Menggali Hukum Tanah dan Hukum Waris Minangkabau.* Edited by Mochtar Naim. Padang: Center for Minangkabau Studies.
Harvey, Barbara S. 1977. *Permesta: Half a Rebellion.* Monograph Series. Ithaca, N.Y.: Modern Indonesia Project, Cornell University.
Hasbi, Mohammad. 1971. "Perkembangan Lembaga Kerapatan Adat di Nagari-Nagari Minangkabau: Uraian Tentang Perkembangan Lembaga Kerapatan Tradisionil Kearah Lembaga Kerapatan Demokratis Nagari." M.A. thesis, Institut Ilmu Pemerintahan, Malang.
Hesse, Elias. 1931. *Gold-Bergwerke in Sumatra 1680–1683.* The Hague: Martinus Nijhoff.
Huitema, W. K. 1935. *De Bevolkingskoffiecultuur op Sumatra: Met een Inleiding tot Hare Geschiedenis op Java en Sumatra.* Wageningen: H. Veenman en Zonen.
Jahja. 1968. "Hukum Waris dan Tanah dan Praktek-Praktek Peradilan." In *Menggali Hukum Tanah dan Hukum Waris Minangkabau.* Edited by Mochtar Naim. Padang: Center for Minangkabau Studies.
Jaspan, M. A. 1964. "From Patriliny to Matriliny: Structural Change among Redjang of Southwest Sumatra." Ph.D. dissertation, Australian National University.
Johns, Anthony H. 1958. *Rantjak Dilabueh: A Minangkabau Kaba.* Data Paper no. 32. Ithaca, N.Y.: Southeast Asia Program, Cornell University.
Josselin de Jong, P. E. de. 1952. *Minangkabau and Negri Sembilan: Socio-Political Structure in Indonesia.* The Hague: Martinus Nijhoff.
Junghans, K. H., and J. Budianto. c. 1974. *Agricultural Production System (Small Holders).* Report of West Sumatra Regional Planning Study. Bonn and Jakarta: West Sumatra Regional Planning Study.
Junus, Umar. 1964. "Some Remarks on Minangkabau Social Structure." *Bijdragen tot de Taal-, Land- en Volkenkunde,* 120:293–326.
———. 1971. "Kebudajaan Minangkabau." In *Manusia dan Kebudajaan di Indonesia.* Edited by Koentjaraningrat. Djakarta: Djambatan.
Kahin, George McTurnan. 1952. *Nationalism and Revolution in Indonesia.* Ithaca, N.Y.: Cornell University Press.
Kahn, J. S. 1974. "Economic Integration and the Peasant Economy: The Minangkabau (Indonesia) Blacksmiths." Ph.D. dissertation, University of London.

——. 1976. "'Tradition,' Matriliny and Change among the Minangkabau of Indonesia." *Bijdragen tot de Taal-, Land- en Volkenkunde,* 132:64–95.

Kantor Sensus dan Statistik Propinsi Sumatera Barat. 1971. *Sensus Penduduk 1971: Hasil Pentjatatan Sensus Lengkap Bulan September 1971 di Propinsi Sumatera Barat (angka sementara).* Padang: Kantor Sensus dan Statistik Propinsi Sumatera Barat.

Kathirithamby-Wells, J. 1969. "Achehnese Control over West Sumatra up to the Treaty of Painan, 1663." *Journal of Southeast Asian History,* 10:453–479.

——. 1976. "The Inderapura Sultanate: The Foundation of Its Rise and Decline, From the Sixteenth to the Eighteenth Centuries." *Indonesia,* no. 21 (April), 65–84.

——. 1977. *The British West Sumatran Presidency, 1760–1785: Problems of Early Colonial Enterprise.* Kuala Lumpur: Penerbit Universiti Malaya.

Kato, Tsuyoshi. 1978. "Change and Continuity in the Minangkabau Matrilineal System." *Indonesia,* no. 25 (April), 1–16.

——. 1980. "Rantau Pariaman: The World of Minangkabau Coastal Merchants in the Nineteenth Century." *Journal of Asian Studies,* 39:729–752.

Kemal, Iskandar. 1964. *Sekitar Pemerintahan Nagari Minangkabau dan Perkembangannja.* Padang: Pertjetakan Daerah Sumatera Barat.

Kementerian Penerangan. c. 1954. *Republik Indonesia: Propinsi Sumatera Tengah.* n.p.

Kennedy, J. 1962. *A History of Malaya A.D. 1400–1959.* London: Macmillan.

Kiyono, Kenji. 1943. *Sumatora Kenkyu.* Tokyo: Kawade Shobo.

Legge, J. D. 1964. *Indonesia.* Englewood Cliffs, N.J.: Prentice-Hall.

Lekkerkerker, C. 1916. *Land en Volk van Sumatra.* Leiden: E. J. Brill.

Loeb, Edwin M. 1972. *Sumatra: Its History and People.* Kuala Lumpur: Oxford University Press. (Originally published in 1935.)

McNicoll, Geoffrey. 1968. "Internal Migration in Indonesia: Descriptive Notes." *Indonesia,* no. 5 (April), 29–92.

Mahkota, Ambas. c. 1962. *Anggun nan Tungga Magek Djabang.* Bukittinggi: Pustaka Indonesia.

Mansoer, M. D., et al. 1970. *Sedjarah Minangkabau.* Djakarta: Bhratara.

Maretin, J. V. 1961. "Disappearance of Matriclan Survivals in Minangkabau Family and Marriage." *Bijdragen tot de Taal-, Land- en Volkenkunde,* 117:168–195.

Marsden, William. 1830. *Memoirs of a Malayan Family.* London: Oriental Translation Fund.

——. 1966. *The History of Sumatra.* London: Oxford University Press. (Originally published in 1783.)

Meilink-Roelofsz, M. A. P. 1962. *Asian Trade and European Influence: In the Indonesian Archipelago between 1500 and about 1630.* The Hague: Martinus Nijhoff.

Moeis, Abdoel. 1967. *Salah Asuhan.* Djakarta: Balai Pustaka. (Originally published in 1928.)

Mossman, James. 1961. *Rebels in Paradise: Indonesia's Civil War.* London: Jonathan Cape.

Nahuijs, Kolonel. 1827. *Brieven over Bencoolen, Padang, het Rijk van Menangkabau, Rhious, Singapoera en Poela-Pinang.* Breda: F. B. Hollingerus Pijpers.

Naim, Mochtar, ed. 1968. *Menggali Hukum Tanah dan Hukum Waris Minangkabau.* Padang: Center for Minangkabau Studies.

Naim, Mochtar. 1971. *Merantau: Causes and Effects of Minangkabau Voluntary Migration.* Occasional Paper no. 5. Singapore: Institute of Southeast Asia Studies.

———. 1972. *Merantau dan Pengaruhnja terhadap Pembangunan Daerah Sumatera Barat.* Padang: Center for Minangkabau Studies.

———. 1973a. *Penghulu di Minangkabau (Penghulu as Traditional Elite in Minangkabau).* Working Papers no. 14. Singapore: Department of Sociology, University of Singapore.

———. 1973b. "Merantau: Minangkabau Voluntary Migration." Ph.D. dissertation, University of Singapore.

Nasroen, M. 1957. *Dasar Falsafah Adat Minangkabau.* Djakarta: Bulan Bintang.

———. 1968. "Hukum Waris dan Tanah dalam rangka Bhinneka Tunggal Ika." In *Menggali Hukum Tanah dan Hukum Waris Minangkabau.* Edited by Mochtar Naim. Padang: Center for Minangkabau Studies.

Nazaruddin. 1971. "Masalah Hibah dalam Hukum Adat Minangkabau." M.A. thesis, Fakultas Hukum dan Pengetahuan Masjarakat, Universitas Andalas.

Neumann, J. H. 1972. *Sedjarah Batak-Karo: Sebuah Sumbangan.* L.I.P.I. Seri Terdjemahan Karangan Belanda no. 2. Translated by Siahaan-Nababan. Djakarta: Bhratara. (Original work published in 1926–27.)

Nitisastro, Widjojo. 1970. *Population Trends in Indonesia.* Ithaca, N.Y.: Cornell University Press.

Noer, Deliar. 1973. *Modern Muslim Movement in Indonesia: 1900–1942.* London and New York: Oxford University Press.

Nuzhadi. 1971. "Latar Belakang Sedjarah Terwudjudnja Adat Bersendi Sjarak di Minangkabau." M.A. thesis, I.K.I.P., Padang.

Oki, Akira. 1977. "Social Change in the West Sumatran Village: 1908–1945." Ph.D. dissertation, Australian National University.

Parlindungan, Mangaradja Onggang. 1964. *Pongkinangolngolan Sinambela gelar Tuanku Rao.* Djakarta: Tandjung Pengharapan.

Pemerintah Daerah Propinsi Sumatera Tengah. c. 1955. "Monografi Adat dalam Propinsi Sumatera Tengah." Padang. Mimeographed.

Radjab, Muhammad. 1950. *Semasa Ketjil Dikampung (1913–1928): Autobiografi Seorang Anak Minangkabau.* Djakarta: Balai Pustaka.

————. 1964. *Perang Paderi di Sumatera Barat (1803–1838)*. Djakarta: Balai Pustaka.

————. 1969. *Sistem Kekerabatan di Minangkabau.* Padang: Center for Minangkabau Studies.

Raffles, Sophia, 1830. *Memoir of the Life and Public Services, with some of the Correspondence, of Sir Thomas Stamford Raffles, F.R.S.* London: John Murray.

Rasjid Manggis, M. Datuk Radjo Penghulu. 1971. *Minangkabau: Sedjarah Ringkas dan Adatnja.* Padang: Sri Dharma.

Reber, Ann Lindsey. 1977. "The Private Trade of the British in West Sumatra, 1735–1770." Ph.D. dissertation, University of Hull.

Robequain, Charles. 1958. *Malaya, Indonesia, Borneo, and the Philippines: A Geographical, Economic, and Political Description of Malaya, the East Indies, and the Philippines.* 2d ed. Translated by E. D. Laborde. London: Longmans, Green.

Rusli, Marah. 1965. *Sitti Nurbaja: Kasih Tak Sampai.* Djakarta: Balai Pustaka. (Originally published in 1922.)

Sa'danoer, Amilijoes. 1971. *Pola-Pola Kewarisan di Sumatera Barat Dewasa Ini.* Padang: Fakultas Hukum dan Pengetahuan Masjarakat, Universitas Andalas.

Saleh, Moehammad, gelar Datoek Orang Kaja Besar. 1965. *Riwajat Hidup dan Perasaian Saja.* Edited by S. M. Latif. Bandung: Badar.

Samah, S. 1950. *Hikajat Si Malin Kundang.* Bandung: G. Kolff.

Schneider, David M. 1962. "Introduction: The Distinctive Features of Matrilineal Descent Groups." In *Matrilineal Kinship.* Edited by David M. Schneider and Kathleen Gough. Berkeley and Los Angeles: University of California Press.

Schnitger, F. M. 1939. *Forgotten Kingdoms in Sumatra.* Leiden: E. J. Brill.

Schrieke, B. 1955a. "The Shifts in Political and Economic Power in the Indonesian Archipelago in the Sixteenth and Seventeenth Century." In *Indonesian Sociological Studies: Selected Writings of B. Schrieke, Part One.* The Hague and Bandung: W. van Hoeve.

————. 1955b. "The Causes and Effects of Communism on the West Coast of Sumatra." In *Indonesian Sociological Studies: Selected Writings of B. Schrieke, Part One.* The Hague and Bandung: W. van Hoeve.

————. 1973. *Pergolakan Agama di Sumatera Barat: Sebuah Sumbangan Bibliografi.* L.I.P.I. Seri Terdjemahan Karangan Belanda no. 31. Translated by Soegarda Poerbakawatja. Djakarta: Bhratara. (Original work published in 1920.)

Sheehan, J. J. 1934. "Seventeenth-Century Visitors to the Malay Peninsula." *Journal of the Malayan Branch, Royal Asiatic Society,* XII, Part II, 71–107.

Sihombing, Herman. 1968. "Pembinaan Hukum Waris dan Hukum Tanah di Minangkabau." In *Menggali Hukum Tanah dan Hukum Waris Minangkabau.* Edited by Mochtar Naim. Padang: Center for Minangkabau Studies.

Sjafei, Sjafri, et al. 1971. *Monografi Kabupaten Solok.* Padang: Fakultas Pertanian, Universitas Andalas.

———. 1972. *Monografi Kabupaten Sawahlunto/Sijunjung.* Padang: Fakultas Pertanian, Universitas Andalas.

Sjafnir, A. N., et al. 1973. *Seri Monografi Adat dan Upacara Perkawinan Minangkabau.* Padang: Kantor Pembinaan Permuseuman Perwakilan Deparmen P. dan K. Propinsi Sumatera Barat.

Suleman. 1973. *Ilmu Bumi Kabupaten Kampar dan Kotamadya Pekan Baru.* Payakumbuh: Eleonora.

Sutan Mangkuto, A. Adnan. N.d. "Masjarakat Adat dan Lembaga Minangkabau." N.p. Mimeographed.

Sutan Pamoentjak, M. Thaib. 1935. *Kamoes Bahasa Minangkabau–Bahasa Melajoe-Riau.* Batavia: Balai Pustaka.

Sutter, John O. 1959. *Indonesianisasi: Politics of a Changing Economy, 1940–1955.* Data Paper no. 36-1. Ithaca, N.Y.: Southeast Asia Program, Cornell University.

Szekeley-Lulofs, M. H. 1954. *Tjoet Nja Din: Riwajat Hidup Seorang Puteri Atjeh.* Translated by Abdoel Moeis. Djakarta: Chailan Sjamsoe.

Tanner, Nancy. 1971. "Minangkabau Disputes." Ph.D. dissertation, University of California, Berkeley.

———. 1974. "Matrifocality in Indonesia and Africa and among Black Americans." In *Woman, Culture, and Society.* Edited by Michelle Zimbalist Rosaldo and Louise Lamphere. Stanford: Stanford University Press.

Teeuw, A. 1967. *Modern Indonesian Literature.* The Hague: Martinus Nijhoff.

ter Haar, B. 1948. *Adat Law in Indonesia.* New York: Institute of Pacific Relations.

Thamrin. 1972. *Masalah Merantau Orang Minangkabau.* Padang: Kantor Gubernur Propinsi Sumatera Barat.

———. 1973. *Lapangan Kerdja Penduduk Sumatera Barat.* Padang: Kantor Gubernur Propinsi Sumatera Barat.

Thomas, Lynn L. 1977. "Kinship Categories in a Minangkabau Village." Ph.D. dissertation, University of California, Riverside.

Travellers' Official Information Bureau of Netherlands India. N.d. *Sumatra.* Batavia: Travellers' Official Information Bureau of Netherlands India.

Tsubouchi, Yoshihiro. 1980. "Formation of the Settlements along the Komering and the Lower Musi Rivers in South Sumatra." *Tonan Ajia Kenkyu,* 27:480–506. (In Japanese with English summary.)

Usman, Zuber. 1961. *Kesusasteraan Baru Indonesia: Dari Abdullah bin Abdulkadir Munsji Sampai Kepada Chairil Anwar.* Djakarta: Gunung Agung.

van der Veer, K. 1946. "Rijst." In *Landbouw in den Indischen Archipel.* Vol. IIA. Edited by C. J. J. van Hall and C. van de Koppel. The Hague: van Hoeve.

Verkerk Pistorius, A. W. P. 1871. *Studien over de Inlandsche Huishouding in de Padangsche Bovenlanden.* Zlat-Bommel: Joh. Noman en Zoon.

Vlekke, Bernard H. M. 1942. *Nusantara: A History of Indonesia.* Brussels: A. Manteau.

Volkstelling 1930, Volumes 1–8. 1933. Batavia: Departement van Economische Zaken.

Watson, James L. 1975. *Emigration and the Chinese Lineage: The Mans in Hong Kong and London.* Berkeley: University of California Press.

Watson, William. 1958. *Tribal Cohesion in a Money Economy: A Study of the Mambwe People of Northern Rhodesia.* Manchester: Manchester University Press.

Westenenk, L. C. 1969. *De Minangkabausche Nagari.* Translated by Mahjuddin Saleh. Padang: Fakultas Hukum dan Pengetahuan Masjarakat, Universitas Andalas. (Original work published in 1915.)

Willinck, G. D. 1909. *Het Rechtsleven bij de Minangkabausche Maleires.* Leiden: E. J. Brill.

Wolters, O. W. 1970. *The Fall of Srivijaya in Malay History.* Kuala Lumpur and Singapore: Oxford University Press.

Yasunaka, Akio. 1970. "Basic Data on Indonesian Political Leaders." Translated by Kenichi Goto. *Indonesia,* no. 10 (October), 107–142.

Index

MATRILINY AND MIGRATION

Designed by Richard E. Rosenbaum.
Composed by The Composing Room of Michigan, Inc.
in 10 point Sabon V.I.P., 2 points leaded,
with display lines in Sabon.
Printed offset by Thomson/Shore, Inc. on
Warren's Number 66 Text, 50 pound basis.
Bound by John H. Dekker & Sons, Inc.
in Joanna book cloth.

Library of Congress Cataloging in Publication Data

Kato, Tsuyoshi.
  Matriliny and migration.

  Bibliography: p. 253
  Includes index.
  1. Minangkabau (Indonesian people)—Social life and
customs. 2. Matrilineal kinship—Indonesia. 3. Migration,
Internal—Indonesia. 4. Indonesia—Social life and customs. I. Title.
DS632.M4K37   305.8'9922   81-66647
ISBN 0-8014-1411-3   AACR2